PEACE, JUSTICE, AND JEWS

PEACE, JUSTICE, AND JEWS

RECLAIMING OUR TRADITION

EDITED WITH AN INTRODUCTION BY
MURRAY POLNER AND STEFAN MERKEN

B&B

BUNIM & BANNIGAN

NEW YORK CHARLOTTETOWN

Published by Bunim & Bannigan, Ltd.
PMB 157 111 East 14th Street New York, NY 10003-4103
Bunim & Bannigan, Ltd.
Box 636 Charlottetown, PEI C1A 7L3 Canada

www.bunimandbannigan.com

Manufactured in the United States of America

Design by Jean Carbain

Cover photograph: "Prayer at the Wailing Wall (Western Wall), Jerusalem, Israel"
Copyright © Aron Brand
Courtesy of Shutterstock

Interior photographs courtesy of Jesse Abrahams, Leah Green, Tal Hayoun,
Avi Hirshfield, Stefan Merken, Deborah Rohan Schlueter, Paul Tick, and Linda Wolf.

Library of Congress Cataloging-in-Publication Data

Peace, justice, and Jews : reclaiming our tradition / edited by Murray Polner & Stefan Merken.
p. cm.
Includes bibliographical references and index.
ISBN 978-1-933480-15-2 (trade hardcover : alk. paper) 1. Peace—Religious aspects—Judaism.
2. Social justice—Religious aspects—Judaism. 3. Pacifism—Religious aspects—Judaism.
4. War—Religious aspects—Judaism. 5. Arab-Israeli conflict—Religious aspects—Judaism.
6. Pacifists—United States. 7. Pacifists—Israel. 8. Judaism—Doctrines. I. Polner, Murray.
II. Merken, Stefan, 1945- II. Title.

BM538.P3P43 2007
296.3'8—dc22

007012809

Hardcover

ISBN: 978-1-933480-15-2
ISBN-10: 1-933480-15-7

135798642

First edition 2007

Dedicated to the memory of
Naomi Goodman and Rabbi Michael Robinson

Whose lives and good works help us all to reclaim our
Jewish tradition of peace and justice

CONTENTS

REVERENCE FOR LIFE 77

OUR HERITAGE

"Defenders of the Status Quo" (created by Mike Shapiro)

Acknowledgments

For permission to reprint the selections in this volume, grateful acknowledgment is made to those named below. Every effort and all possible care has been made to obtain appropriate permission from the copyright owners to print material included in this book. Any errors or omissions are unintentional and will be rectified in any future printings upon notification to the editors, who wish to express their gratitude for permission to reprint material from the following sources:

Jesse Abrahams allowed us to use his photograph "Another Grandpa for Peace." Claudia Dreifus' "Berlin Diaries" appeared originally in *Ms.* Magazine, and is reprinted with Ms. Dreifus' permission. Jerry Elmer's essay is from his book *Felon for Peace: the Memoir of a Vietnam-Era Draft Resister* and Copyright 2005 by Vanderbilt University Press. Reproduced by permission. Edward Feder's "Will There Ever Be Another Holocaust?" appeared originally in Murray Polner and Naomi Goodman, editors, *Nonviolent Activist: The Heart & Mind of Edward Feder* (Jewish Peace Fellowship, 2002) and is reprinted with the permission of Jerry and Seth Feder. Helen Fein allowed us to use "Reading the Second Text: Meaning and Misuses of the Holocaust." Dorothy Field's "Khirkha" and "Not That It's So Much Easier" appeared originally in her *Leaving the Narrow Place,* published by Oolichan Books of Lantzville, B.C., Canada. Naomi Goodman's "In the Heady Seventies of the Woman's Movement" is from her *On Borrowed Time: Poems of Two Centuries,* Fithian Press, 2005, and also appears with the permission of Joel & Rachel Goodman. We also thank Tal Hayoun for her photograph for Ruth Hiller and Sergeiy Sandler's essay. Susannah Heschel's "The Loneliness of a Prophet" appeared originally in the *Jewish Week* [N.Y.] January 9, 1998, and is reprinted with Susannah Heschel's permission. Rabbi Abraham Joshua Heschel's "A True Story" is also reprinted with Susannah Heschel's permission. Avi Hirschfield allowed us to use his photographs accompanying Nina Natelson's essay. Ira Katz's "Remembrance of War" appeared originally in www.LewRockwell.com and is reprinted with its permission and that of Ira Katz. Herbert C. Kelman's essay, "Anti-Semitism and Zionism in the Debate on the Palestinian Issue: Personal Reflections" is Copyright © 2006 by Herbert C. Kelman. This paper is based on a presentation at an international workshop on "Perceptions of the Middle East: Between Anti-Semitism and Islamophobia," held at the Hebrew University of Jerusalem in May 2005. Professor Kelman is grateful to John Bunzl, organizer of the Jerusalem workshop, for permission to use the material here. We also thank Deborah Rohan Schlueter and Linda Wolf for permission to use their photographs for Linda Green's essay. Mike Shapiro granted us permission to use his cartoon, *I really wish you guys would knock that off.* Thanks too to Peretz Kidron for material from *Refusenik*, published by Zed Books, London and Paul Tick for his photographs. Milton Viorst's "Descent into Violence" is excerpted from his book, *What Shall I Do With This People?* © Milton Viorst, reprinted by permission of the Wylie Agency. Richard Schwartz's "Social Justice" is reprinted with permission by Lantern Books from *Judaism & Global Survival* by Richard Schwartz, Ph.D. (Lantern Books, 2002). Lawrence Wittner's essay on Joseph Rotblat is printed with his permission and the www.historynewsnetwork.org., where it initially appeared. Michael Young's essay "Facing a Test of Faith: Jewish Pacifists in the World War II" appears by permission of Blackwell Publisher Inc.

Introduction

Peace, Justice, and Jews: Reclaiming Our Tradition is our response to a world that in recent years seems to have grown ever more dangerous and irrational and our response to those of our fellow Jews who believe they can ignore others' legitimate grievances, as well as the limits of power, and that might makes right. This book also questions: 1) a mass media that has, sadly, become increasingly irrelevant to a democratic and informed citizenship, 2) governments that manipulate and propagandize, and 3) the American neoconservative mentality that has encouraged governing elites in the United States and Israel to rely on preemptive war as their best defense. "War does not bring Peace," a sign at an Israeli peace rally once poignantly reminded us. It never has. *Peace, Justice, and Jews* is our way of saying that all people, Jews and non-Jews alike, would benefit from a commitment to and respect for human rights and justice, in a world in which we do not do to others that which we would not have done to ourselves.

We Jews have a peace tradition. Biblical and Rabbinical Judaism permitted self-defense, but as Jewish law evolved, acts of retribution, revenge, and violence were hedged with all sorts of restrictions. Thus, we deliberately emphasize peace because we believe it reflects the most basic attitude in our Jewish heritage. Peace has been the idea, the messianic dream, which we have hoped and prayed for, and the goal for our future generations. Religious and secular Jews have historically always been prominent among the skeptics, reformers, and rebels fighting despotism and tyranny. This derives from the purest and highest in our morality: the belief in Shalom, which encompasses much more than the absence of war. Shalom is best defined as wholeness, grace, and truth: ethical values which when married to the concept of justice define what being a Jew—or anyone—can and should be, not merely in opposition to war makers, but equally to the way we treat the most vulnerable among us: animals, prisoners, conquered people, military conscripts, and all victims of cruelty, indifference, and violence.

Our contributors are not all pacifists, nor do they all agree with one another. Some have served in the military. Some like Rabbi Albert S. Axelrad remain "pacifoids," those who would reluctantly accept warfare should Israel's existence be genuinely threatened. One, Scott Kennedy, is not Jewish, yet he, like the others in this volume, shares a common faith best described as the acceptance and recognition that moral ends (many hardly moral) cannot justify immoral means, and that violence can never—indeed has never—brought lasting peace, nor injustice given birth to a fairer, more just society. All of the contributors, we believe, would respond favorably to Rabbi Leo Baeck—the former Berlin rabbi and courageous defender of his fellow German Jews facing Nazi persecution—who told his fellow inmates in Theresienstadt in 1944, one the worst years in that dark and murderous era, that our prophets "turned against the sort of politics that creates its own moral code, they objected to any justification of right by victory." In that improbable and ominous setting where he and his fellow internees were alone and abandoned by the world, Baeck defined the guiding principle of Jewish life: "True history is the history of the spirit, the human spirit, which may at times seem powerless, but ultimately is yet superior and survives because even if it has not got the might, it still possesses the power, the power that can never cease."[1]

Our book is an alternative forum celebrating the fact that we Jews "are defined by neither doctrine nor credo," as Henry Schwarzschild, a refugee from Nazi Germany and later a prominent civil rights and anti-war activist and longtime opponent of the death penalty memorably reminded us. "We are defined by *task*. That *task* is to redeem the world through justice." And, we might add, by *ethical behavior* growing out of our Jewish tradition and our historical and cultural experiences. Nor are we Jews "passivists" as the noted feminist and pacifist Naomi Goodman always insisted, but are instead *activists* dedicated to defending and preserving life as best we can.

None of us has easy answers to highly complex ethnic, economic, religious, or tribal conflicts. We cannot offer simple solutions to historic hatreds and resentments; but neither can the hawks and neoconservatives in the United States or elsewhere, who rely on force and the threat of force in our troubled world. If the twentieth century was the bloodiest in recorded history, the twenty-first century threatens to be even worse with nuclear proliferation and with the very profitable manufacture and sale of incredibly destructive conventional weapons continuing unabated.

Beginning with the savagery of World War I, where millions died in defense of failing empires, to the 60 million dead in World War II and the Holocaust; from Vietnam and Iraq to all the wars by and against Israel; to the continuing carnage in Asia, Africa, the Balkans, and Latin America—the butchery goes on, leaving shattered populations and ruination in its wake, while in most instances war crimes go unpunished, and the guilty are rarely held accountable. When bloody conflicts finally end, the hope is that violent means can be discarded and ethical behavior can return once more. But it never works that way, as an astute Edward Feder once wrote: "The goal is flawed; one war follows another. A problem solved by war is not a problem solved, and the dustbins of history are full of causes and ideologies turned sour, because the means used to achieve them were evil."[2]

We offer in this collection an "alternative vision," as Rabbi Sheila Peltz Weinberg puts it in her essay "Judaism, Feminism, and Peace in the Nuclear Age." We are impractical visionaries and dreamers, we are told by friends and critics alike, who fail to understand how the "real world" works. There are always "enemies" out there, we are regularly reminded, today more than ever. Thus, torture and perpetual conflict are accepted by far too many frightened citizens. Our way, however, reflects the *Avot's* powerful imagery: "The day is short, the task is great.... It is not your duty to complete the task, but you are not free to desist from it…"

In that "real world," opponents, whoever they may be, are demonized as creatures of unmitigated evil with no moral qualities. "Worst case" scenarios are disseminated endlessly and widely to convince people that an enemy is always coiled to strike. It is not difficult to scare people who have been indoctrinated from an early age in schools and in a popular culture that mythologizes past wars and crusades. It is hardly surprising, then, that families willingly send their loved ones off to battle their latest "enemies."

Above all, our contributors give evidence of the enormous variety of Jewish experience in the United States. From shtiebl to suburban temple to secularists, from the left, center, and right, we are a diverse people with no locus of infallible authority. Our writers are unafraid to take sides, even in the face of majority—often disapproving—opinion. This is evident in our chapter on the Middle East and Israel, which calls to mind a major—if, sadly, largely forgotten—figure of the Jewish past: Ahad Ha'am (Asher Ginzberg) whose prescient essay "This Is Not the Way" warned that a future Jewish nation would not succeed if it emulated colonialistic thinking. "The main point, upon which everything depends, is not how much we do but how we do it," he wrote in *The Truth from Palestine* after he arrived home in Odessa from Palestine in 1891. He also cautioned the Jewish settlers in Palestine to consider the rights of Arabs living there. "We think," he wrote, "that the Arabs are all savages who live like animals and do not understand what is happening around. This is, however, a great error."

Throughout modern history there have always been peaceful and more enlightened policies available to our leaders. Certainly we know very well why wars begin and how hard they are to stop once underway—when propaganda and uncritical patriotism drown out criticism and stigmatize dissenters as unpatriotic, traitors, and supporters of terrorism. We know the roles that greed, massive expenditures on munitions, imperial hubris, diplomatic myopia, and incompetence, hypocrisy, lies, and ideological and religious fanaticism play. That we know and recognize all of these things is one thing; that relatively few of the world's powerful elites care enough about peaceful alternatives and "alternative voices" is quite another.

Murray Polner & Stefan Merken
February 2007

Notes

[1] Albert Friedlander, *Leo Baeck: Teacher of Theresienstadt* (New York.: Overlook Press, 1991), p.216.

[2] Murray Polner and Naomi Goodman, editors, *Nonviolent Activist: The Heart & Mind of Edward Feder* (New York.: Jewish Peace Fellowship, 2002), p.2.

WHAT WE BELIEVE

Joe had been a conscientious objector during the war,
doing alternative service working in a mental
hospital. I had never heard of conscientious objection
but the moment Joe explained it to me, I knew that was
what I was, am, and should have been all along.

—Rabbi Michael Robinson, "Living Nonviolently"

Ethics, Victimhood, and Power

Ira Chernus

When I was a youngster in the 1950s, I believed that being Jewish was all about having a special set of religious values, a special way to find God. Years later, I learned that this made me different from most of the American Jewish adults around me. When sociologists of that era asked them what set them apart from their Gentile neighbors, the answers they got rarely mentioned God. And they rarely mentioned any special affinity for Israel. In fact, most people said that there was no special value or belief or behavior that set them apart from non-Jews. The only thing that made them different was a social fact: all their friends were Jews.

Back then, American Jews didn't talk much about anti-Semitism and the Holocaust either. Many of them had experienced significant anti-Semitism in the pre-World War II days. They knew that things were far better now, and they looked forward to even more social acceptance in the future. So it made sense to overlook the vestiges of anti-Semitism, to assume it would keep on diminishing until it gradually disappeared.

That all changed in a matter of a few days during the second week of June 1967, when Israel and its Arab neighbors fought the Six-Day War. Jews flocked to their synagogues, not necessarily to find God, but to show unprecedented support for Israel. Though they did not know it, they were creating a new form of Judaism. The eminent historian of Judaism, Rabbi Jacob Neusner, has called it "the Judaism of Holocaust and Redemption." It rests on four basic beliefs, which combined to create a sort of vaguely defined creed:

- Anti-Semitism is, always has been, and always will be a threat to Jews everywhere.

- Jews have a special relationship with the land of Israel.

- Only as long as the Jewish state exists, with a Jewish majority population, can Jews everywhere feel safe and redeemed from the threat of anti-Semitism.

- The secure existence of Israel is the one and only symbol of the secure existence of Jews and Judaism, forever.

As a college student majoring in religion and thirsting for religious experience, I was rather baffled by this new turn. Where was God in all this fervor, I wondered?

By 1973, when Egypt attacked Israeli troops occupying the Sinai, the doctrines of "the Judaism of Holocaust and Redemption" had become a fixed dogma. I drove my closest friend to the El Al terminal at JFK airport in New York so he could fly back to rejoin his Israeli army unit and serve in the war. A couple of Hasidim walked around the waiting room, urging all the men to put on *t'fillin* and *daven*. The young Jewish soldiers in the terminal treated them as a curious anachronism, if not an outright annoyance. For the soldiers—and for most American Jews, it seemed to me—God had little to do with it. Everyone was simply rooting for Israel to win another smashing victory.

But I didn't see it that way. I suggested to friends that Israel would do best by declaring defeat. "What do the Egyptians want?" I reasoned. "Nobody really wants the Sinai. It's pretty worthless. Mostly, the Egyptians want to regain their wounded pride. So Israel should fall back to its 1967 border and declare defeat. Then everyone can go home and be happy, and no one will die." It all made perfect sense to me. Yet it was hard to find many other Jews who agreed.

Those few of us who did not cheer for Jewish military victory were as concerned as anyone else to insure Israel's survival. Indeed, we felt that we showed more concern than anyone else for Israel's peace and security. We argued that it made little sense to seek secure survival and peace by pursuing the risks of war, when other options were surely available. Yet we were bitterly attacked by right-wing Jews, who managed to commandeer the label "pro-Israel." Now that label meant "pro-Israeli power and might," a meaning it has kept in mainstream public discourses ever since.

A year later I was teaching courses on the history of Judaism to college students. I had to explain to them why the Six-Day War had sparked the new "Judaism of Holocaust and Redemption." There were no scholarly studies to guide me, so I developed a rudimentary theory, one that I've refined over the years. Here's what I've come up with:

By the mid-1960s there was a kind of emptiness in American Jewish life, an unconscious longing for some distinctively Jewish values. By 1967, many people in the US were beginning to explore new possibilities for individual meaning and group identity. African-Americans were asserting their right to equality more powerfully than ever before. Some Jews had expressed their Jewish identity by working with the civil rights movement. By 1967, with the rise of the black power movement, they were no longer sure that the cause of racial justice had any place for white people. Yet they could see that it was becoming acceptable in liberal circles to assert one's ethnic identity. Latinos, Asians, and Native Americans were following African-Americans in standing up as oppressed people, demanding their rights.

As white people, the Jews could easily be classed with the oppressors. This was an uncomfortable feeling, of course, especially for the many Jews who genuinely sympathized with the cause of people of color. At the same time, the growing anti-war movement was asking whether the United States itself was not the oppressor in Vietnam. By 1967, there was a new sense emerging that every person was either with the oppressors or the oppressed. It was the most fundamental moral choice, and no one could avoid making it. How could Jews be sure that, when oppression arose, they were on the right side?

One possibility was to depict themselves as perpetual victims of anti-Semitism, always among the oppressed. However, American Jews did not want to believe that they would always be threatened by anti-Semitism simply because they lived in the Diaspora. They wanted to live fully and freely as Americans. How could they feel fully accepted, yet still count themselves among the oppressed?

The Six-Day War solved that problem. By picturing Israel as a small, weak, victimized nation, and then identifying themselves with Israel, Jews could see the US as a place where Jews were increasingly accepted, yet still view themselves as victims of persecution. Then they could not be among the persecutors. So American Jews "discovered" a special, almost mystical tie between every Jew and the Holy Land.

But Jewish victory brought with it a new problem. Israel now occupied not only Jerusalem, but also all of the West Bank and Gaza. In the Jewish community, it seemed obvious that this was something to celebrate. Yet if Israel was so powerful, could Jews still be sure they were on the side of the weak and the oppressed?

This problem was especially acute for American Jews, who could not express their tie with Israel in political terms. They had to express their Jewishness as a religious or cultural identity. So they had to make support for the political state of Israel a religious or cultural value. For virtually all of them, that meant making support for Israel a moral and ethical value. They could not celebrate Jewish power and military victory as good in and of itself. They had to give it an ethical meaning.

Power could have an ethical meaning as long as it was used only to fight oppression. Jews could give Israel's power a moral value as long as they viewed Israel as a victim of aggression. They could celebrate Israel's military victory as long as they believed it a justified and necessary act of self-defense. By identifying with an innocent and persecuted Israel, they could participate in that act of power and feel perfectly moral at the same time. But identifying with Israel meant making Zionism the center of Jewish life. It meant equating the fate of Israel with the fate of every Jew everywhere.

It is no coincidence that, just when American Jews "discovered" their unbreakable bond with Israel, they also "discovered" the unique importance of the Nazi Holocaust in every Jew's life. The Holocaust was offered as crucial proof that anti-Semitism is indeed eternal, that Jews are indeed perpetually threatened by irrational hatred and oppression. This, in turn, became the supposed proof that all Arabs were motivated by the same hatred that had moved the Nazis to their murderous project. Once this premise was accepted, there could be no doubt that Israel's military victory was a necessary act of self-defense and therefore absolutely morally justified.

"The Judaism of Holocaust and Redemption" resolved the conflict between power and morality. When it claimed a permanent bond between every Jew and the land of Israel, it allowed all Jews to participate in Israel's power and thus overcome the shame of Jewish weakness. When it claimed that every action taken against Jews anywhere is an act of anti-Semitism, and another Holocaust looming on the horizon, it turned every act of Jewish power into an act of morally justified self-defense. The slogan "Never Again" seemed to justify every kind of Jewish violence.

Was the Six-Day War necessary to preserve Israel's existence? Was Israel a victim of an unprovoked attack? Careful historians still hotly debate the question, and the debate will probably never be settled. Nor is there any clear answer to the question of the Arabs' motives. There certainly was, and is, far too much anti-Semitism in the Arab world. Yet it is too simplistic to see every Arab leader as another Hitler.

Since 1967, though, most American Jews have overlooked these complexities of fact so that they can embrace a simple story and a distinctively Jewish set of values. They still do not have to live differently from their Gentile neighbors, which might make them potential targets of stigma, discrimination, and oppression. Yet in order to sustain their new-found form of Judaism, Jews must exaggerate or overestimate their own experience of anti-Semitism. Many seem eager to trade stories of anti-Semitism and hear their leaders do the same, as if they enjoy hearing bad news. That is how they convince themselves that Israel's motives are always pure and innocent, which means that Jewish power is always morally justified—even when the facts on the ground (or, more precisely, viewed on television) seem to raise troubling questions about the morality of Israeli policies.

For the same reason, American Jews must believe that Israel is always threatened. That means Israel must always have an enemy. The name of the enemy hardly matters. So it is not surprising that it is always changing. At first the enemy was a generic faceless mass called "the Arabs." Once Israel made peace with Egypt and clearly had peaceable relations with Jordan, the enemy was reduced to specific Arab states. During the 1980s, the sense of enmity focused more on the Palestinians. After the 1993 Oslo agreements, the enemy became Hamas, Hezbollah, and other Islamist groups. In 2001, Yasir Arafat and his ruling circle were put back in the category of enemy, along with Saddam Hussein. After Arafat died, the scope of the enemy was refocused on the Islamists in neighboring lands, and Iran joined them at the top of the list. As the political situation changes in the future, the name of the enemy will no doubt change, too.

Regardless of who is labeled the enemy, though, every act of that enemy is counted, by definition, as a threat. Within the terms of the dominant doctrine, every threat must be countered. Fighting back is a way to prove both that Jews are being victimized and that Jews have power. Since Israel has the most powerful military in the Middle East, when it responds to threats it usually uses major force. Naturally, this evokes angry, sometimes violent, responses. Jews take those responses as proof of threat and a reason for even more forceful response. Military conflict serves as a kind of ritual performance, a way to act out their beliefs and confirm their basic premise that Jews, the perpetual victims, always use their power in a morally justified cause.

Tragically, this performance is a ritual sacrifice in which far too many real people die. Most of them are Arabs. Some are Jews. This hardly makes Israel more secure. On the contrary, it perpetuates the physical facts of insecurity. Here in the US, as well as in Israel, it also perpetuates and exacerbates the psychological facts of fear, anxiety, and defensiveness in Jewish life. It demands a sense of perpetual victimhood. It creates a culture of victimization. This is a high price to pay.

Yet many Jews have been, and still are, willing to pay that price. Perhaps this tells us that human beings find security not in physical safety, nor in freedom from fear, but in beliefs that offer a firmly fixed, immutable, unquestioned sense of meaning and identity. As long as "the Judaism of Holocaust and Redemption" gives them meaning and identity, Jews will cling to it and repeat its ritual performances, regardless of the price.

For me, the price has always seemed too high to pay. "The Judaism of Holocaust and Redemption" has produced a legitimation of Israeli violence that still strikes me as senseless and self-defeating. If there were any doubt about that, the disastrous Israeli attack on Lebanon in July 2006, should put that doubt to rest. The worldwide moral outrage at Israel's disproportionate violence has done more damage to Israel than any Kassam or Katyusha rockets ever could. And that outrage was, in this case, well deserved. Eventually Jews everywhere must confess this truth and somehow try to come to terms with it. But all the needless killing has inflicted a moral wound on the Jewish people that will take a long, long time to heal.

I had reached many of these conclusions by the late 1970s. When I spoke my thoughts in public, the institutional Jewish community where I lived made it clear that I was not welcome as a member. Sadly, the feeling was mutual. I had little desire to be part of a community that could watch itself bleed morally and its victims bleed physically, yet act as if it had no responsibility. As I look back over the past quarter-century from the vantage point of advancing age, I think perhaps I made a mistake. Perhaps I should have fought for my values and my place within the community. I know of others who did; but it took an enormous emotional strength that I simply didn't have.

And I know so many others who also did not have that strength, or simply did not care. Jewish-American leaders today spend much of their time bemoaning the long, gradual demographic decline of American Jewry. The numbers indeed tell an ominous story. They blame it mainly on intermarriage. Do they ever stop to think about all the thoughtful, morally sensitive Jews who have decided, since 1967, that they simply could not in good conscience be part of such a community? How much energy and talent might have enriched American Jewish life if the organized community had been willing to accept the kind of debate that is commonplace in Israel, where Israeli government policies are subject to radical criticism every day?

The blame for this loss falls partly on right-wing supporters of Israel's policies, who react hysterically to the slightest suggestion that Israel shares some responsibility for prolonging the conflict and the bloodshed. But some of the blame must fall on the huge community of politically moderate American Jews. They cannot completely shut out the images they see on television from the Occupied Territories. Neither can they completely give up the beliefs that have shaped their Jewish identity for so long. Caught between two competing psychological demands, they are confused and paralyzed. They hesitate to say anything about Israel's current policies. Whatever they might say seems, to them, a half-truth at best, and quite possibly just wrong. So they censor themselves and remain silent, leaving the strident right as the only voice clearly heard in the organized Jewish community.

Fortunately, there is a growing voice of moral dissent within American Jewry. This offers tremendous comfort to those of us who have been voicing the same concerns for decades. It may be especially important to those who (like me) live in smaller cities. We were often the lone voice pointing out the moral wound that Jews were inflicting on themselves. We often had to bear the exclusion from Jewish life, the angry recriminations, the senseless charges of "anti-Semitism" and "Jewish self-hatred," pretty much alone. Over the years, many thoughtful Jews have thanked me for speaking out, confessing that they shared my views but were afraid to take a public stand.

Now, as more and more people of good conscience take that stand for peace and justice and human rights in Israel and Palestine, there is reason to believe that American Jewry's moral wound may some day begin to heal. It is never too late for *t'shuvah*: to reverse course and do the right thing. That is the only way to heal a moral wound. But our community will still carry a terrible scar, one that may last forever. Perhaps it should. We can only hope that when our children's children see that scar they will forgive our generation for having gone so far astray from our highest moral values, and the words "Never Again" will mean something wholly different to them than they mean today.

Where the World of the Human Spirit Meets the World of Everyday Events

Ken Stanton

My parents escaped from Nazi Germany. Although they lived within a few blocks of each other in Berlin, they first met as students at San Francisco City College. In 1942, shortly after they married, my father was drafted. He returned to Germany during the war as a sergeant in the US Army. My parents lost aunts, uncles, cousins, and grandparents in the Holocaust.

My mother was a pacifist and an atheist. She was very assertive, without being aggressive, and believed one should never tolerate abuse or threats. She believed that most organized violence was caused by people who subordinated their personal moral responsibility to religious or political ideologies. She was very open about being Jewish, and she had German friends. She did not believe that Germans were more likely than anyone else to massacre or oppress ethnic and religious minorities.

My father's parents converted to Christianity and attended the church of Pastor Niemoeller in Dahlem. After attending the Lutheran church for several years, my father joined the Unitarian church, where he felt more at home. He currently belongs to a Reform Jewish congregation. He spent his career as a civilian employee of the US Air Force. His experiences during the war had convinced him that US military power was a force for good in the world.

I was born in Sacramento, California, in 1948, and graduated from high school in 1965. After I left home, I decided that I was Jew. The Germans had murdered my relatives because they were Jews; I determined that I would, *davka*, do my part to assure that my descendents would live as Jews. I married a Jewish woman and we have raised our children as Jews.

At the age of eighteen, I registered for the draft as a conscientious objector and requested 1-A-O ("draft eligible—objector") status. This was a difficult decision. Though I am not a pacifist, I was morally opposed to the war in Vietnam. At the same time, I felt I owed a debt of honor to the US Army, which had allowed my father to return to Germany as a soldier, enabling him to live his life thinking of himself as a fighter rather than a victim. My thinking on this issue was also guided by my reading of Gandhi, who organized an Indian medical unit to serve in the British Army during the Zulu uprising. Obtaining a 1-A-O classification was not difficult. The local draft board had a monthly quota to fill and a draft eligible conscientious objector counted towards that quota.

After two years at University of California at Santa Cruz on a student deferment, I took a leave of absence from the university and volunteered for the draft. I felt oppressed by the knowledge that our country was fighting a war while I was avoiding it. I believed that avoiding the war on a student deferment was somehow an injustice towards those who could not—or would not—obtain these deferments. I have always favored a universal military draft. I believe that, if our own children have to serve, the American public will be less likely to support wars that are not in the public interest.

I was drafted in September 1967, and was sent to Fort Sam Houston, Texas, for a special basic training program for conscientious objectors. About half of our basic training class consisted of young men who were opposed to the war on personal moral grounds; the other half were religious objectors, primarily Seventh Day Adventists. I was always treated well in the Army and was accepted without comment, both as a conscientious objector and as a Jew. However, I did have a brief run-in with our First Sergeant one Saturday as I left the training company to attend *Shabbat* services. Knowing I was not a Seventh Day Adventist, and having no idea that Jews observe the Sabbath on Saturday, he had assumed I was trying to avoid a work detail.

After basic training, I went on for advanced training at the Army Medical Training Center, also at Fort Sam Houston, and qualified as a Medical Aidman in January 1968. Upon graduation from training, I was issued orders for Vietnam and given a leave of absence.

While skiing on leave, I dislocated my shoulder. When I reported to Fort Lewis, Washington, in February 1968, I was sent to the orthopedic ward at Madigan Army Hospital for an operation. I remained at Madigan from February to July 1968. Because the war had resulted in a shortage of medics, I was asked if I would assist as a medic on the ward, and was given light duty for three to four hours each day. The hospital had a library with a very good collection of anti-Communist literature. Beginning with Crossman's *The God That Failed*, I went on to read the works of Silone, Koestler, Wright, Camus and other left-wing writers. I was attracted by their commitment to thoughtful engagement, as well as their reluctance to subordinate their own moral responsibility to an overriding ideology.

After convalescing from surgery, I was again given orders for Vietnam. I arrived in Vietnam in early August 1968, and was assigned to be an infantry medic. I spent most of my tour with the 9th Infantry Division at Dong Tam, in the Mekong Delta.

During Rosh Hashanah services the chaplain told us we had been given leave to stay in Dong Tam for the entire ten days until Yom Kippur. However, my unit was beginning to make contact, so after the holiday service, I hitched a ride on a re-supply helicopter and went back to the field. On September 26th I was shot in the arm while helping to rescue two wounded men. I was awarded a Purple Heart and a Bronze Star with "V" device ("for valor") for that engagement. As it turned out, I was back in Dong Tam for Yom Kippur services.

Initially, I was perceived as naïve by other soldiers. When I first arrived in country, the quartermaster became enraged when I refused to accept an M-16 along with the rest of my field gear. He felt that I was either naïve or a coward. The day after I was wounded, I requested a complete re-issue of my field gear, which I had dumped as soon as we came under fire, keeping only my medical aidbag and my helmet. The quartermaster cheerfully gave me what I needed. Apparently, he had decided that I was neither naïve nor a coward.

On another occasion, shortly after arriving in the Mekong Delta, I was riding in the back of a truck with other young men in my unit. I looked at the landscape around us—green rice fields nearby, tropical treeline in the distance and, overhead, a great, blue sky with large white clouds—and I commented on the beauty of the scene. I was startled at the reaction this elicited from my new buddies. They cussed me out, thoroughly and energetically. I was told that I was naïve, that no one who had been in combat could possibly consider the scene beautiful, and that I would soon learn that there was nothing to like about treelines.

A few weeks later, after having been under fire with the others, and having been wounded, I once again found myself riding in the back of a truck with members of my platoon. Not thinking about the previous reaction my remarks had elicited, I commented on the beauty of the countryside through which we were passing. There was a long and uncomfortable silence. Then one of my buddies said, "It's not beautiful, but you've been there, and you can say anything you want to say."

In October 1968, I transferred to the battalion clearing station in Dong Tam. From December 1968 until June 1969 I served as the non-commissioned officer in charge of the emergency room. Because I had been to college, I had been offered the position of company clerk, a job with many perks. I declined respectfully, explaining that I could only justify to myself being in the war if I were working as a medic. During the spring of 1969, we experienced forty-five days and nights of rocket and mortar attacks.

While in Dong Tam, I taught conversational English to an advanced class at a girl's high school in My Tho, the nearest city. I also trained village health workers who had completed their classes and were sent to us for their clinical practice. On a number of occasions I had the opportunity to care for civilians who were sick and injured, as well as wounded prisoners of war.

Shortly before returning to the States, I was in the orderly room. I had told everyone that I was going to be studying at the University of California at Berkeley. That was just after the anti-war protests in the spring of 1969, which had been thoroughly covered by the Army newspaper, *The Stars and Stripes*. A couple of the older men, career sergeants, said they thought it was a pity that I would be going to Berkeley. Someone said, "You're a good man. You don't want to hang out with those hippies and radicals." I said, "Please don't take this wrong, because I like you men, and I respect you, but I'm one of them, not one of you. You only think I'm one of you because I have a short haircut, and I'm wearing these green clothes."

I returned home and was separated from active duty in June 1969. I went back to UC Santa Cruz in the fall of 1969. In October, I was invited to speak at the local Moratorium Day demonstration. Since then, I have avoided demonstrations. For the next three years, I worked two nights a week as an orderly at the local county hospital, dropped out of the university twice, completed the nursing program at a local community college, and completed my B.A. However, I spent most of my time reading, sculpting, and drinking with friends.

In June, 1972, I met my future wife, Rivka Greenberg, in a summer class at UC Santa Cruz. After Rivka's graduation from UC Berkeley, in June 1973, we were married and moved to San Francisco. Rivka had been an anti-war activist and she still marvels at the irony—and copes with the difficulties—of being married to a Vietnam veteran. In the autumn of 1973, Rivka began a master's degree program in special education at San Francisco State University, and I entered a master's degree program in public health at UC Berkeley.

On *Yom Kippur*, in October 1973, shortly after we returned from services, I received a phone call from my mother. She said that she had heard on the radio that Israel had been attacked and the situation did not sound good. That was on Saturday; by Tuesday, I had arranged leaves of absence from UC Berkeley, and from my nursing job at San Francisco General Hospital. I said good-bye to my new wife, and flew to Israel. I arrived in Tel Aviv on *Erev Shabbat*.

My first assignment was in the emergency room at Ashkelon Hospital.

After a week, when it became clear that most of the wounded were being flown past Ashkelon directly to definitive care further north, we received a call for volunteers to work at a hospital for prisoners of war. I volunteered for the assignment, and spent the next four weeks taking care of wounded Egyptian soldiers.

After a brief time in the emergency room, I started to frequent the wards. I had spent almost half a year on an orthopedic ward as a soldier, and felt that I would be useful there. In the army—any army—wounded soldiers are both patients and staff. With the help of an Egyptian officer who spoke English, I organized the patients into teams and taught them basic nursing skills. Ambulatory patients bathed those who were confined to bed, changed the bed linens, and assisted with feedings; I did dressing changes and dispensed medications.

After about a week, the Egyptian officer, a young man my own age, said to me, "You and I are friends." I answered, "No, we're not friends. You are a patient and I am your nurse. If we had met in Sinai a few weeks ago, you would have tried to kill me. That doesn't meet my definition of a friend." Being a noncombatant who takes care of prisoners of war is a difficult role to maintain. Having clear boundaries has enabled me to do what I thought was right in ambiguous circumstances.

When I asked an Israeli officer at the camp why, as a lawyer in civilian life, he had defended Palestinians accused of terror attacks, he said, "For the same reason that you take care of wounded Egyptian soldiers, because it is our professional responsibility."

Six weeks after the war began, the truce was signed, the prisoners in our hospital were repatriated, and I flew home.

During the next eight years, Rivka and I spent half a year in Mexico and Guatemala, two years in Tel Aviv, and four years in London. Since then, we have lived in Michigan and in the San Francisco Bay Area. We completed our master's degrees and Ph.Ds, and have worked in our respective fields as direct service providers, administrators, consultants, and university teachers.

We have three daughters, Hadara, Shira, and Mayan, who were born in Tel Aviv, Ann Arbor, and Oakland, respectively. Our daughters attended Jewish day schools and all of them travel widely, both with us and on their own. All of them have spent time in Israel, including extended visits with Arab Christians in Nazareth, who are relatives of Rivka's by marriage. Through Rivka, our daughters have had opportunities to participate in work for peace, justice, *Tzeddakah*, and interfaith dialogue. All of us are involved in Jewish community activities.

In 1997, I spent two weeks as a consultant for a Catholic charity, working with a group of Palestinian physicians and business people in Ramallah and Bethlehem to develop an operational plan to re-open a former charity hospital. Because our team of consultants and local contacts included Christians, Muslims, and a Jew, we agreed at our first meeting to take Friday, Saturday, and Sunday off each week. I used the time to visit my relatives in Israel. My first stop was at the home of my eldest cousin in Jerusalem. Her husband is a long-time Likud activist and her whole family gathered for my visit. They held a long discussion about whether or not it was right for me to be working with Palestinians. Finally, her eldest son, a career army officer, settled the matter by saying, "It's a good thing. We don't want our neighbors to be hungry, sick, or uneducated." After that, I was welcomed in all of my relatives' homes.

While riding in a Jerusalem taxi, I received a lecture from the driver on the current situation. He explained to me that ultimately there had to be peace between the Israelis and the Palestinians. "After all, we're stuck here together; we will have to get along." His concern was internal conflict among the Jews. He worried that the left and right, the religious and secular, the Ashkenazim and Sephardim, would be unable to find a middle ground of compromise and cooperation. I found his pessimism quite reassuring. It reminded me of a passage from Sholem Aleichem that I had read in Vietnam: "But enough of this depressing talk. What news is there of the cholera in Odessa?"

* * *

Reflecting on these events, I have tried to understand why my life has taken the course it has. As a child, I heard stories of my family's experiences in Nazi Germany and during the war, and of my relatives' experiences in Israel. I always wanted to have adventures. That is probably the underlying reason I felt I had to drop out of college and go to war—history was happening in Vietnam and I did not want it to pass me by. That is probably also the reason I went to Israel during the Yom

Kippur War. My parents taught us liberal values. Perhaps more important, they taught us to think and argue and read. The only acceptable reason for leaving the dinner table before the meal was over was to find a reference for a discussion in progress. Of course, coming of age in the 1960s had an impact. The civil rights movement and the war in Vietnam dominated the news, and everybody talked about them.

I recognized at an early age that my views were often different from other's. By the time I left for college, I had determined that, while I was happy to be in agreement with others, I was comfortable when I was not. My mother told me once that I have the unusual quality of seeing people for who they are. I tend not to be concerned about age, gender, race, religion, or other characteristics that frequently create barriers between people. Even when I disagree with someone, I am usually able to understand why they think and act as they do. It is hard to have enemies when one understands the other person's point of view.

I have difficulty with ideological labels. I am not a pacifist, but I try hard not to be aggressive in my personal life. I believe that, as a society, we should ensure that our neighbors are not hungry, sick, or uneducated. I believe that the Jewish community of the Diaspora should support Israel, and should support the development of a viable Palestinian state. Sustaining these beliefs, and making them part of my life, is more difficult than simply aligning myself with a particular ideological position. I believe that I am free to choose my friends, but I do not have to allow my friends to choose my enemies.

I do not consider myself an activist, but I try to align my actions with my beliefs. I currently work in a community hospital emergency department where I try to be of use to those individuals whom I encounter in the course of each day. I try to be both thoughtful and practical, and to live my life in the place where the world of the human spirit and the world of everyday events meet.

Why I Won't Go to Israel

David Howard

Introduction

I am a Jew and a pacifist. I was born in 1947, two years after the Holocaust and a year before Israel became an independent nation. I speak Hebrew. I also know Yiddish and Ladino and I've read a thousand books by Jewish authors. My rabbi as a child was a Holocaust survivor and noted Talmud scholar. I've spent my life among fellow Jews. Yet I've never set foot in the Promised Land. No Yad V'shem. No Western Wall. No Carmel, no Negev, no Galil.

It's not for lack of opportunity, interest or proximity. I've lived on the Mediterranean coast and been as close to Jerusalem as Crete and Cairo. I once got as far as the Israeli Embassy in Mexico City, to inquire about *aliyah*. But I've always hesitated, on the brink. This, then, is the story of a presence to Jewish spirituality, culture, language and identity and absence from Eretz Yisrael. In passing, it is also the story of a journey from violence to pacifism. Israel, mostly through its failings, has helped teach me the lessons of peace I believe all humanity must learn. For that I am grateful.

* * *

I acknowledge that a pilgrimage to Israel would touch the soul of any Jew. I acknowledge that declining to go may be perceived as lazy, sanctimonious or cowardly. Speaking out from a distance risks being excessively cerebral and detached, failing to reach the heart of the matter: *am yisrael chai*, the living Israeli people. I want to honor the pilgrim, the immigrant, and the refugee, and I admit that a trip to Israel would be spellbinding. I've encouraged my own daughters to take "Birthright" trips, provided by the benefactors of the Jewish state. But personally, I abjure the Israeli spell. I won't be bound. I won't go. The daughters of Palestine also have birthrights. Instead, I long to break the spell: Shoah, Nakba. Nakba, Shoah. Law of Return, Right of Return. *Shalom Alechem, Wa 'Alaikum Salaam.*

Israeli Law of Return

"Every Jew has the right to come to this country. The rights of a Jew under this law . . . are also vested in a child and a grandchild of a Jew, the spouse of a Jew, the spouse of a child of a Jew and the spouse of a grandchild of a Jew."

If we renounce Law of Return, we renounce triumphant prophecy, ancient nostalgia, tribalism, and dispossession. We renounce Next Year in Jerusalem. This is a choice we Diaspora Jews are empowered to make, perhaps morally obliged to make, before it's too late.

We can say, in the words of Bob Dylan, "It ain't me, babe. It ain't me you're lookin' for, babe." We can make this simple gesture of goodwill and good faith without bitterness or rancor, in loving kindness. Like reciting a blessing. *Shalom u'vracha.*

An "it-ain't-me" psalm of liberation goes like this: I understand our suffering, our historical desperation, our refugee salvation. But this Zion turns out not to be a very good idea, after all. This army of Occupation and its compulsory military servitude—not a good idea. This secret stockpiling of 200 nuclear bombs— not a good idea. This second-class citizenship for Arabs, this Jewish chauvinism—not a good idea.

It ain't me, babe.

Shema, Listen

Let's reclaim our most sacred prayer—a prayer held hostage by armed men. *Shema Yisrael*, Listen, Jewish people. Our God is one God.

If we listen, we will hear the voice of our Palestinian twin. Her God, our God. His land, our Land. One God. One Land?

May our sons and daughters fall in love, make love, make peace. I wish you,

Israeli Jew, a Palestinian bride. I wish you, Palestinian Arab, a Jewish groom. You have my blessing. For God's sake, let's miscegenate.

We can do this. It is not cultural suicide; it is not betrayal. Our love will prevail over roadblocks, checkpoints, barriers, and prisons.

Love trumps flags.

Right of Return

In 1948, several hundred thousand Palestinian natives fled or were expelled from what became the Land of Israel. This Exodus is called the Nakba, the "disaster."

In 1950, Israel passed the Absentee Property Law. Palestinian property was confiscated, villages were demolished, and ownership was transferred to Jews. The victims in exile are called "absentees." The Israeli "Custodian of Absentee Property" estimates 70% of Israel's territory belonged to "absentees." The Jewish National Fund says it's 88%.

In nearly sixty years the Palestinian refugee population has grown to some 4,000,000 people. There are fifty-nine refugee camps in Gaza, the West Bank, Jordan, Lebanon, and Syria. Many started as tent cities. Now they are vast urban ghettos. Another million or so Palestinians live outside the region, in the Palestinian Diaspora.

Palestinian Right of Return is based on the Universal Declaration of Human Rights, the Geneva Conventions and UN Resolution 194.

Point of No Return

"The term point of no return originated as a technical term in air navigation, to refer to the point on a flight at which, due to fuel consumption, a plane is no longer capable of returning to its airfield of origin. . . . the phrase implies an irrevocable commitment."

Please donate my right under Law of Return to a Palestinian victim of the Nakba. Consider this offering a prayerful question: Have we not yet reached the point of no return?

The State of Israel is not worth killing for. Palestine is not worth killing for. Bombing a bus full of Jews or torturing West Bank prisoners are borders we must not transgress, points from which there is no moral return.

In the five-year Intifada between September 29, 2000 and March 2005, Israelis killed 723 Palestinian children. Palestinians killed 121 Israeli children. Their names are Nora, Yusif, Ibrahim, Khalil, and Hani; Rachel, Gal, Danielle, Tiferet, and Yonatan.

Awakening

Sometimes a Zen master poses a koan, a Zen riddle, and slaps his disciple in the face to awaken him. Here are five slaps in my Jewish face.

1

1961. There is a new student at Weaver High School in Hartford, Connecticut. His name is Sammy, an Israeli who speaks English with a thick Eastern European accent. Sammy's parents survived Auschwitz, tried to make a go of it in Israel, and ended up broke in Hartford.

"What's Israel like?" I ask him.

"Like here," Sammy answers. "Only they have Arabs instead of niggers."

2

1971. I hitchhike from New York to San Francisco with Jacob, a hippie psychologist whose uncle was once a bodyguard for Ben Gurion. Over a joint and a Wonder Bread cheese sandwich Jacob tells me, "Whatever you say about the Israelis, they've given us dignity. Before Israel, we internalized the goyishe stereotype of the Jewish male as a pimply faggot with gefilte fish breath. Now, nobody fucks with us."

3

1973. Chabad has sent a young missionary rabbi to feed, clothe, and preach to the Jewish heathens of California. Rabbi Isaac is a black-bearded cherub on a mission from God. He cruises the psychedelicized Berkeley streets in a *mitzvahmobile*. He marches into smoky anarchist coffeehouses, once frequented by Allen Ginsberg and Huey Newton, to blow the shofar, lest a Jew not hear it on Rosh Hashanah. He brings tefilin to assimilated Jews who don't know phylacteries from prophylactics. He lights Shabbat candles.

"Why do you do this?" I ask Rabbi Isaac, 3,000 miles and a couple of centuries from Crown Heights.

"For *Ahavas Yisrael,* the love of the Jewish people."

He means it. The Chabad House door is open day and night. Jewish junkies and war resisters sleep on the floor next to the Ark of the Torah. When I had surgery to remove a benign tumor from my lung, Rabbi Isaac and his wife Rivka climb seven floors—it's a sin to ride an elevator on Shabas—to visit me.

Yet Isaac has done a tour in the IDF. He's fired an Uzi. "The Rebbe says even Damascus is part of Eretz Yisrael."

4

2000. Intifada. War correspondent Chris Hedges reports from the Khan Youni refugee camp in Gaza: "Yesterday at this spot the Israelis shot eight young men, six of whom were under the age of eighteen. One was twelve. This afternoon they killed an eleven-year-old boy, Ali Murad. . . . I have never before watched soldiers entice children like mice into a trap and murder them for sport."

My friend, Paul, who spent four years in Israel, denies every Israeli atrocity. "IDF soldiers are just Jewish kids. Like us. They could no more murder somebody than you or I could."

5

2004. Malka comes to Ojai for her nephew's Bar Mitzvah. She lives on an experimental kibbutz in the Negev. It is devoted to mystical values, full of Israelis who have been to India, taken Ecstasy, danced to trance music, practiced yoga. It's a wonderful community. Sababa. Nifla. The real Israel. Vegetarian, organic, liberated.

"Do you have to be Jewish to live there?" I ask.

"What do you mean?" she replies. "In Israel, everyone is Jewish."

Enough

After nearly sixty years, the polemics of Zion are tedious, enervating, paralyzing, and terminal. *Dayenu*. Enough already. The sanitized founding myth—a land without a people for a people without a land—remains a lie, an unrepentant lie.

Your Turn

Ani maamin, I believe with perfect faith, that all people must eventually climb the Mount Sinai of pacifism. There is no greater calling. World peace is our paramount sacred responsibility. The Shoah of bloody conflicts perpetually raging around the world is ultimately one Shoah, humanity's Shoah.

Many paths lead to this Sinai's summit. I have walked my own path in sin and folly. I have learned my lessons from committing acts of violence; witnessing, supporting, and fomenting the violence of others; believing in causes that relied on violence; failing to pursue peace zealously enough.

But it is never too late or too early to wash the blood from our hands, to forgive, and ask forgiveness, to listen and heed the call.

I entrust you with the task of climbing this mountain, Israeli and Palestinian children, sons and daughters of Hagar, Sarah, and Abraham. I cannot take you by the hand. Your peace and justice pilgrimage must be walked alone and often in darkness.

The old men will not pass you a torch. They have extinguished the light unto the nations. Instead, they will pass you a loaded Uzi, a pile of nukes, and a pack of lies. Pass that up. They are looking for someone who will die for them and more.

It ain't you, babe. It ain't you they're lookin' for, babe.

A Dreamer's Sojourn in the Holy Land

Kenny Freeman

Is there an alternative? Can Jews and Arabs live together in peace and harmony, with all knowing that justice has been achieved? That brotherhood and sisterhood can be achieved by two peoples who share one core belief—that the Land itself is a Holy Land, and is the homeland of them both.

This is like asking, "Will the Messiah come? And when?"

I've got a lot of reasons to believe in Jewish-Arab togetherness going back to grandparents who had been in the Bund in Russia and became communists in America, but also lovers of Zion who thought Palestine should become socialist.

I was born in 1942, so that my childhood was in the context of the Holocaust and how it affected my family in America. Then I started with the civil rights movement in Washington in 1959, and finally became a full-time "freedom worker" for CORE in North Carolina in 1964. The KKK tried to assassinate me when I lived in Durham County in 1967. After a long involvement in the anti-Vietnam War movement, studying Gandhi and nonviolence along the way, my attention turned to Israel, where in 1976 students at Bir Zeit University were flying Palestinian flags in front of Israeli Border Police, and in turn being attacked with clubs.

I had never questioned the depth of my own fondness for Israel. In 1952, my childhood rabbi had just returned from Israel. He had, he announced, seen the fulfillment of the words of Isaiah, and his faith was contagious. My adult rabbi in Washington, DC was an active member of an Israeli kibbutz. But by 1976, when I saw the Israelis beating the Palestinians on television, I faced the dilemma of having supported Israel while having had the experience of being clubbed myself while protesting segregation.

So, I began studying Israeli history and Jewish history along with reading Scripture, which I'd been doing for a while. I also began negotiating with the Jewish Agency, exploring becoming a new immigrant. I guess they thought I was an impulsive, perhaps crazy, radical, and so they delayed giving me a ticket to Israel. Naturally I proved them right by buying my own ticket; I arrived in Israel in 1978, and immediately changed my status to "new immigrant."

I kept looking for a place that would take us in. I was with my wife and youngest daughter and had two children by a previous marriage whom I expected to come to Israel and eventually join us. And, I was still an impulsive radical—perhaps crazy? My own belief in my sanity was maintained by a group who read everything I wrote and who advised me—the most influential being Daniel Berrigan, the Jesuit priest and anti-war activist, whose blessing I've sought on all my ventures to this day.

I searched through Jerusalem (Yeshiva Diaspora), talked with people in the peace movement (Abie Nathan) and with kibbutzim that were once radical (Hazorea, Mishmar HaEmek). In the end, I was convinced that I needed a previously agreed upon starting place in Israel, with the backing of the Jewish Agency, and much more money that I'd had. So we returned to America.

After two years, we had the money, and the Jewish Agency gave us a choice as to where to go. Wishing to live among Arabs, we chose Nazareth Illit, a tiny Jewish town attached to Nazareth, the largest Arab city in Israel.

I spent nearly a year in Nazareth. I worked on my experiment: We became totally absorbed into a Christian Arab family in the old "Kasbah" section of the city; we became very close to a Muslim Arab family from a village just north of Nazareth; I started the only joint Jewish/Arab business venture in Nazareth, with the approval of the Mayor's Office, printing and distributing prayer books for peace as souvenirs for the tourists who were otherwise buying small bottles of "water from the Sea of Galilee."

I had spent about a week walking around in Nazareth before a short man in a tiny grocery store called out to me, "Hey, American." This was Elias, who operated the store and lived above it with his wife, three sons, and two daughters. I had come to Israel because I believed in coexistence and wanted to test it. Elias had been born near Acre to an old Palestinian family, and was forced to move to Nazareth by the Israeli Army in 1948. The conditions they lived in might have been considered primitive—no telephone, a kerosene heater for the winter, a living room that became the bedroom at night—but these were the same conditions we ourselves lived in the entire time we were in Israel.

What I learned was that coming together is done through family, not through political organizations. I was in touch with several people in what was then the Israeli peace movement, especially Father Bruno in Jerusalem, who was our introduction to Neve Shalom, to people at *New Outlook* magazine in Tel-Aviv, and more.

In local elections in Tel-Aviv, I voted Communist (Hadash), in national elections for Begin, and then Shamir (Herut). I told people I was the extreme left wing of Herut: for a unified country (Greater Israel) with justice and equality within it. But this was politics. When Elias first invited me for coffee, served by his wife, who brought it downstairs to meet me, that was a milestone beyond politics. Then we were invited to dinner at their house with the whole family.

I began teaching their eldest daughter how to type, so she was a constant visitor to our flat in the Absorption Center. Elias had a brother who was an official in the Labor Organization in Haifa, and he came to Nazareth to meet us.

After nearly a year we had to move to the Manshiyeh quarter in old Tel-Aviv, between the Shuk HaCarmel and the Sea. Since neither of us had a telephone or a car, we ended up visiting each other by bus, spending several days sleeping in each other's flats. Elias was two blocks from the Church of the Annunciation; I was two blocks from the Mediterranean. We visited back and forth, and our children even more so. When my parents came we took them to Nazareth.

Once you have reached the place where "my house is your house" quite literally, you knock on my door with five people, and I'll feed you and bed you and make you feel at home the same way you do for me in Nazareth, in our 1 1/2 room flats, then you have achieved the goal—your two families have blended into one intentional-family.

Elias and I both had the same dream: Jews and Arabs getting along together. We'd gone as far as seeing whether Neve Shalom would accept us as a "package," two families at once, one Jewish, one Palestinian. When we finally all arrived together, the community was in the middle of a "sexual scandal." We left.

We were absolutely convinced, our two families, that Jews and Arabs living together was not only possible, it was pleasurable, and mutually advantageous: while I taught his daughter Elianor to type, his wife, Nada, taught my wife how to make pita Arab style, and *enjeddra*.

Now, not only was I different, a relatively radical American Jew, but Elias was also different in that he was a Christian Arab.

That's why Mohammed and Khalid were so important—they were the Muslim part of the Nazareth experiment. Mohammed was my age, forty. He had a restaurant in Nazareth Illit, specializing in falafel and humus. He was the only

Arab operating a business that I knew of in Jewish Nazareth Illit; Khalid was his younger brother. Because they sold falafel, and we were vegetarians, they were the first people we met in the little town of Nazareth Illit.

I think at first Khalid just wanted an opportunity to improve his English by spending time with us. But we became very close friends; in the evening, when he closed the restaurant, Khalid would bring the leftover food to our apartment, where we would feast and talk late into the night.

Khalid was younger than Elias and more adventurous—he and two cousins took us camping on the shores of the Sea of Galilee, nights with campfires, incredible food, no one else near us, nights for singing and trying to fit six people into a two-person tent. Amid lots of laughter while returning home in a crowded taxi, we were caught up in a wedding procession in Kfar Cana, the bride on a white horse, everyone celebrating, traffic moving on the road between Nazareth and Tiberias at a horse's pace.

When we moved to Tel-Aviv, Khalid visited, and was the first person to get me to swim out to the breakwater in the sea, both of us nearly drowning in the rip tides. After that we were closer—we had shared a life and death experience. He was like a younger brother to me as well as to Mohammed.

What did I find out? That Christian and Muslim Palestinians could share my dreams.

When I left Nazareth, there were multiple reasons. The police and the officials of the Absorption Ministry were harassing us for associating with Arabs, to the point where my own family was being put at risk. Armed "civil guards" came to our apartment when we had Arab visitors, especially Khalid. We hadn't found jobs in the Galilee, and my wife was offered a position at Tel-Aviv University. I'd always loved Tel-Aviv.

But foremost in our decision to leave was the awareness that our so-called political activities were going to lead to more harassment, discrimination, and eventually arrest. Nazareth was too small, and my companions and I were too noticeable. To the Israeli police I was a communist organizer, just like I'd been twenty years earlier in North Carolina.

How I loved Tel-Aviv. For me it held a whiff of the atmosphere of left wing, half-crazy revolutionary Jews who'd lived in Tsarist Russia. In Tel-Aviv everyone was free to be whoever he or she wanted to be. It was uninhibited, very lively, and I felt completely at home on Rehov Daniel for over three years, more so than any place I've ever lived. I could walk down the sidewalk weeping, or out in the street yelling, and no one cared. It was understood on some level that we were all crazy, with good reason.

Jewish nationalism prevents the Kingdom from being realized; but how can we not be its victims? After the Holocaust, that any place in the world would still be Jewish was a miracle, and had to be preserved. I loved Nazareth, and loved Arab culture, and was very happy to have been absorbed into the part of the Arab community in Nazareth that accepted me.

But I was also in need of a connection to Jews. The first morning I was in Tel-Aviv I had to get milk for our baby. I met an old man laying tefilin in his grocery store, a number tattooed on his arm, who got me the milk after he'd finished *davening*.

The memories of my youth, which I thought had been erased, I found again in Tel-Aviv. I know my own view of the city is too unique for others to understand, but for me it was far more Orient than West, and I loved it. I lived two blocks from the Hassan Bek Mosque. A Jew threw a hand grenade into it, no one was injured, but the explosion frightened the whole neighborhood. I also witnessed the Border Police attack two innocent Arabs waiting for a bus in front of my building.

I was offered a job as a writer by the Jewish doctor in charge of the health system in Gaza under the Civil Administration in 1984. He built Sheba hospital in Gaza and encouraged Arab physicians. He asked me to visit all the Arab medical facilities in Gaza and Khan Yunis and write about them, as well as compose papers on public health issues such as poliomyelitis in Gaza and infant rehydration, that is, when children were dehydrated from diarrhea they were treated with infant rehydration formula, which is basically Gatorade.

In Gaza I met Eyad. And with Eyad it was like with Elias; first we ate together, got to know each other, then he took me home to meet his wife and children; then he took me to dinner at his father's house, with the whole family in attendance. We also visited a brother in his store in Gaza. But Eyad was not typical of Gaza, the same as Elias was not typical of Nazareth. Is that important, doesn't the meeting between unusual people count as much as that between ordinary people?

On the other hand, I knew doctors who took me throughout Gaza, to hospitals, clinics, well-baby programs, and I never met anyone who wasn't welcoming and gracious. Back in 1984 I, obviously an unarmed Jew, could walk alone into the main Shuk in Gaza to buy pickled turnips, and everyone was polite, and no one was hostile. But I never saw an Israeli settler, not even once in Arab Gaza, and it was two years before the first Intifada when I left.

Still, I think my own experience is valid: it is possible for a Jew to live among Arabs, for Jews and Arabs to be close friends, and for their families to meld into each other.

Perhaps, in terms of Arab-Jewish relations, it was the best of times, but nevertheless, what is possible is possible.

I am an Israeli citizen by choice. I love Israel from top to bottom, and this is totally related to my Jewishness. I love Jewish culture, Jewish history, the Jewish religion, and the Scriptures.

I believe Jews and Arabs could live together in one country if their primary allegiance was to a unified Holy Land, rather than to their own nationalist needs. Both peoples need a homeland, a refuge from a world that doesn't want them—the Right of Return has to apply to both peoples, the Jews *and* the Palestinians.

For me, Elias, Mohammed, Khalid, and Eyad were all part of a country I loved. Not because we were Jews and Arabs together proving something—because we were people who liked each other—our "politics" was to eat together, to visit each other; and back then, we all had faith in the future.

In the fall of 1985, my wife was offered a job by the US Government that was ten times her salary in Tel-Aviv; and I had three children getting ready for college. So in December we returned to the US where I spent fourteen years doing outreach to the homeless and mentally ill for the DC government. Then a set of personal circumstances led to my becoming the director of a Catholic Worker House in DC

I believe in my heart that the need for a Holy Land on this earth is even greater than the need for a Jewish homeland, or the need for a Palestinian homeland. I believe that if we don't turn Israel and Palestine into a truly Holy Land, than mankind may be doomed, but certainly the Jewish presence in Israel.

In my life, G-d has only spoken to me once in a dream. This is the dream:

I had gone up to Jerusalem. I was walking in the Old City. All around me were the little synagogues, the yeshivas, little clusters of ten-Jews in the vendors' stalls in the narrow alleyways, and all the groups of Jews were praying, and they were smiling, and they were happy. And I could see into the Churches, and the Christians were all singing and smiling and happy. And through it all was the song of the Muezzin, and all around me were Muslims walking to the Mosque, and laying out their prayer-rugs right there in the alleyways. And it is very narrow in the Jerusalem Old City alleyways, and with all these people engaged in their praying and singing and grouping together, everyone was pushed against each other, and I was easing my way through the crowd, as one does in the Old City.

And I found myself suddenly standing next to an elephant—I was standing next to this large gray leg, and as I looked up I saw it was an elephant, right there in the Old City.

And then I saw that there were four elephants, standing in a square, nose-to-tail, and that they had a canopy above them on which was a deck, with a person seated on it, and above it, supported on four golden rods, was another layer, with another four elephants, and another person seated, and another layer of four elephants, and the people were throwing flower petals out onto all the people in the Old City below them, and I was very close to the elephant and I kept looking up to see the top of the column of elephants, only it seemed to go up forever.

And I said, "What is going on here?"

And I was answered, "What, did you think the Hindus wouldn't be here too?"

The Loneliness of a Prophet: Abraham Joshua Heschel: A Daughter Remembers

Susannah Heschel

Even after twenty-five years, my father's presence remains vivid to me and my memories of him are visceral. When I think of him, my first memories are either of his humor and playfulness, or of his gentle, quiet conversations with me. I remember his delight in my childhood games, playing school or house or zoo with me, down on the floor with my dolls and toys.

When he was little, he said, he didn't play; he studied; so my games was a new world to him. At my childhood birthday parties, he loved to make up games for the children to play (sometimes to my annoyance, since he usurped the center of attention!), and our most frequent after-dinner family activity was reenacting my day at school: I was the teacher with my mother and father playing the mischievous pupils.

But what I miss most is his sensitivity to me, his attentiveness to all my worries and insecurities, his hugs and kisses; his holding my hand when we took walks on Shabbat afternoons, his enthusiasm when he first saw me at the end of a day at school. I was always amazed that he understood my adolescent insecurities and sympathized with all the frustrations I felt being a teenager and being a woman in a sexist society. Somehow he always said the right thing, whether responding to my joys or worries.

More than sympathizing, he took a stand, asking me to make *kiddush* and *havdalah,* lead *birkat ha-mazon,* or have an *aliyah,* and it was originally his idea that I apply to Rabbinical school. I suppose I was surprised at his openness because he was so much older, and had been raised in a very different culture, in Hasidic Warsaw, but his responsiveness grew out of his deep commitment to justice, and to his rejection of *halakhic* absolutism. Like the Kotzker rebbe, whom he wrote about in his last, two-volume Yiddish book, my father insisted on authenticity and felt that God loves novelty. To repeat oneself, the Kotzker taught, is to commit forgery. All of us are obligated not to imitate the Judaism of our grandparents, but to create new meanings that reflect our generation. Imitating the Judaism of the past is not authenticity, but what he called "spiritual plagiarism."

Although my father embraced all Jews, in a true reflection of the spirit of one of his ancestors, the Apter Rav, known as the "Ohev Yisrael," the lover of Israel, he himself remained a lonely figure. He was very close to his Hasidic relatives, particularly to his brother-in-law, the Kopitzinitzer rebbe, who lived in New York City, yet he was never invited to speak at Orthodox synagogues. His criticisms of the Reform and Conservative movements left many of its leaders uncomfortable. Among his faculty colleagues at the Jewish Theological Seminary, he was the only one invited constantly to lecture and teach at universities around the world and yet he was never asked to give a sermon at the Seminary services, as were other faculty.

Despite his isolation, my father retained his equanimity. He believed in what he was doing, convinced that his calls for a deeper spiritual life and a greater engagement in social issues were crucial for the survival of the Jewish people. After all, our survival, he taught, depended on our own behavior: Prayer will not save us, he wrote, prayer may make us worthy of being saved. Sometimes my parents would laugh as they read attacks on my father in the Jewish press, because the claims were so absurd and false. I remember feeling hurt and angry; I couldn't understand how anyone could fail to see the goodness of my father. Perhaps, I thought, they were fulfilling the Hasidic teaching that you are only capable of seeing in others those qualities that you have in yourself.

The most beloved of my father's books is *The Sabbath,* which evokes the atmosphere that my parents, together, created in our home. Only when he met my mother, Sylvia Straus, was my father able to produce his theological writings. Indeed, if you really want to understand a person most intimately, consider whom he or she has chosen as a life partner.

My father's political activism was very personal. His anguish over Vietnam permeated our home. My mother and I often found him up in the middle of the night unable to sleep. When Israel was threatened in the spring of 1967, the terror was palpable. Even when he was attacked (as he often was) in the Jewish press, he maintained his strong convictions. When he first spoke out on behalf of Soviet Jews, there was outrage in Jewish circles—we weren't supposed to mix in. The government of Israel tried to make him cease his efforts against the war in Vietnam, but that did not stop him. Orthodox rabbis attacked him for trying to convince the Vatican to issue a ban on conversion attempts of Jews, but he was delighted when his efforts succeeded, in *Nostra Aetate*. He always preserved his integrity and his belief in doing what was right, regardless of the lonely position in which he found himself. He did not bow to pressure, but always kept his moral position. His Judaism was not shaped by social pressures, nor by demographic concerns, but by fundamental moral convictions and religious beliefs.

Too often these days we are warned about the dire statistic of intermarriage and assimilation, but it is rare to hear voices like my father's that articulate the principles, moral and spiritual, that Judaism exemplifies. Those principles are the true reason for being Jewish. To be a Jew, my father wrote, is not simply to be, but to stand for. Every Jew must be a representative of the Jewish spirit. He was such a representative.

People mourn my father's death for many reasons. His voice of moral leadership is missed sorely today, as is his engagement in social and political issues. His scholarship on medieval Jewish philosophy and Hasidism was unique, and his theological writings gave voice to the most profound religious experiences that most of us assumed could never be articulated. But more than anything, I mourn him for his human qualities, his kindness and empathy. I have come to realize how very few good people exist, and how truly precious my father was.

So much of what Jews have created in the last twenty-five years stems from Heschel's inspiration: the Havurah movement, socially-conscious political activism, the revival of Jewish spirituality, renewed interest in Hasidism, creative Jewish theology, the renewed pride in being Jewish. *What we are missing today, however, is the voice of moral leadership that we heard with Heschel.* His prophetic tradition has been replaced by voices of witness that describe anti-Semitism, voices of doom that decry statistics of assimilation, and voices of anger that insist on narrow definitions of Judaism. They leave us with a cynical taste in our mouths; none gives us the transcendent religious vision we need.

In celebrating my father's memory, we have to bring to life the joyful and thoughtful aspects of Judaism he taught and exemplified: that we are all made in the image of God, that God's creation is filled with wonder and awe, and that God needs us as partners in caring for our fellow human beings and for all of creation.

Not That It's So Much Easier: A Poem

Dorothy Field

For me, being a Jew among Jews—Fridays I stand at the intersection dressed in black holding a sign END THE OCCUPATION protesting what Israel does in our names—razing olive groves, bulldozing homes, annexing land that was given to others.

In Israel, Women in Black get cursed, pelted with garbage. Here in Canada they're more polite. Still, we know what they say behind our backs: *Traitors, finishing what Hitler started.*

Then going home to light the candles.
There wasn't much Jewish when I was a child, still
A few words lodged—

You shall not oppress the stranger
(Remember we were strangers)
When strangers reside with you, you shall not wrong them
(We were slaves in Egypt)
Or the orphan or the widow
(Remember how we left, how we roamed the desert)
You shall teach your children

Growing up I never heard a blessing.

At home a huge Christmas tree took up most of the living room, so tall it scraped the ceiling, a six-pointed tinfoil star on top, hung with glass ornaments hand-blown in Germany—they'd been in my mother's family for generations. My parents were easier with the enormous Christmas tree than the Hanukkah menorah on the mantle.

I knew what it was to be assimilated.
It took a long time to learn to be Jewish.

Reading Sholem Aleichem, Irena Klepfisz, Kadia Molodowsky, Primo Levi, Abraham Joshua Heschel, Martin Buber. Very Jewish to learn from the pages of books.

Visiting synagogues and cemeteries: Bombay Hong Kong Rangoon New Delhi Prague Budapest Morocco Mexico City New Orleans Alabama Mississippi Paris Rome Kensington Market Lower East Side . . .

Every year at Pesach my father read these words
    From the Hagaddah:
You Shall not Oppress the Stranger
Words that held me, touched me in a way I didn't
    Understand?

I felt I was the stranger, never Jewish enough among Jews, no religious training, knowing no Hebrew, imitating the cantor's *SHEMA YISROEL* in the carpool home from Sunday school, his high-pitched wail, words we didn't know, no one explained. Bereft of culture, knowing just the few Yiddish words my parents used, the same ones radio hosts love—*schmooze schmatte schlemiel.*

Still I was a Jew. Wherever I went they knew me. In Florence at fourteen a man knocked on the car window, gave us directions to the synagogue. In Merida a French tourist picked me out. Kayaking off Vancouver Island a woman from Michigan found me.

You know the feelings of the stranger

Me, always the stranger, too Jewish for the rest of the world, trying to buy Passover matzohs in my local supermarket: *Oh, you mean maz-toes, no, we don't have them.*

Looking for secret Jews in Abiquiu, descendants of anousim who followed Columbus. Searching for scattered Jews in tiny pastel *shuls* south of Bombay. A derelict synagogue in Memphis, now a derelict jazz club, a Star of David above the cracked neon. In small towns across Oklahoma, Arizona, a hot springs resort in Arkansas.

Learning to find the old Jewish businesses in small towns across the American South, traces of Jewish merchants, middlemen to rural planters—classic brick buildings, names emblazoned on the fronts, small towns, bigger cities . . . the Jews long gone.

Remember we were strangers . . .

Unseen, misunderstood. Startled by offensive comments no one else thought twice about: The auctioneer at the farmers' market selling a lot of calves, when the bidding got slow: *Oh, the Jews from Sooke are here.* The old lady across the street, a woman I loved—every Sunday she dressed in her Salvation Army uniform, went off to church. When I told her I was Jewish: *You didn't have to tell me that, Dear. You must be good with money, Dear.*

Now Tuesday evenings I study Hebrew, learn to read the letters, right to left, sing the blessing over the candles, Friday mornings I braid challah, prepare for Shabbat . . .

Maybe because my father read:
And you shall teach your children

Though how much he wasn't sure—certainly not the old customs his parents had abandoned: the Seders at his grandparents', the long table stretching the length of the flat, his grandfather reading every prayer, his uncles begging him to hurry, my father with the other kids under the table, giddy on homemade wine. My family's Seders were tiny and dignified, no relatives, no chaos—

And no singing. We were the latest in a long story: shrimp cocktail at my Brooklyn grandmother's, sailing on Rosh Hashanah, eating our way through Yom Kippur. My mother remembered only one childhood Seder at some relative's, her embarrassment when she asked for butter at a meat meal, stuffing too-hot horseradish into her bloomers—it left a purple stain.

The sword comes into the world because of
    justice delayed

Never again, we say, meaning different things:
Never again to Us, or Never again to Anyone.

You shall welcome the stranger and those who
    are in need

As I do, welcoming Jewish strays, those whose families never observed, those who've just found a Jewish grandmother in Denmark, a father whose father was a Cohen in Scotland . . .

Because I know what it is to be shamed
for not knowing, shamed for being . . .

the wrongly imprisoned, the beggar in the street

Waiting eagerly for Pesach, the table laden with food, long evenings with friends telling stories, creating our own ways to be Jewish, making space for love and grief and . . .

The widow and the orphan

Bite of beet-red horseradish

Together they shall be . . . .

Tang of apples walnuts sweet wine

Let all who are hungry . . .

Reminding me to set the table, put out the candles,
my Seder plate from a Palestinian pottery in East Jerusalem.

Come and eat . . .

Olives, dates, pomegranates
gefilte fish, kugel
golden soup flecked with *schmaltz*

And I will bring you into the land . . .

Jerusalem, next year

I open the door for Elijah

Glossary:

Hagaddah: (Ha-GUD-ah, in Yiddish; Ha-gad-DAH in Hebrew) text read at the Passover or Pesach Seder (PAY-Sa(c)h SAY-der). The word "Seder" means "order". The word "hagaddah" means "the telling". It tells the story of Moses and the Pharaoh, the plagues, and the crossing of the Sea of Reeds (the Red Sea), tells us when to say each blessing and taste each symbolic food—wine, matzoh, bitter herbs, etc. The Haggadah's text is ever evolving. Some have been written by women for women's Seders, some to address Black people's struggle for justice, some center around the conflict in the Middle East. Pesach is primarily a home ritual; no rabbi is needed. This is one way Jews have been able to maintain our customs even while scattered in tiny pockets around the world. All we've needed was memory and one or two other Jews.

Elijah: the prophet of peace. We always have a glass of wine on the Seder table for Elijah.

At a certain point in the Seder we open the door to welcome him. In women's Seders there is also a cup for Miriam, Moses' sister, who led the Jews in singing and dancing after they crossed the Sea of Reeds.

Christian, Jews, and Muslims: A Personal Journey

Scott Kennedy

I have been a peace activist since my conscientious objection to the Vietnam War in the 1960s. My peace work has focused on changing US foreign policy to more clearly reflect the values that most Americans hold dear, such as human rights and the rule of law over brute force.

This commitment to change our nation's foreign policy has led me to work for nuclear disarmament and against US intervention in other nation's affairs. I'm often asked why a large part of my work focuses on the Israeli-Palestinian conflict. Sometimes this question reflects curiosity at the life choices of a longtime activist. Other times it's a thinly veiled accusation of anti-Semitism for the "singling out" of Israel.

My life journey includes challenges and opportunities that shaped me as a young man and inspired me to take on peace work as a vocation. Interactions with three very different individuals helped pull me into this work. One was a Christian who identified deeply with Jews. The second was an Orthodox Jew who revered Jesus. The third, a rabbi whose Jewishness led me to a lifelong commitment to nonviolence.

As a college freshman in 1968, it was my good fortune to travel to Israel with Episcopal Bishop James A. Pike, one of the most widely recognized progressive church leaders in the 1950s and 1960s.

Pike was deeply affected by Hitler's attempted extermination of European

Jewry—especially through his recognition that Christian theology often justified a pervasive and pernicious anti-Semitism and that the Church abetted the Holocaust. Pike, therefore, was devoted to building ties with the American Jewish community. He was strongly pro-Israel and prized a "State of Israel Commendation Award" he had received—a collection of archeological "lamps" in an olive wood box for "Exemplary Leadership in the Cause of Friendship between the USA and Israel."

I later learned that several prominent Palestinian Christian clergy had been influenced or helped by Bishop Pike at various stages in their vocations. But Pike dealt with them as individual cases of kindliness, rather than within a political or national context. I have a photo from 1968 of Jim Pike in the market of the Israeli Arab town of Nazareth. A rivulet of sewage makes its way down the middle of the street. Pike commented about the backwardness of the Palestinians without any apparent appreciation for the structurally unequal allocation of public resources that continues to cripple Palestinian municipalities in Israel. The Palestinians as a people were essentially invisible to him, reflecting the Eurocentric attitude that continues to dominate American perceptions of the Palestinians and their national cause. I struggled to overcome this racist attitude.

Bishop Pike and my sister Diane Kennedy invited me to travel to Europe and Israel with them in the 1968. I tagged along as their "gofer," carrying bags, making notes, and typing manuscripts while enjoying their company. Their research convinced them that the meaning of Jesus' life and teachings was most clearly understood through the lens of the inter-Testamental period of Judaism from the Maccabean Revolt in 165 B.C.E. to the time of the Bar Kochba Revolt 132–135. Jesus lived, preached, and was executed during a period of tremendous religious and political ferment when Jewish Palestine bristled under and periodically revolted against foreign rule.

Diane and Bishop Pike married in 1968. I spent early 1969 working with them as their "life of the historical Jesus" took shape. In September 1969, while enjoying a belated honeymoon, Bishop Pike died in a tragic accident in the desert East of Bethlehem. It took five days to find his body. I flew to Jerusalem to be with Diane and was with Israeli trackers when we first spotted Jim, dead from heat exhaustion and a fall on the cliff of a deep canyon above the Dead Sea. Israeli police carried his remains from the desert in a metal coffin. Diane and I buried his body in Jaffa.

During that first trip, we traveled to religious sites in Jerusalem, Bethlehem, Nazareth, and the Galilee, and to the Golan Heights and Gaza. We met extraordinary Jewish Israelis, including David Flusser, Professor of Comparative Religion at the Hebrew University.

Flusser was born in Vienna, grew up in Prague and identified fully as a Czechoslovakian. By age twenty, with WWII on the horizon, Flusser fled to Palestine as a Jew in fear for his life, a self-described "de facto Zionist."

Flusser was a practicing Orthodox Jew. He mastered Hebrew, Aramaic, Latin, Greek, and Arabic and became one of the foremost experts on the Jewish roots of Christianity. He amply demonstrated the Jewishness of Jesus through his voluminous writings. He also engendered greater communication and mutual understanding of Jews and Christians. Flusser's scholarship and his person were deeply respected in both Jewish and Christian scholarly and religious circles.

David Flusser believed that a deeper appreciation of Jesus would help Jews, Christians, and others live better lives. He often reflected on what Jesus' message might mean for how we live today. Though he thought self-defense justified in extreme situations, Flusser saw Jesus' example influencing us towards pacifism.

It is no wonder Jim Pike eagerly sought Flusser's insights and cultivated his friendship.

During the search for Jim, Anglican Archbishop George Appleton of Jerusalem conducted a special mass on Friday night at St. George's Cathedral. As the service ended, Diane and I were shocked to see Flusser sitting quietly several rows behind us in the otherwise empty church. He'd walked a considerable distance from his home to be with us.

A year later, Diane and I found the madness of the Vietnam War and the growing violence of the anti-war movement crazy-making. We left California and rented rooms in a small pension in Arab East Jerusalem in 1970. There we completed the book Jim and she had begun (*The Wilderness Revolt*, Doubleday, 1972). The innkeepers were Palestinian Christians who lost property in West Jerusalem in 1948—during what Israelis call "the War for Independence" and Palestinians "the Disaster."

The 1970 civil war in Jordan cast a pall over our lives. Our hosts could not believe that we studied Hebrew and had so many Jewish friends. Jewish friends, who often bragged about how safe Jerusalem was compared to American cities, were afraid to come to the Palestinian side of town.

Several months in Jerusalem had begun to turn my interest from the history of Palestine and Judaism at the time of Jesus to the contemporary politics of Israel and Palestine. I started reading about current events and sought out those few brave souls from the peace movement delving into Middle Eastern politics. My support for Israel from Jim Pike was rounded out by exposure to Palestinian views. Studies of Jesus and contact with Flusser strengthened my awareness of the common foundation of Jewish and Christian peacemaking.

This shift in my interest was cemented at a gathering of the War Resisters League in 1974 where I met Allan Solomonow, a Jewish pacifist active in the Jewish Peace Fellowship who also headed the Fellowship of Reconciliation's (FOR) Middle East Program. Fueled by our shared interest in Middle Eastern politics, Allan and I struck up a friendship and collaboration that lasts to this day. At his invitation, I joined an FOR 1975 delegation to Lebanon, Syria, Jordan, Egypt, Israel, and occupied Palestine.

Our delegation met remarkable Israeli Jewish pacifists such as Joseph Abileah and Yeshayahu Toma Sik. I worked with them for many years and felt a particular responsibility for building on such contacts. My extensive exposure to Jewish Israelis and their views of the conflict was matched by living on the Palestinian side. My ties to the area were strengthened by the powerful experience of loss of a loved one. I thought that someone motivated by deep appreciation for both Palestinian and Israeli peoples would have a contribution to help build a constructive role for the American peace movement.

I saw a huge blind spot in the views of many Americans. The very values that prompted social activism for human and civil rights, against the war in Vietnam, intervention in Central America, in favor of the United Nations, arms control, nuclear disarmament, nonviolence, and the rule of law over brute force, were not applied to the Israeli-Palestinian conflict. Our individual and organizational kindred spirits in the region were not known or actively supported by Americans committed to human rights and peace. Allan and I set out to change this situation by introducing American peace and justice activists to the realities of the Israeli-Palestinian conflict and enlisting their aid in changing American policy.

For three decades, we have organized delegations to Israel and the occupied Palestinian territories. We bring Israeli and Palestinian speakers to the US to advocate a two-state solution to the lengthy conflict. We encourage individuals and organizations committed to peace, justice, and human rights, to bring those principles to bear on the policies and practices of our government in the region. A fundamental change in American policy is necessary to achieve a sustainable resolution to the Israeli-Palestinian conflict.

Such groups as Gush Shalom, New Profile, Coalition of Women for a Just Peace, Yesh G'vul, the Families Forum for Bereaved Parents, and the Israeli Committee against House Demolitions have grown dramatically since those days. The

Internet makes it much easier to lend encouragement to Jews working in this country and in Israel for a political settlement that takes Palestinian rights and aspirations into account.

Still, too few people are aware that many American and Israeli Jews promote and practice nonviolence with respect to the Israeli-Palestinian conflict. Jewish peacemakers' clarity about the need to end the Israeli Occupation for the sake of both Israelis and Palestinians, persistence in the face of sometimes withering personal attack, and courage in going against the contrived consensus promoted by the media, sustain me in my work for a more just American foreign policy and help me weather false accusations of anti-Semitism.

Rabbi Michael Robinson was one such peacemaker. We served on the FOR National Council together for twenty years. Mike was a pillar of the Jewish Peace Fellowship and played a critical role in transforming the FOR from a strictly (and mostly Protestant) Christian organization into an interfaith organization. While he always cared deeply about issues, Rabbi Robinson kept the sanctity of persons foremost in his work and speech. He often said: "I'm not pro-Palestinian and I'm not pro-Israel. I'm pro-humanity."

Mike and I traveled to Israel and Palestine in 1989 during the first Palestinian Intifada as part of the Middle East Witness, a nonviolent program.

We stayed overnight in the El Bureij Refugee Camp in Gaza Strip. A 24-hour curfew was in place and strictly enforced by Israeli army patrols that stalked the narrow and deserted alleyways. Our Palestinian guides snuck us into the crowded refugee camp and hustled us along a walled corridor. Hurried knocks yielded an open metal door and we were spirited inside a walled compound, the home of an aged Palestinian woman named Sarah. We talked late into the night. A string of visitors vaulted over the high wall in the moonlight to sit cross-legged on the hard floor, sip tea, and talk with us about their life under Occupation. Mike and I slept on Sarah's concrete floor.

We also responded to a call by the townspeople of Beit Sahour, the industrious West Bank Palestinian town famous for its olive wood products, for international support on December 9, 1989, the second anniversary of the Uprising. Beit Sahour had waged a "no taxation without representation" civil disobedience campaign to protest the Israeli Occupation. Their tax resistance precipitated a crackdown by the Israeli military and seizure of lathes and other woodworking equipment and personal property. The town was closed off from the rest of the West Bank for weeks at a time. Daily demonstrations were met by swift repression by Israeli forces.

US passports allowed us to pass without difficulty through Israeli military checkpoints into Bethlehem. Soldiers stopped us on the outskirts of Beit Sahour, however, where an officer explained that the area was "closed." No one could enter or leave the town.

Rabbi Robinson wouldn't settle for "No." Approaching the soldiers, speaking Hebrew, he identified himself as a Rabbi. He returned shortly, with evident disappointment, dumfounded that his entreaties were to no avail. The soldiers barred our entry for our "own safety."

We took another route and entered Beit Sahour by foot. The streets were eerily empty. An occasional face glanced past a parted curtain or from a second story window. The townspeople were fully aware of our presence. We wondered who else was tracking our movement.

At one point, several dozen Palestinian women crossed our street a half-block ahead. Women were the heart of the first Intifada and women of Beit Sahour were known for their militancy. Our guide warned that Israeli soldiers would soon follow. A doorway unexpectedly opened and a man gently took my arm and pulled me into a modest but well kept home. Mike quickly joined me just before Israeli soldiers charged past the house.

An hour later we set off for overnight stays with Palestinian families. The next morning my host and I visited homes and businesses completely stripped of furniture and equipment. A familiar rhythmic clapping and chanting soon greeted my ears as a crowd of women moved down a narrow street toward the intersection where we stood. The demonstrators began leaving and my host motioned for me to step into a nearby shop. I decided to openly witness the goings on as soldiers arrived. I was alone on the street and immediately confronted by two soldiers.

The officer in charge of the roadblock the day before arrived. "Didn't I tell you yesterday that you couldn't be here? Where's the Rabbi?" he demanded. I said I had no idea. The officer motioned to a young soldier to place me in the back of a truck. The soldier climbed onto the bench across from me. Would I please tell him the Rabbi's whereabouts? I demurred. He then simply moved on, asking me about the California earthquake two months earlier and commented how scary it must have been.

I motioned to the scene outside, "You've had your own earthquake." His voice suddenly softened. He used to bring his family to picnic nearby on the Sabbath, but they come no more. "And now," he shrugged, rifle resting across his knees, "here I am like this." Clearly he thought the Israeli army had no place chasing women through the streets.

As we wound our way through town, I peered out the open back of the truck.

It might be a long time before I'd see Beit Sahour again. Passing through a small town square, my eyes fixed on a group of Palestinian men by a church. All wore the traditional checkered scarves over their heads. One man straightened up and flashed the two-fingered "V" sign, the symbol of the Palestinian Uprising.

There he was—the Rabbi!

Wearing a *kufiyeh* and looking every bit a relative to the Semitic Palestinian cousins surrounding him, Rabbi Robinson blessed my departure with a wave of his hand and a broad smile.

Within the hour, I was back in Jerusalem. After observing the Intifada from the other side of the barricades, Rabbi Robinson came out of Beit Sahour a day later.

Later we met with a dozen representatives of various Jewish peace groups. At one point, a self-congratulatory tone entered the conversation when an Israeli described weekend picnics in Beit Sahour to support their tax resistance. An active war tax resister since the Vietnam War, Mike asked: "Wouldn't you better honor the Palestinians' tax resistance, not by applauding their efforts, but by refusing to pay taxes to support the Occupation?" A shocked silence covered the room.

Rabbi Robinson's commitment to a just peace in Israel and Palestine was deeply rooted in his Jewishness and manifested in his active and profound belief in nonviolence. He worked shoulder to shoulder with Palestinian Arabs and Christian Americans as well as Jewish Israelis.

I often think of the contrast between my life and lives led by the people of Beit Sahour and the young Israeli soldiers now staffing roadblocks or chasing young demonstrators. Santa Cruz has recovered from its 1989 earthquake, but the shifting geopolitical tectonic plates constantly convulse Israel and Palestine.

A dozen years after Mike Robinson and my adventure in Beit Sahour, Palestinians were nine months into the "Al Aqsa Intifada," the second uprising named for the third holiest shrine of Islam where protest erupted in September 2000.

This Uprising was far more violent, women's leadership was far less evident, and there was widespread use of weapons and suicide bombings by the Palestinians. The preponderance of casualties on both sides were civilians, many of them children.

The first Intifada ushered in a hopeful period of peace talks and first-ever mutual recognition by Israel and the P.L.O. The Al Aqsa Intifada, in contrast, symbolized the collapse of the peace process and exhaustion of earlier hopes for coexistence of the two peoples.

In 2001, while on my way back to Beit Sahour, the town was again sealed off from the world by the Israeli military. I carried in my heart the image of Rabbi

Robinson, his face framed by the kufiyeh, standing with Palestinian villagers, flashing the sign of the Uprising as Israeli soldiers hauled me away.

He could have been Sarah's son. And Sarah would have been proud of this remarkable rabbi.

Rabbi Michael Robinson embodied for me the possibility of finding common ground with people whom others insist are enemies, the possibility that Jews and Arabs, Israelis and Palestinians, Middle Easterners and Americans can overcome the Occupation and build a future together.

Christians, Jews, and Muslims.

A Peace of Mind

E. James Lieberman

When her family left Odessa for America in 1905, Mom once said it was a time when Jewish men were willing to amputate a toe in order to avoid the tsar's military service. Dad's family emigrated around that time from Gorodok, Kovel, in Russian Poland. In part, then, my two grandfathers emigrated to avoid soldiering; shared fate brought them to Milwaukee where ultimately there were five children on Mom's side and eight (of eleven born) on Dad's. Our elders spoke Yiddish among themselves at times; we kids absorbed only a few words.

Grandpa L., a fur trapper in the old country, became a peddler in Wisconsin, while Grandpa P. got started in the furniture business. Dad and only one brother went through college; most of Mom's sibs did. Having thought of becoming a rabbi, Dad instead went to medical school and was in practice when my parents married in 1930. Despite three children and a busy practice he volunteered for the US Army in 1942 to join the fight against Hitler. After stints in Florida and Pennsylvania, he was sent to Oakland, preparatory to being sent overseas to fight Japan. Only seven at the time, I fought WWII vicariously at the movies, went to college and medical school in the 1950s, and was too old for the Vietnam War, by which time I was a psychiatrist by training and a pacifist by a process I can only surmise.

In the summer of 1943, Mom packed up our stuff and drove from Milwaukee to Oakland with Marcia, eleven, Edith, five, and me, eight. Dad's orders to ship out never came, however, and he served at the Oakland Army Hospital, and we stayed in the States for "the duration." I saw *Bataan* and *Corregidor* along with lots of cowboy serials on Saturday afternoons, identifying with the heroes but feeling vulnerable, too. Some of Dad's patients were German and Italian prisoners. My eldest cousin and youngest uncle were also in uniform, somewhere. Mom and Dad were liberal, attuned to the news, generally calm. I was startled one April day coming home to find Mom crying because Franklin Roosevelt had died.

We settled in Oakland after the war. Tech High was our neighborhood school; though only twelve percent of students were "college prep" there were good teachers in all subjects—academics, music, typing, drama, shop, and athletics. The student body was diverse: Black, Latino, Japanese (just-returned from wartime detention), Chinese, Italian, Portuguese, and a handful of Jewish kids in a class of 600. The California School for the Blind mainstreamed students there. I learned to offer (not grab) an arm to help a blind classmate and to respect their special skills—reading braille, wrestling, playing piano and chess. Our chess team, half-blind, was good enough to be invited to San Quentin Prison, where we mostly lost to players who didn't look like dangerous criminals. I took wrestling seriously, a good nonviolent contact sport for a small guy, competing alongside blind teammates to win the city championship. My parents, too skittish to watch, just tolerated my love of going to the mat. I mastered chopsticks and enjoyed the strangeness of offbeat Chinese restaurants with Puey-Chong, an immigrant from Taiwan. We graduated in 1951; I lost a classmate in the Korean War but only found out about it at my 25th reunion.

We attended annual Seders, usually hosted by family friends, but I did not become Bar Mitzvah: wartime dislocation enabled my parents, who seemed indifferent, to let it drop. We joined a Temple where I was confirmed, having sung in the choir and learned about Judaism and other religions. Unfortunately I recall only one inspiring teacher in three years, and a higher proportion of disruptive classmates than at Oakland Tech (I was a quiet, respectful kid.) Mom was a good violinist who loved playing string quartets. She seemed to prize her non-Jewish friends: she had a yearning for general acceptance along with doubt that non-Jews could be trusted.

Going along to get along—non-confrontation—was my modus operandi then. In fourth grade I accepted a piece of bread at a friend's house after school, realized it was Passover, and consumed it with guilt rather than try to explain. Years later, on a walk home from an orchestra rehearsal (I played cello) a new kid (trumpet) from Vermont said he liked California, except that there were too many Jews. A decent guy, he obviously didn't know I was Jewish; I said nothing. Mom and Dad were alarmed but I shrugged it off. Though shy, I kept girls in focus. I took a girl from confirmation class (not a Tech student) to senior prom, dated mostly non-Jewish women in college and medical school, and then married within the faith.

Bouncing around the country as an Army brat, I became a letter writer and saver, stamp collector and geography buff. In my teens, international postal chess came naturally, where each of seven in a group plays the other six simultaneously. Each tournament took at least a year by airmail. Mom knew German and French and enjoyed translating cards and letters from a few eager correspondents who didn't know English. One of them was Paul Schulte, a German family man with three children who was twenty years older. Later we learned—it should have been no surprise—that he had served in Hitler's army.

Starting UC Berkeley, apolitical, barely aware of the loyalty oath controversy that had racked the campus, I cared more about the championship Golden Bears football team. As a pre-med student German was my choice of language. In compulsory ROTC we learned to carry, shoot and clean rifles, and read topographic maps—which I knew well from backpacking in the Sierra. The wrestling coach welcomed me. Thanks to Professors Sears Jayne and Mark Schorer I came to love literature. After doing a paper on religion for which I read some freethinkers, I turned agnostic. Pacifica Radio's KPFA-FM brought, among others, talks by Milton Mayer, a feisty Jewish pacifist and regular contributor to *The Progressive*. My father got me to read a biography of Dr. William Osler, the great, original teacher of bedside medicine who married late in life and had one son who was killed at the end of World War I. A poem by Walt Whitman, *Come up from the Fields Father*, captures and conveys for me the shock and grief of such a death.

In 1954, after junior year, I planned my first trip abroad. Herr Schulte, who had encouraged a visit, sent a letter saying he assumed I was Jewish, that he had fought in the war, and was deeply apologetic. He offered the "du" pronoun instead of "sie" along with a plea that I visit him and his family in their home. Mom and Dad feared things were going too far, that my eagerness to accept was understandable but immature. Mom's beloved German professor from Wisconsin had moved to Stanford and I'd met him. He—B.Q. Morgan—read the letter and concluded that Paul was offering genuine friendship. A storm brewed as my plan became known. At that time many Jews refused to buy German products, speak German, play or even listen to music by Wagner. Cellist Leonard Rose, a family friend, would not perform in Germany after the war, and urged me not to cross that boundary.

Still, I went on my own by student ship to Europe, stayed in youth hostels, rode an English bicycle and relied on trains for longer jaunts. After London,

Paris, and northern Italy I spent a few days in Yugoslavia, the first Iron Curtain country to allow Americans in, and discovered that Esperanto was a working international language. (I heard of it first from a Finnish postal chess player.) Ludwig Zamenhof (1859–1917), "Dr. Esperanto," the Polish-Jewish physician who developed the international language, became world famous in his time. He was a peacemaker concerned with linguistic rights of minorities and his spiritual mentor was Rabbi Hillel.

Senator Joe McCarthy and his ilk fostered rampant anti-Communism in those days. The Austrian in our chess group was supposedly a Communist, but, invited and undaunted, I spent a pleasant night at his house.

Although it was nine years since the end of World War II, signs of its destructiveness persisted in Europe. There were still city blocks of rubble, pockmarked countryside, and many, many amputees. In their modest house in the industrial city of Hagen, the Schulte family welcomed me, crowding themselves to give me my own room and bath. Paul handed me a pack of toilet tissue saying "*nur für dich* [only for you]" while they were using newsprint. He took me for a walk the first day. Pausing near a bomb crater, one of many, he said, "*Wir sind kriegmüde* [we are war-weary]." There was no mention of Allied air raids in one of which they lost a three-year-old daughter. When it comes to bombs, it hardly matters whose they are. The results on the ground are the same. After three days of total immersion in German, in the bosom of a loving family, I left for Denmark. Rita, fourteen, in tears, gave me a farewell hug. Over my protest, Paul stuffed his prized pocket chess set into my bag.

In September, after a restful voyage home, I started medical school—with human anatomy and cadavers. For a semester, at each of twenty metal tables, four students studied and dissected a body. Most of us had never seen a dead person, much less a whole platoon of them. I had come from a war zone to a death chamber. From then on I morphed into a pacifist.

The details are lost, but I read Gandhi and Lincoln Steffens, found a Friends Meeting where someone said, "Live as though you'll die tomorrow; learn as though you'll live forever." Milton Mayer's *They Thought They Were Free* came out in 1955, telling stories of ten Germans he knew in pre-war Germany whom he interviewed after the Holocaust. Among them I recognized people like the Schultes, but also patriotic Americans who approved of placing Japanese-Americans into internment camps and were also ready and willing to incinerate cities—if necessary, whole countries!—with atom bombs.

I spent the summer of 1956 working at the Sonoma State Hospital for the mentally retarded. The dedication of the staff to society's castoffs impressed me; caring for them is a worthwhile expenditure of time, effort, and money for a civilized people. I could not and cannot say the same for "national defense." I supported Linus Pauling, the American Friends Service Committee, and the campaign against nuclear testing. Adlai Stevenson received my first vote for President.

Torn between psychiatry and public health as career choices, I luckily found a mentor in Brock Chisholm, M.D., who came to the University of California at San Francisco (UCSF) to lecture. A Canadian psychiatrist, retired brigadier general, and first head of the World Health Organization, he combined the two fields, presenting a personal, non-bureaucratic approach to public health, and a visionary yet practical social psychiatry. In 1957 I attended the annual world Esperanto congress in Marseilles and became convinced that the language worked beautifully, and that its failure to catch on as a universal second tongue is due not to any linguistic fault but to societal inertia, nationalist jingoism, and disdain on the part of uninformed intellectuals, especially academic linguists. As G. K. Chesterton said about Christianity, it hasn't been tried and found wanting—it hasn't really been tried.

In April 1958 I spent two weeks living with a doctor-mentor near Carmel, the home of Milton Mayer. When we met, I asked whether I would be doing more good proceeding with an internship or applying for CO status, or both. He recalled an exchange between William Penn and George Fox, his Quaker mentor. Penn supposedly wondered whether, despite his station in life that dictated he wear a sword, he should put it away in concert with Quaker principles. Fox answered, "Wear it as long as thou canst." Mayer, the radical, counseled moderation. There was no urgency to make a statement. Mayer himself answered a question about converting from Judaism to a faith (Quakerism) more supportive of his views: "If I can't be a good Jew, why should I be a bad Christian?"

The UCSF campus weekly, *Synapse*, published "An Open Letter to My Draft Board" May 23, 1958, my parting shot. Noting that Selective Service Boards required medical students to check in within five days of graduation, I contrasted the ethics of healing—caring for all sufferers with equal concern and regard—versus an ideology which tolerates, even encourages, war and capital punishment. Grateful that doctors could perform national service in the Public Heath Service (PHS), I explained that I came to my peace commitment without a traditional CO religious background. One sentence is both dated and timely: "Since the end of the Korean war we Americans have spent over $200 billion for defense against

Communism, which continues to make headway in a world where half the people are still hungry."

I interned at the US PHS Hospital, Staten Island, in New York City, and wore a naval uniform. In November 1958 there was a crisis in Lebanon and the PHS was suddenly on standby. For a few days I was not sure whether to refuse if called for military duty but we were not called up. But I remember at least two of my fellow interns being understanding and supportive. That spring I applied for residency in psychiatry at the Massachusetts Mental Health Center (MMHC) in Boston, and UCSF as a "safety." I was accepted at MMHC but not UCSF, and wonder if my anti-war letter to *Synapse* had cost me.

Employment at MMHC required taking a loyalty oath for state employees. That bothered me. Dr. Jack Ewalt, its Chief of Psychiatry, said I could work for free or try to get someone in the State House to excuse me from taking the oath. I met with an assistant state Attorney General briefly to satisfy him that I did not want to overthrow anything by force or violence, so approval to pay me came through. But there was yet another oath. MMHC was a teaching hospital. The new residents received notice of appointment as Teaching Fellows, the lowest rank at prestigious Harvard University. Two of us from California sent the papers back unsigned, because a teachers' oath was required. Dr. Ewalt called us in for a scolding and asked us to resign. Already somewhat surprised that all Harvard faculty (all teachers in the state, public and private) had been signing the oath since 1935, we were stunned, and said we wanted to stay. It was a horrible moment. We were also told we would teach (medical students) without a title, but if we ever communicated with the Harvard Corporation again without approval we would be fired. We readily accepted that. There was a story in the *Harvard Crimson* about this incident and I later wrote an article, "The Oath as a Political Defense."[1] In 1967 the Supreme Court ruled the oath to be unconstitutional.

That was my first civil disobedience and active nonviolent confrontation. As a young psychiatrist I was impressed by Gandhi's psychological sophistication. He said that he wanted people in his "army" who were capable of violence but who chose to be nonviolent, thus screening out pacifists whose fear of their own aggression was unresolved. In the next few years I heard Martin Luther King, Jr. speak, joined groups demonstrating at Groton, Connecticut, against Polaris submarines and at Ft. Detrick, Maryland, against germ warfare. Active in Physicians for Social Responsibility, I wrote on pacifist themes. Peace candidate H. Stuart Hughes engaged many of us in a futile campaign for the Senate against Ted Kennedy in 1962. After residency and a year of public health we moved to Washington, DC, where I could fulfill my service obligation at the National Institutes of Mental Health. The boss there told me that he put in a good word for me in response to a security query from a Government agent about my past. I extended the required two years to seven—President Kennedy had launched a national mental health program calling for 2,000 community mental health centers by 1980. Sadly, by 1970, President Johnson's Vietnam War had drained much of the funding away. I refused the telephone tax imposed to support the war, but the Government, rather than take us to court, garnisheed the small amounts from my bank account.

Along the way I met Rabbi Abraham Cronbach, a co-founder of the Jewish Peace Fellowship, in Indianapolis in 1961, and heard an inspirational television interview of Rabbi Abraham Heschel by Carl Stern.[2] My wife and I joined a Temple where a liberal rabbi did not respond to my offer to give a seminar on nonviolence after King's death. I visited Israel in 1974, and found it both inspiring and troubling. Most Israelis are not religious, yet the Orthodox have disproportionate influence. I was and am still troubled by the dependence of Israel on American foreign and military aid, by the power of American Israel Public Affairs Committee (AIPAC), and by the emphasis on militancy by the Israeli right and its Christian fundamentalist supporters.

Pacifism is to war as public health is to medicine, where costly pharmaceuticals pretend to compensate for what is often failed prevention. The Government never acted on my CO application, finding it easier to extend my student deferment. I am not an absolute pacifist. The war in Bosnia to stop Milosevic seemed worth fighting, but I want to choose my battles, while soldiers follow orders. Most wars are wrong and most are preventable. Our government behaves as though procuring ever more armaments is a sure way to peace rather than a temptation and spur to make wars, big and small.

Psychotherapy, my pseudo-Rabbinical career of forty-five years, resonates with nonviolence. It is the opposite of "shoot first; ask questions later." In this, asking the right questions in the right way means you never have to shoot. Therapists help sufferers observe and address themselves, including their worst thoughts and impulses. Gandhi might call that part the "opponent." He would join with Freud to insist that the internal opponent be treated with respect in our effort to win it over to the way of peace and the goal of justice.

Notes

1 "The Oath as a Political Defense," UCSF *Synapse,* May 23, 1958 and *Harvard Crimson*, November 27, 1959.

2 NBC-TV, February 3, 1973. See Heschel, A.J., *Moral Grandeur and Spiritual Audacity,* edited by Susannah Heschel, New York: Farrar Straus Giroux, 1996, pp. 395–412. See, too, my articles such as Grinspoon, L. and Lieberman, E.J., "Escape from the Bomb," *The New Republic*, September 4, 1961 and Lieberman, E.J., "Psychochemicals as Weapons," *Bulletin of the Atomic Scientists* 18:1:11-14, 1962.

Jewish Secularism

Bennett Muraskin

"Merely to be gentle is not yet to be good. . . . If pacifism is purely a blend of lemonade and empty rhetoric, it cannot be what democrats believe it should be: the active unconditional resistance of human reason. It is imperative to distinguish between struggle and war."

Ernst Bloch (1885–1977)

Growing up as a red-diaper baby and a secular Jew during the 1960s and 1970s, I was not too keen on pacifism. The major milestones of progress, I was taught, were violent revolutions—the French and especially the Russian. We admired the Red Army both for its success in the Civil War that brought victory to the Bolsheviks and in World War II. Because of its role in defeating the Nazis, the lefty Jews in my Yiddish *shule* depicted it as the savior of western civilization in general and the Jewish people in particular. Our heroes were the volunteers of the Abraham Lincoln Brigade who fought Franco's fascist armies in Spain, and the Jewish resistance fighters who led the Warsaw Ghetto uprising. The partisan hymn, *Zog Nit Keynmol* (Never Say) inspired us with hope and courage, one line proclaiming that it "was sung with weapons in hand."

The Marxism I embraced in my youth preached class struggle and the necessity of violent revolution. Although we had already rejected the Soviet model, many of us saw Red China or Cuba as beacons of socialism and both nations were not shy about glorifying military prowess. During the Vietnam War, we ardently supported the National Liberation Front, admiring its fighting skills against overwhelming American firepower. With the emergence of the Black Panther Party in the mid 1960s, which glorified armed resistance to police—aka "pigs"—and used an automatic weapon as one of its symbols, we signified our solidarity by chanting "Revolution has Come; It's Time to Pick Up the Gun."

I was aware of the role of pacifists in the anti-war movement, especially A. J. Muste and David Dellinger, but they could not hold a candle in my imagination to Che Guevara spreading revolution throughout South America through guerilla warfare. I admit to not even knowing of the existence of the Jewish Peace Fellowship during that era, and I am fairly certain that I was typical of radical Jewish youth.

It has often been said that a disproportionate number of white civil rights activists were secular Jews, but they did not articulate a Jewish ethic for their activism. Stanley Levison, a leftist secular Jew, became a close advisor to Martin Luther King, Jr. Yet King's nonviolence came from the Christian tradition and from Gandhi, a Hindu. Theodore Bikel was the exception in this regard. He once sang a Yiddish socialist song in the original and in his own English translation to a mass meeting held in a Black church in Birmingham Alabama.

I have come to the conclusion that secular Jews of East European ancestry have not played a significant role in the pacifist movement or in support of the pacifist cause. The *Encyclopedia of the American Left* has numerous entries about secular leftist Jews and the institutions they founded or led, but only two Jewish names appears in its entry on "Pacifism"—poet Allen Ginsberg and Paul Goodman. True, Ginsberg was a child of East European immigrants, but his pacifism derived from his Buddhism. Maurice Isserman has a chapter, "Radical Pacifism," in his book, *If I Had a Hammer. . . The Death of the Old Left and the Birth of the New Left*. He discusses the role of Norman Thomas, A. J. Muste, Bayard Rustin, David Dellinger, etc., but the only Jew he names is the very unconventional Paul Goodman.

Why this under-representation, when East European Jews and their descendants were so over-represented on the left in general? Secular Jews in Eastern Europe were rebels against the Jewish religious establishment. The rabbis' secret to Jewish survival was, of course, adherence to Jewish law, but just as important, submission to Gentile power. As long as Jews did not cause trouble for Gentile rulers, they would be allowed to regulate their own affairs. Should anti-Semites threaten the Jewish community, the tried and true strategy was to appeal to the highest Gentile authorities and seek their protection, often through bribery. If Jews kept their heads down and rolled with the punches, they would outlast their enemies and in God's good time, the Messiah would arrive and return Jews from exile to the Land of Israel. It was this traditional Jewish version of "pacifism" that secular Jews rejected. It appeared as an excuse for passivity.

In place of religion, the most politically active among secularized East European Jews adopted either socialism or Zionism. The former, with its emphasis on class struggle and social revolution had no use for pacifism. Jewish socialists opposed "capitalist" and "imperialist" wars, but not class war. It was impossible to convince them that the tyrannical anti-Semitic Tsarist regime could be toppled by nonviolent means. Zionists sought to create a new Jew—a pioneering nationalist—who would settle a new land and be willing to defend it against the native population. Their heroes were Jewish warriors: the Macabbees and Bar Kochba. Pacifism was the last thing on the Zionist agenda.

There were exceptions among the Zionists, but they tended to be German in origin. Two out of three most prominent Zionist advocates of Jewish pacifism (and Arab-Jewish equality) were religious humanists: Martin Buber, who initially supported Germany in World War I and Rabbi Judah Magnes, who opposed it from the beginning. Buber came from Germany; Magnes was the American-born child of Polish and German immigrants. The best known German-Jewish pacifist by far, Albert Einstein, "religious" only in Spinoza's sense of the term, vigorously condemned World War I, but like the others supported the Allied war effort in World War II.

Perhaps the best known East European Jewish Zionist pacifist was A. D. Gordon, the spiritual father of the kibbutz movement. An immigrant from Russia who came to Palestine in 1904, he personally advocated cooperation with the Arab population. However, his embrace of the "conquest of labor" provoked Arab resistance by insisting that Jewish employers hire only Jewish workers. His beloved kibbutzim barred Arabs and were often built on the site of former Arab villages.

Non-Zionist or anti-Zionist Jewish pacifists from Eastern Europe or of East European origin include the religious Natan Hofshi and the secular Toma Sik, both of whom were active as advocates of nonviolence and conscientious objection in Israel, and American violin virtuoso Yehudi Menuhin. But more typically, they were German Jews—Marxist humanist philosopher Ernst Bloch, anarchist, martyr and intimate of Martin Buber, Gustav Landauer and the German-born Israeli peace activist Uri Avnery, all secular Jews. The anarchist Rudolph Rocker, a non-Jew who learned Yiddish, lived among Jewish workers and became the charismatic leader of Jewish anarchists in England and the US, was also from Germany. Only

Hofshi is featured in the book *The Challenge of Shalom,* which traces the Jewish tradition of peace and justice. Menuhin is briefly mentioned, but none of the others. As far as I know, all suspended their pacifism during World War II.

Why did most pacifist Jews come from Germany? Was it the influence of the *Haskalah* or Jewish Enlightenment that originated with the German Jew Moses Mendelssohn who was inspired by his encounter with European liberalism? Or perhaps their affinity for the Christian pacifist tradition within Central Europe begun by the 16th century Anabaptists and continued by their Mennonite descendants? Many German Jews, including Buber and Einstein, were familiar with Christianity and fascinated by the personality of Jesus, who can legitimately be considered a pacifist.

I have long wondered what is there in Jewish tradition to sustain leftist secular Jews in their anti-war or pacifist positions. The Torah itself is a very militaristic text: The ancient Hebrews are on a mission from God to conquer Canaan by force and are explicitly commanded to exterminate the native inhabitants. The subsequent books of the Jewish Bible are no better. Joshua, Judges, Samuel, and Kings are full of violence and warfare. The Prophets provide many lofty sayings, including "Not by Might, Nor by Power, But by My Spirit Saith the Lord," but the prophets' dedication to peace is highly conditional. If the Jews obey God's laws, as interpreted by the Prophets themselves, swords will be beaten into plowshares and nations will study war no more; but if the Jews disobey, plowshares will be beaten into swords and God will exact horrific punishment. Selective quotation is a tricky business that, in my opinion, should be approached with great caution.

I plead guilty myself to being influenced by prophetic literature. I entitled my book of biographies of secular/humanist progressive Jews *Let Justice Well Up Like Water*, a quote from Amos 5:24, but I believe that the prophets were more authentically committed to social justice than to peace. For example, Jeremiah advocated submission to the Babylonians, not out hatred for war, but out of a conviction that foreign conquest was necessary to punish the Jews for their sins. Above all, the Prophets were fanatical in their insistence on religious conformity and, therefore, terrible role models for progressive Jews.

Talmudic sources are equally ambiguous. The Talmud is so massive that diverse and conflicting opinions on a seeming infinite variety of subjects abound, but the sad fact is that the prevailing Rabbinic opinion was that the injunction to "love your neighbor as yourself" did not apply to non-Jews. The famous quote that concluded *Schindler's List* and appears in so many books about Judaism, "Whoever kills one soul is as if he destroyed mankind. Conversely, whoever saves one soul is as though he has saved the whole world" is actually the less authoritative version of *Mishnah Sanhedrin 4:5* and *Talmud Sanhedrin 37a*. Both add the words "in Israel," after "soul," thereby limiting its scope to Jews only. Jewish law *(Halakha)*, the preponderance of the Talmud, does not treat non-Jews with respect.

Agada, the non-legal portions of the Talmud, consisting mainly of folklore, as well as the folklore that comprises much of the *Midrash* are a more fertile source for progressive humanistic ideals, including pacifist ones. For example, the earliest invocation to *tikkun olam* comes from *Agada*, in particular *Pirkey Avot*, a tractate from the *Mishna* in which Rabbi Tarfon says: "It is not your obligation to complete the task [of perfecting the world], but neither are you free to desist [from doing your part.]" Hillel's familiar ethical maxims (What is hateful to you do not do to your fellow etc.), so fundamental to humanistic values, come from the same source.

If there is any Jewish sage who could be cited in support for pacifism, it would be Yohanan ben Zakkai, the rabbi who opposed continued resistance to Rome during the 68–72 C.E. rebellion that resulted in massive bloodshed and the destruction of the Second Temple. He faked his death so he could be smuggled out of Jerusalem. He then obtained Roman approval to establish a Rabbinic academy. His nonviolent approach, rather than the fanatic belligerence of the Jewish rebels, is often credited with ensuring the survival of the Jewish people. Hans Kohn grew up in Prague and lived in Paris, London, and Palestine before making his way to the US in 1933. A critical scholar of modern nationalism, he joined Magnes and Buber in advocating a bi-national state in Palestine. Kohn claimed to draw inspiration from Yohannan ben Zakkai's pacifism in advocating international cooperation as an alternative to war.

Two books of the Bible, Ruth and Jonah, stand out for their messages of respect and compassion for the non-Jewish "other," an essential precondition for peace and justice. In fact, they are among the very few books of the Bible where no one is killed by God or man.

The Moabites are reviled in the Torah, but in the Book of Ruth, these putative enemies of the Jewish people welcome a Jewish family fleeing famine. Contrary to Jewish law, the two sons in this family married Moabite women, one of them Ruth. When they died, Ruth chose to return to Judah with Naomi, her mother-in-law. By affirming her love for the Jewish people, Ruth was accepted as a Jew. No indoctrination or conversion ceremony was required. And she did not become just any Jew, but the great grandmother of King David.

Jonah is a reluctant prophet who flees from God rather than accept an assignment to preach repentance to the Assyrians of Nineveh. To make his escape, he boards a ship, but God sends a storm to cause a shipwreck. The non-Jewish sailors seek to save Jonah and only agree to throw him overboard when Jonah insists. The whale or big fish swallows him and spits him out at Nineveh. In short order, the people of Nineveh repent and God forgives them, but Jonah is upset because he fancied himself a prophet of doom. God answers: "And should not I care about Nineveh, that great city, in which there are more than a hundred and twenty thousand persons who do not yet know their right hand from their left (referring to the children) and many beasts as well!" Here God extends his compassion to non-Jews, men, women and children, who prove capable of moral redemption. There is no other book of the Bible where non-Jews are depicted so favorably, where God concerns himself with their fate and where He uses peaceful persuasion, rather than threats and violence, to teach a lesson in universal human dignity.

Drawing on the Yiddish tradition, my favorite source of humanistic values, I have found two folktales that clearly embrace the concept of nonviolent civil disobedience:

> The story is told that the leading men of the community were unsatisfied with the work of the caretaker of Rabbi Yoshe-Ber's Rabbinical court in Brisk. They held a meeting and decided to fire the caretaker. Then they gave the task of dismissing him to Rabbi Yoshe-Ber, but he refused.
>
> "Why not, Rabbi?" the community leaders asked. "You're the rabbi and he's your employee."
>
> "I'll tell you," Rabbi Yoshe-Ber replied. "Since you read and know the story of the sacrifice of Isaac, you know that when the Blessed Name commanded Abraham to sacrifice Isaac, we find that it is written that He Himself spoke as follows: 'Take now thy son, thine only son . . . ' But when He commanded Abraham to spare Isaac, God sent an angel, as it is written, 'And the angel called unto Abraham . . . '
>
> "This poses a question. Why was it that the Blessed Name did not send an angel at the beginning? The answer is that He knew very well that no angel would have accepted the assignment. Each of them would have said, 'If You want to command death, You had better do it Yourself.' "
>
> (*Yiddish Folktales,* ed. by Beatrice Silverman Weinreich)

And one on the lighter side:

> To a Rabbinical school in Old Russia, the military came in search of recruits. The entire student body was drafted.
>
> In camp, the students amazed their new masters by their marksmanship on the rifle range. Accordingly, when war broke out, the Yeshiva youths were ordered en masse into the front lines.
>
> Shortly after the contingent arrived an attack began. Far in the distance, in No Man's Land, an advancing horde of Germans appeared. The Tsarist officers called out, "Ready . . . aim . . . fire!"
>
> But no fire was forthcoming.
>
> "Fire!" yelled the officers. "Didn't you hear? Fire, you idiots, fire!"
>
> Still nothing happened.
>
> Beside himself with rage, the commanding officer demanded, "Why don't you fire?"
>
> One of the youths mildley answered, "Can't you see . . . there are people in the way. Somebody might get hurt."
>
> (*A Treasury of Jewish Folklore*, ed. By Nathan Ausabel)

I included these stories, as well as others from *Agama* and *Madras*, in my book, *Humanist Readings in Jewish Folklore*, which I wrote for the express purpose of introducing secular Jews to the humanist elements in Jewish tradition.

Where are the secular Jewish pacifists and anti-war activists in the US today? Howard Zinn is a pacifist. Noam Chomsky may not identify himself as such, but his anti-war record is without blemish. Yet I would argue that their Jewishness is peripheral to their public life. Bikel is still with us, a strong voice for peace and reconciliation in Israel/Palestine, active in Meretz USA. Of the three explicitly secular Jewish organizations in North America, the Workmen's Circle, the Congress of Secular Jewish Organizations and the Society for Humanistic Judaism, the first two have long demonstrated strong anti-war commitments, extending to support for a two-state settlement in Israel/Palestine and opposition to the US invasion of Iraq.

All three draw on humanistic elements in both the socialist Yiddish and left Zionist traditions. Yiddish writer I. L Peretz's poem, *Ale Mentchen Zaynen Brider*

(All Men are Brothers), put to the melody of Beethoven's Ninth symphony, the Bundist unity song, *Ale Brider* (All Brothers) and Yiddish poet Avrom Reisen's inspirational *Dos Naye Leed* (The New Song), along with the Hebrew *Bashana Haba'ah* (Soon the Day Will Arrive), *Hiney Ma Tov* (Oh, How Good), derived from Psalm 133:1 and *Lo Yisa Goy* (Vine and Fig Tree) (derived from Isaiah 2:4 and Micah 4:4) are frequently heard at their gatherings.

Jewish Currents, a magazine edited by Lawrence Bush, represents the intellectual and literary legacy of the secular Jewish left. As the combined voice of the Workmen's Circle and former Jewish communists, it is broadly sympathetic to a pacifist agenda. And progressive Jews of all persuasions work together in organizations like B'rit Tsedek v'Shalom, Americans for Peace Now and Jews for Racial and Economic Justice.

I still cannot say that I consider myself a pacifist. On a case-by-case basis, however, I find myself having a harder and harder time justifying war. Some wars start out looking "good," but the "cure" turns out at least as bad as the disease. For example, in the case of Kosovo, the war launched by NATO in 1999 succeeded in stopping the Serbs from expelling Albanians, but resulted in Albanians expelling Serbs. Furthermore, the bombing of Belgrade did far more harm to civilians than to the Yugoslav government or military. The classic "good war," World War II, which I still think was necessary, ended with the incineration of over 200,000 Japanese and involved other grave war crimes committed by the anti-fascist coalition.

In Israel/Palestine, a complete cessation of violence on both sides, as part and parcel of a comprehensive negotiated two-state solution, may sound utopian, but in the final analysis is the only rational alternative to more suffering and misery.

At the end of the day, secular Jews are also secular humanists. Humans are social by nature and find meaning in relationships. Humanists long for and strive toward a world of mutual care and concern, free of cruelty and its consequences, where differences are resolved cooperatively, without resorting to violence.

Humanism's Yiddish counterpart, the poem *Dos Naye Leed*, mentioned above, is also clearly compatible with pacifist ideals:

> And though delayed may be the day when love and peace join hands,
>   Yet it will come, for it must come, no dream; it's our command.

> I hear the song of mighty throngs, the song of peace in chorus.
>   And each voice sings, as each note rings: "The sun is rising for us."

And end to night, the world grows bright with hope, with joy and giving.
I hear the sound, it's all around: "To courage, strength and living!"

(Translated by Hershl Hartman)

The joining of individuality with interdependence enriches our lives, encourages us to enrich the lives of others, and inspires hope of attaining peace, justice, and opportunity for all.

Living Nonviolently

Rabbi Michael Robinson

When I was seventeen I was a student at North Carolina State College follow-ing my lifelong dream of studying to become an architect. World War II was on. It was a difficult time to be a student. Daily, we heard of the advancing German armies and the threat of extermination of European Jews. We Jews had canonized Franklin Delano Roosevelt and were naïve enough to believe that saving Jewish lives was a central objective of the war. That Roosevelt and the US allies did noth-ing to stop the killing of the Jews, much less to rescue them, has been documented in Arthur Morse's book, *While Six Million Died*, and in David Wyman's *The Aban-donment of the Jews*, which reported that in the face of overwhelming evidence of the Holocaust, the United States (and Great Britain) refused to help rescue the victims until very late in the war.

I did not know this then. I shared the common wisdom that Hitler must be stopped. It was as if I had heard the first half of Gandhi's statement—that one must resist evil—but had not heard the second part: that the ideal way to resist evil is nonviolently. So, caught up in the war fever all around me, I enlisted in the Navy. I served in the Navy's amphibious forces in the southwest Pacific on an LST—Landing Ship Tank—disgorging vehicles or men right onto beaches. Be-cause I was an electronics technician I never fired a gun, thank God.

One time we had our cargo deck filled with Japanese prisoners taken, I be-lieve, on one of the Halmahera Islands. We would go below deck to look at them squatting in a position we in the mountains of North Carolina called "hunkering down." We had heard about the Japanese fighting men in the propaganda we were fed, yet they seemed not too different from us—quiet, passive, waiting. Language barriers kept us from speaking with them.

We had all heard that a Japanese would rather commit *hara-kiri*, or suicide, than accept dishonor. One of my buddies got the idea of leaving a hunting knife on the ledge in the tank deck, right in view of our prisoners. After several days when we delivered our prisoners, the owner recovered his knife. Not one of the 150 prisoners had been moved to use it to escape the dishonor of being captured. We learned, much to our disappointment, that the things we were taught about the enemy were not necessarily so.

When the war was over, I was not rotated home on the basis of my point-count because I was the only one aboard the ship who could repair the movie machine. By the time I returned home near the end of April 1946, the world had changed. Hardly a month later I received a letter from the Navy offering me a bonus and advancement in rank if I reenlisted to protect my country against the Soviet menace. Just a few months before the Soviets had been our allies and the heroic defenders of Stalingrad, but now they were enemies. My growth continued. I have never since allowed the government to tell me who is my enemy and whom I am supposed to hate. In fact, I have learned to hate injustice, cruelty, violence, and suffering. As the ancient rabbis taught: hate not the wicked but the wickedness.

Dog watches, midnight till 4 A.M., had given me time to think about what my life would be like when I returned home. Though I never knew anyone who had become a rabbi and was never close to a rabbi, the calling grew in me, yet kept trying, unsuccessfully, to run from it. To prepare myself I went to Cincinnati to apply to the Hebrew Union College for the Reform rabbinate. The college agreed to postpone entrance exams for me until September. In the summer of the 1946, while preparing for entrance exams at HUC, I met Joe Felmet, who lived in my town and who I had never really known, although he had appeared in community theater with one of my sisters. Joe had been a conscientious objector during the war, doing alternative service in a mental hospital. I had never heard of conscientious objection but the moment Joe explained it to me, I knew that was what I was, am, and should have been all along.

While I spent my summer learning enough Hebrew to translate the book of Genesis and identify all the verb and noun forms, Joe spent his summer going through the requirements to take bar exams. He had read for the law after graduating from the university and had been on the first Freedom Ride, arrested in Chapel Hill, North Carolina, on a technicality and served time on a chain gang. Of the twenty-three states that accepted reading for the law not one would permit anyone convicted of a felony to take the bar exam. In the Southern states, violating segregation laws was a violent affront to the accepted standards of the people and a serious felony. Joe, therefore, never got to practice law. We were good friends that summer and when I left for Cincinnati he gave me the names of two people, members of the Fellowship of Reconciliation and of that first Freedom Ride, who became co-conspirators in the beginning of my lifelong career of nonviolent resistance to laws, which I believe on the basis of my religious faith to be unjust and wrong. Meeting Joe Felmet was a step in changing my life.

At HUC I discovered the Jewish Peace Fellowship, which was founded in 1941 to support Jewish conscientious objectors during World War II and whose very existence was a witness to the legitimacy of conscientious objection as a an authentic expression of Judaism, a position which the Central Conference of American Rabbis had affirmed in the 1930s. I learned that one of the professors at the seminary, Rabbi Abraham Cronbach, was one of the three founders of the JPF (the others were Rabbi Isidor Hoffman and Jane Evans) and I became a member of the small group that met from time to time at his home. Rabbi Cronbach lived his teachings. During World War II German prisoners of war were housed in Cincinnati. Crony used to raise money in the Jewish community for gift packages to take to these young men, imprisoned far from home. I don't need to tell you that the local Jewish community pressured the college to get rid of this man who—they believed—carried his unwillingness to hate too far, and his insistence that love is the ultimate way. Many years later I learned of Edda Servi Machlin's family and the German soldier they befriended. Edda, a member of my former congregation and the author of the book *The Classic Cuisine of the Italian Jews*, was from the village of Pitigliano, Italy, where her father was the Orthodox rabbi. When the Germans occupied Pitigliano there was a German soldier, a young man far from home, who her parents made a member of the family, frequently having him as a guest for dinner. That German soldier was the one who came and warned them that the Germans were rounding up Jews and was therefore responsible for saving their lives. They responded to him in humane way, and he to them.

The Bible itself, the root of all of this, is not a consistent document. It is a people's self-understanding of its origins. It is a human document. Much of it flows, as Martin Buber taught, from the human encounter with the Divine. Everything is in it. We have one strain in the Bible, the self-account of his feisty people, fighting its way through history, claiming all the time that its battles to displace the Canaanites from their land was the will of God. (Aside: In my religious school eighth-grade class, Mark Davidoff asks me to come in. He's upset because the kids in the class raise questions about whether the Israelite conquest of Canaan wasn't similar to the European conquest of the Americas, pushing the indigenous peoples off their lands. I compliment them on their moral sensitivity and their unwillingness to say something is okay just because our ancestors are the ones who did it and claimed their conquest was God's will.)

Martin Buber, while still in Germany, met with a group of German theologians and declared his absolute commitment to nonviolence. One of them demanded of him: "What about Saul and Agag the King of the Amalekites?" You remember the story: Samuel tells Saul to take no prisoners when going into battle with the Amalekites, led by their king Agag. Saul identifies with the king and takes him alive. Samuel admonishes him for not following the will of God, takes Saul's sword and kills Agag. Again, the question "What about Saul and Agag the king of the Amalekites?" Buber with tremendous respect for the Bible remains silent. Again: "What about Saul and Agag?" And Buber replies: "I do not believe Samuel understood the will of God."

However, alongside the story of the people fighting their way into Canaan is another biblical story that begins with Abraham.

Abraham was a desert sheik—a very prosperous sheik. He and his nephew had large flocks. Remember the story of Abraham and his nephew Lot when they entered the land? There is a quarrel or fight between the herdsmen of Abraham. Abraham simply tells Lot and his herdsmen to choose first. If you go to the left, we will go to the right. If you go to the right, we will go to the left. In other words, Abraham says that the best land and the most water are not worth fighting over.

Yet another scholar, Martin Bergmann, in his book *In the Shadow of Moloch*, has agreed that the story of the binding of Isaac, which we read on Rosh Hashanah was, in the first instance, intended as a strong protest against human violence, a rejection of violent aggression which in ancient days among Semites took the form of the ritual murder of children. When the Divine voice pleads with Abraham, "Lay not your hand upon the child," it represents a new, emerging consciousness moving beyond violence.

When Moses spends forty days and forty nights on the mountain of God, time which I believe he spent in mediation, he has an encounter with God. Whether it be a Christian mystic, a Hindu or Buddhist mystic, the path to the experience is culturally conditioned. But on top of the mountain the experience is identical. It is out of time. It is out of space. And it is wordless. But words flow from the experience. For Moses and for many Jews that followed him through the centuries, from that experience flows the knowledge of what I must now do. The culmination of the words that flow from Moses' experience culminate in Thou Shalt Not Kill. Several centuries later, after King David completes the conquest of the land, the Book of Chronicles tells us that David is not allowed to build a Temple of God because David was a man whose hands were bloody from battle. The Bible is telling us that violence, even the violence of the state and its armies, comes under the judgment of God. The Torah had already told that no iron could be used in preparing the stone of the altar. Iron is used to make weapons of war, to injure and to kill. The altar of God Israel is a place to ask forgiveness for acts of violence.

The Rabbinic Judaism of the Talmud and the Midrash is much clearer in its rejection of violence in all forms, including capital punishment, another form of communally sanctioned violence, which the Bible itself sanctions for certain crimes, though there is no evidence that it was ever carried out. In contrast to the claim of the Christian scriptures that the Sanhedrin condemned Jesus to death, the rabbis declared that a Sanhedrin that sentences one person to death in sixty years shall be known as a bloody Sanhedrin.

The rabbis had great respect for the Bible but they were not guilty of making an idol out of a literal interpretation of the Bible. It is when the Psalmist implores God to destroy the wicked that the rabbis tell us we are to read not *harasha*, the wicked, but we are to read *resha*, wickedness. In the Bible the Israelites are commanded to make war against the seven Canaanite nations. In response the rabbis repeat that this is a mandatory war in which every Jew must participate. There is just one detail: none of the seven Canaanite nations existed any longer in the time of the Mishnah and Gemara. We were commanded to engage in war against non-existent nations.

During the Vietnam War both my wife Ruth and I spent a great deal of time working with COs. Young men called, wrote, and came to see me from all over the country. Our job was to help them in identifying the spiritual roots of their conscientious objection to participating in war in any form. It was a matter of questioning, and over and over again the young men would return to the biblical affirmation that humans were created in the image of God, and that life—all life—is sacred. This is what is taught in Mishnah Sanhedrin, when the question is asked why God began the creation of humanity with one man, Adam. The rabbis responded that, "One person alone was brought forth at the time of creation in order to teach us that one who destroys a single human soul is regarded as the destroyer of the whole world, while one who preserves a single soul is regarded as the preserver of the whole world." In the same passage from Tractate Sanhedrin, in dealing with the question of why creation began with one man, Adam, it states that, "one man was created the common ancestor of all so that the various human families should not contend with one another saying that my ancestors are better than yours."

During the Vietnam War I was also called as witness at a number of courts martial when a young man seeking discharge from the military as a CO was being tried by a court of military officers for refusing to obey orders. I remember one particular trial at Fort Dix, New Jersey. The young man had refused to board a plane for a *second* tour of duty in Vietnam after having filed for discharge as a CO and being turned down. The presiding officer of the court martial asked me, as the expert witness, if there was anything in the Jewish religion that would demand that a man refuse to obey orders.

I responded that we are taught that there are three things that a person cannot do even to save his own life: commit incest, idolatry, or take a life. The prohibition against incest is an old and strong one. Idolatry at the time of the Mishnah (as in Mattathias's time) was to give obeisance to the emblem of the state, to worship the nation. To do that is to blindly follow orders, to ignore your conscience. We are required to do as Mattathias did: refuse to bow to the state even at the risk of our lives. If someone were to hand you a gun (or a sword) and order you to kill another or be killed, the Talmud bids us to accept death rather than to take a life. "Who is it to say," the rabbi asked, "that my blood is redder than his?" I must tell you that my testimony did not save the young man from prison. You will be interested to know that for several years after his release from incarceration and his "dishonorable" discharge from the army, he worked on an Indian reservation, *serving others.*

Jews like to believe that Jesus' calling upon the people to love their enemies (which is certainly difficult to do) is Christian, so it gets us off the hook. I don't know what Christians do to get themselves off the hook, but I do know what Judaism teaches. In the book of Proverbs there is a command, "If your enemy hungers, feed him, if he thirsts, give him to drink." In other words, branding someone or some group the enemy does not eliminate your human responsibility to him; in fact it doesn't get you off the hook at all, and is hardly different from your responsibility to those you love. This is biblical Judaism, hardly different it seems from the Jew Jesus' teaching. It is the way of nonviolence. And every Passover we need be reminded of the Midrash of the Israelites crossing the Red Sea.

After the Israelites crossed the Red Sea, according to the biblical story, the Egyptian armies drowned. In a very graphic ancient song in the 15th chapter of Exodus, the Israelites celebrated the victory, their redemption and the demise of the enemy. In most incredible language, God is referred to as *Ish milchamah*—man of war. The Midrash tells us that when the angels in heaven heard the Israelites singing they joined with them. God then rebukes the angels and asks them why they are singing. They respond: "We are singing because your children, the children of Israel, have been saved." *"Do you not know,"* responds God in this midrash, *"that the Egyptians who drowned this day are also my children?"* It was impossible for most of the rabbis of the Talmudic-Midrashic period to envision violence as a legitimate Jewish option. Compassion for the enemy is expressed to this day in the Pesach Seder when the plagues are read. Because Egyptians suffered from these plagues, wine is removed from the cup of redemption as each is read.

The teaching of nonviolence continued in our tradition all the way to the present. Aaron Tamaret, a Polish rabbi who was at the first Zionist Congress in Basle in 1906 called for Jews to turn our back on violence. In the Yishuv, as Jews began to settle Palestine, there were those who called not for a Jewish state, but for a binational state where Jews and Arabs would build a country together, with two official languages, without Jewish domination. Chaim Weizmann, a member of this group called Ichud, or unity, wrote in 1929 that it was not even necessary to have a Jewish majority in Palestine. Martin Buber and Judah Magnes, the first president of the Hebrew University, were equally committed to nonviolence. Albert Einstein was offered the first presidency of the state of Israel, but refused so that he would be free to work for peace. Einstein and Buber, incidentally, were both affiliated with the Jewish Peace Fellowship.

Today there are many in Israel who have come to understand that "there is no way to peace, peace is the way." Some of these are the soldiers of Yesh G'vul who have refused to be members of an occupying army and have gone to jail over and again rather than serve beyond the Green Line. There are COs in Israel, where the right to conscientious objection is not recognized by law. Some have been imprisoned, while others have been quietly assigned to alternative service. And in Israel and the US, there are a growing number of people—both Jews and non-Jews—committed to working for economic and social justice and peace through nonviolent means.

Allan Falls Down the Rabbit Hole . . .
And into the Middle East Conflict

Allan Solomonow

In the early 1960s, while I was at UC Berkeley, I declared myself a Conscientious Objector and applied to my draft board for CO status. This was based upon Jewish values, thanks to five years of *heder* (Jewish after-school studies). For reasons I don't know, the draft board declined to act on my request, but at the same time didn't draft me. I think that they might have been unwilling to enter the then uncharted waters of passing judgment over the conscience of non-Christians. This act also brought me into early contact with the national, but admittedly small, Jewish Peace Fellowship.

After graduate school, I moved to New York City. In the summer of 1966 I found myself directing the Counselor-in-Training (CIT) Program of a pacifist summer camp, Camp *Ahimsa* (nonviolence), outside of Voluntown, Connecticut. This was a project of the CNVA, the Committee for Nonviolent Action, which pioneered the idea of civil disobedience in the United States. Being a new idea and at the time of war, a pro-peace summer camp entailed certain risks. I was in charge of the oldest of the campers, those who might choose to become assistant counselors in the following summers. I was about to turn twenty-six, the age at which I would no longer be eligible for the draft

The CITs were responsible for undertaking a summer project. They planned a demonstration at the launching of the "Will Rogers," a nuclear submarine named after an anti-war American Indian! I was invited to speak as part of the brief program. By a quirk, I had two copies of my draft registration card, each neatly signed across the short end. Towards the end of my speech I pulled out one of the cards and carefully tore off the part with my signature, placing the portion of the card without my signature into an envelope, to mail it to what was then the Selective Service System. I wanted to underscore that I was disassociating myself from the draft—and the war. To me this was a harmless, symbolic expression of my free speech. I found out otherwise.

Not long afterward, I stood trial in Connecticut for having "mutilated a Selective Service document." The Assistant US Attorney was a young man by the name of Jon Newman, who argued, "If all young men did as Mr. Solomonow has done, democracy, as we know it, would cease to exist." In spring 1967 I met Ofelia, who became my wife. I was sentenced to serve a year in Allenwood, a federal minimum-security prison farm, which I entered in fall 1968, just after the birth of the first of our two sons. Before entering prison, I made a quiet vow to resume my peace work when I got out—to let the government know that imprisonment would not be a way of deterring my commitment. I spent my prison term serving as a teacher of basic literacy to moonshiners and inner-city Blacks.

On leaving prison in 1969, I met Naomi Goodman, a kind and gentle woman who graciously offered Ofelia and me her summer house near Easthampton, Long Island, where we stayed for a week or two after I returned to the normal space of society. We spent a little over a week there and on our way back to Manhattan in Naomi's car, she asked if I wanted to become the first full-time staff person for the Jewish Peace Fellowship. Naomi explained the JPF's problems: too many inquiries from young men interested in the possibility of applying for CO status were coming in and there was no one who had my experience as a Jewish CO. I quickly accepted and by the fall of 1969, the JPF had staff: first me, and then we added representatives in Chicago and Los Angeles and finally an assistant in New York City.

It quickly became apparent that thousands of young Jews throughout the nation were seeking draft counseling, more that any other religious group in the country. Most of the young Jewish men were finding medical and psychological excuses, other were leaving the country, but few were becoming COs; they felt they couldn't—after all who ever heard of a "Jewish pacifist?" Very little had been written about this topic. In a crash effort that took a few weeks, I managed to edit a 64-page book that included relevant comments from the Orthodox, Conservative, and Reform Jewish traditions, *Roots of Jewish Nonviolence*. It was distributed to all draft boards and became the basis for many Jewish CO claims and remains in print.

Some formidable problems remained. Almost every Jewish man who sought CO status was asked, "What would you have done during the Holocaust?" and "What would you do if the Arab states attack Israel again and begin to slaughter the Jews?" The latter question was particularly vexing; there was virtually no literature in the peace community that threw light on a "peace" let alone a pacifist stance for Jews on the issue of Israel.

As we wrestled with these issues, another dilemma emerged in my effort to expand draft counseling. Almost no synagogues would permit us to do draft counseling in Jewish temples and their other premises. The reasoning was simple; "Israel depends on the US for support, if we Jews criticize the US government over war in Vietnam, then the US will be less likely to support Israel."

Rabbi after rabbi offered us checks, but asked that we not mention their name. Our draft counseling took place at Quaker (American Friends Service Committee (AFSC) and Friends Meetings) and Catholic Worker offices and peace centers. Some of those counseled even included the sons of the very rabbis we had sought out for support. This dynamic troubled me and I wondered whether the principles I was taught in *heder* was being compromised for the sake of Israeli government policy?

With continuing acts of terrorism in the Middle East, the need for a pacifist position became increasingly evident. In fall of 1970, I left the JPF to become the first paid staff for CONAME, the Committee on New Alternatives in the Middle East. CONAME had just been founded by a number of anti-war intellectuals and activists, mostly but not entirely Jewish. Their hope was that the lessons of Vietnam might be applied to the Middle East, so what was then happening in Vietnam would not come to pass in the Middle East.

My personal expectations were simple: I saw this as a momentary diversion; I would work on the Middle East only because it addressed a special need and then return to graduate studies and teaching. Clearly, Americans were far more committed to peace in the Middle East than to peace in Vietnam. By raising the issue, I told myself, others would be moved to form new groups for research, lobbying and action. A concerted American initiative might make a difference in solving the Middle East conflict.

CONAME's Board was drawn primarily from Jewish anti-war leadership (there were also some Quaker and other non-Jewish activists among us). Among the more prominent Jewish names were Robert Jay Lifton, Paul Jacobs, Seymour Melman, Irene Gendzier, and Noam Chomsky. The latter was one of the few scholars who had tried to put the Middle East into some meaningful perspective.

The CONAME principles, quite radical then, now seem more like the statement of a contemporary Arab-Jewish dialogue group. But at the onset of the 1970s mere dialogue felt like a radical and perhaps even unattainable goal.

At the time there was just the beginning of a peace movement in Israel along with a few independent Palestinian voices who were sometimes willing to speak up but would not enter any dialogue with an Israeli. The one thing going for us was a book just published by the Quakers, *Search for Peace in the Middle East.* The book directly addressed the volatile Middle East issues that were pitting Americans against one another. *Search* called on the Arab states to recognize Israel, it affirmed the UN's call for the right of return for the (Palestinian) refugees and prophetically broached the idea of self-determination for the refugees.

I was no less intrigued by the widespread criticism of the book that came from Israel, the Arab states, American Jews, US and Soviet officials. Clearly the Quakers were doing something right! One of my first tasks for CONAME became another booklet, this one on the many responses to *Search for Peace.* Among the team that worked on *Search* were three I came to admire: Rabbi Leonard Beerman from Los Angeles, Prof. Don Peretz who had directed Middle East work for the American Jewish Committee, and a prominent Quaker, Landrum Bolling. Don Peretz, a remarkably thoughtful scholar, remains my informal advisor to this day.

The War Resisters League offered an office and the AFSC provided some initial financial support for ME work. The first year and a half of CONAME were sobering and instructive to me. On the one hand, most of the Arabs we knew were committed to a "unitary, secular democratic state." This seemed like a compelling, principled Western idea except for the fact that to most of the Jewish community it meant the physical destruction of the State of Israel, a "one-state solution." As far as the Jewish community was concerned, all the refugees were terrorists and deserved nothing. If only they would settle in the many Arab states and give up the land to the Jewish people, the problem would be solved. It was virtually impossible to arrange for synagogues to hear moderate Arab voices or Arab groups to listen to Israeli doves.

As I look back at it, 1971 and early1972 were a turning point for me. Not only because I was becoming more deeply interested in the Middle East but because as the Middle East unfolded, it was revealing more and more about the challenges of nonviolence, which I now realized was my abiding passion. "If only I could understand why thoughtful people passionately committed to justice and peace became rabid when it comes to the Middle East then," I told myself "I might find the essence, the Holy Grail, of nonviolence."

Although both sides were resistant, as a Jew, coping with Jewish rigidity was peculiarly painful to me. I believe that the essence of being a Jew is a thirst for knowledge and a dedication to analysis unbridled by dogmatism. Yet almost as one, the most authoritative sources in the Jewish organizational community insisted that the Arab world was pro-Communist, was determined to destroy Israel; that there were no such a people as Palestinians, and so on. How could I convey to the Jewish community that some of the Arabs I knew could easily be their neighbors?

After a little over a year of work, CONAME's board decided that I should go to the Middle East to take stock of the peace community on both sides and to line up possible speakers, Jewish and Arab, to go on a speaking tour in this country. The date was finally set for February 1972, to coincide with an international peace conference being planned Rome by a joint effort of the Socialist and Communist parliamentary leadership. The other American delegate was Paul Jacobs. We had both heard rumors that Israeli peacenik Uri Avnery might attend to meet with PLO representatives in Rome.

The month-long trip was a rousing success. Avnery met with mid-level PLO officials secretly one evening. Many Israelis were active politically in groups like SIAH, the Israeli New Left organization and the more moderate *Shalom u'bitachon,* Peace & Security. Individual Arabs, mostly leftists, were beginning to write articles, but few were willing to come on a speaking tour especially if it meant talking before Jewish audiences. I wound up inviting a young Israeli economist to come and speak later in the year.

By the time I returned home from the trip I was convinced, though I probably did not realize it at the time that my calling was to experiment with and learn about nonviolence as a tool for Middle East understanding. Surely, I thought, American Jews would join in the struggle for peace much as we had in Vietnam.

CONAME invited the first Israeli-Palestinian speaking team, maverick Israeli journalist Amos Kenan and Palestinian journalist Jamil Hamad. The next team included Meier Pa'il, former head of the Israeli Army Staff College and Raymonda Tawil, a Palestinian feminist whose home in the West Bank was a salon for Israeli doves. Later her daughter Suha married Yasser Arafat. Both tours were planned to reach Jewish audiences at campus Hillel foundations and some liberal temples. A program at a well-known temple in Los Angeles was broken up by a smoke bomb. We also sponsored the first tour of an Israeli refusenik. All these tours were extremely difficult to set up and publicize: many rabbis risked their positions by opening their temples to voices of "the enemy."

One premise of CONAME had been that since there was so much resistance to dialogue it was not practical to have a solely Jewish organization. But some members of CONAME felt there *had* to be a Jewish group, and helped form one called Breira or "Alternative," a response to the cry of the Israeli right, "Ein Breira" (no alternative).

In the fall of 1974 CONAME merged into the Fellowship of Reconciliation (FOR), thanks to the ingenuity of Jim Forest, one of the staff. An early project was an interfaith Middle East tour which I led with Tom Cornell who was also on the FOR staff. In June of 1975, nineteen of us left for three weeks in Egypt, Jordan, Israel and Palestine, Lebanon, and Syria.

At the exact hour our plane left Cairo for Beirut, Lebanon exploded into civil war. Our guide, waiting at the Beirut airport, blanched when she saw our Shalom/Salaam pins and told us to take them off. For the next ten days, we were cut off from the world and traveled under dangerous conditions, but were able meet with our contacts as planned and travel in and out of battle areas. Despite the chaos and lack of communications, we even managed (with the help of our PLO contacts) to go to Shabbat services at a Jewish synagogue.

We met with two Palestinian leaders, each of whom spoke to us of a dramatic new direction in PLO policy including dialogue leading to recognition of Israel and negotiations with the US, all heresies at the time. This new direction had been published by *An Nahar*, Beirut's largest and most important newspaper, as a three-part series. After almost two weeks of hair-raising turns and events, we managed to leave Lebanon in an Air France freight plane to Damascus.

On returning home, a small delegation of tour participants went to the Israeli Consulate in New York City. We were anxious to share with the Consul General news that might bode well for Israeli-Palestinian dialogue. His response was discouraging: Who did we think he was—a publicity agent for the PLO? This was a crystallizing moment for me. It brought home how resistant the Israeli government was to any change in its perceptions and how far we had gone in our transformation from the people of the book to a people of a modern militarized state. From *lo v'koach yigbar ish* (not by strength does one prevail) to *rak v'koach yigbar ish* (only by strength does one prevail).

REVERENCE FOR LIFE

I see my Chaplaincy role as caring for the spiritual
needs of the inmates and also their families. When a
Hasidic man was arrested I worked closely with him to
get kosher meals, access to a *tallit* and prayer books. He
received a 12–22 year sentence, which is a virtual death
sentence since he is in his sixties . . .

—Phyllis Taylor, "Binding up the Broken Hearted:
A Prison Ministry"

Binding Up the Brokenhearted: A Prison Ministry

Phyllis B. Taylor

"I'm not going to talk to you. I'm not going to tell you about my brother," she said. "So don't," I replied. "Then what the f... do you do here? You going to talk to me about f... God?" I replied I was there to remind her she was loved and loveable. She then told me she was a hooker and did all kinds of dope. "Still loved and loveable," I said. That was the beginning of my relationship with her and my definition of my ministry in prisons and jails.

I have had a long standing interest in prisons and jails which comes from my Jewish values based on *tikkun olam*, justice, and *gmilut hasadim*, caring for the individual. I can think of no place which reflects racism, class, and poverty so much as our prisons and jails since so many who are incarcerated are poor persons of color. There are also Jewish men and women incarcerated who often don't get the support they need. They and their families suffer because they are "invisible" in the prison system and in the Jewish community.

My work began more than thirty years ago when I volunteered in the Philadelphia Prison System as a Registered Nurse. Because of my ten years experience in working in hospices, I received a call from a nurse in the Philadelphia Prison System asking if I would see one of the patient inmates, a man with widespread cancer. I did, as well as another person with AIDS. This prompted me to go to the Warden and share with him my observation that where prisons and jails used to be filled with young healthy people, now they were increasingly filled with young, very unhealthy people as well as those who were older. I told him about what hospices did, which led to a long relationship that resulted in establishing a Hospice and Comfort Care Program in Philadelphia prisons. I also consulted with Pennsylvania's Department of Corrections to help develop an "Inmate Buddy System," whereby men and women inmates can be "buddies" to frail and dying prisoners.

I was then asked to work with inmates grieving over the deaths of parents, grandparents, partners, children, siblings, and other relatives. Many of the deaths were caused by violence, suicide, drug overdoses, AIDS, and alcoholism. Sponsored by the Board of Rabbis and then the Jewish Chaplaincy and Healing Program it led me to become a Chaplain, a position I now hold. What, then, does it mean to be a Correctional Chaplain? Many things, I believe. But first let me explain the world I've entered into, a world, which the vast majority of Americans neither know, or wish to know.

"Prisons" are places for those who receive sentences of two years or more. They tend to have more programs and stability than jails. "Jails" are for detainees and those sentenced to county time, from one month to twenty-three months. In the jail where I work more than 60% of the more than 7500 inmates have not yet been sentenced. I find that utterly appalling. In a society where one is presumed innocent until proved guilty, if you are poor or have violated probation or parole you are treated as guilty until proved innocent. I have worked with people whose bail is $150 but because they and their families cannot afford to post bail they must sit behind bars for months. Jails are also places where people come and go. In Philadelphia more than 35,000 pass through the gates each year. The instability of the population and the tension of not knowing what is going to happen to you legally create despair, increased mental health issues, and sometimes violence.

Another reality of the jail setting is that people come in right from the street. Many have chronic illnesses like HIV/AIDS, Hepatitis C, TB, cancer, high blood pressure, and heart and lung diseases that were not attended to either because of lack of health care or because of addiction and the lifestyles of the men, women, and adolescents. Many are "dope sick" from withdrawal and a number of those newly incarcerated enter with traumatic injuries from shootings, stabbings, and other results of violence. Sometimes their families don't know where they are, which only increases the stress on inmates and families.

What is the jail I work in like? As I use each one of my senses I am aware of the incredible noise from the blaring of TVs or shouting inmates. The smell of unwashed bodies and unbrushed teeth is pervasive. As I walk through the halls or into the cellblocks I am aware of how many people are from the minority communities. What do I feel? As I watch some of the men and women shuffling down the hall in handcuffs, shackles, and leg irons I am deeply distressed at what we do to people. I have been behind bars so long that most of the time I am not afraid. However, as I hear harsh language and then the sounds of fights, I become deeply upset. I have found myself crying when the violence escalates and I feel powerless to intervene.

To be a Correctional Chaplain I had to go through Correctional Officer training. As difficult as that was for me as an older person, I am very grateful for the experience. The only part of the training I did not have to do was to learn how to fire a gun. Instead, I had extra days of on-the-job training. The first day began with a suicide. It was traumatic for everyone and illustrative of some of the profound problems of the criminal justice system. The man who killed himself was picked up for a parole violation. He had not reported to his Parole Officer years earlier. In those intervening years he had pulled his life together. He became a minister, married, had small children, and was a model in his community. When he went to court he felt, as did everyone else, that he would get "time served." Instead he was sentenced to prison. That night he hanged himself with shoelaces.

The next day was uplifting. We have a juvenile unit. These youth have been charged with committing terrible crimes and are awaiting trial. While waiting to be adjudicated they go to a school organized by the Philadelphia public school system. This day was graduation. Three boys/men were to graduate from the prison high school. The audience for graduation was comprised of other incarcerated youths, two family members, and the jail staff. They had caps and gowns and entered to the music of *Pomp and Circumstance*, which played on a boom box. What a contrast. Death and triumph. Despair and hope. These are emotions and realities I deal with on a daily basis as a Correctional Chaplain.

I have real respect for the staff and understand the security orientation necessary to protect inmates from each other, to safeguard staff, and to prevent escapes. I also know that we were taught to be "fair, firm, and consistent" and to be respectful of other staff and the men and women under our care. Is that ever violated? Yes. However, when I have seen things I believe are unjust, I work the "chain of command" and have found the authorities generally responsive.

What is my job like? I love it. It is just where I feel called to be. In my tiny office (where I have to stand to let the inmate in), I have tried to create a sanctuary. When talking to an inmate I always close the door, which makes the Correctional Officers concerned for my safety. However, the closed door gives the incarcerated person a space where they can feel peaceful and perhaps even relax. Sometimes they come in handcuffed and wearing leg irons if the officer is especially concerned about violence. I wear "body armor," a small box that can be activated if I feel threatened and which will bring help. On the walls I have photos of children, a letter written by a child to his incarcerated parent, scenes from nature and photos of Christians and Muslims in prayer. I also have "shalom" drawn by an inmate placed on the wall. I have spiritual books and magazines so the person can leave with written materials if he wishes. I have ordered birthday, sympathy, get-well and thank-you cards to give to the men and women so they can stay in touch with their families. Each time I enter the jail, I and other staff and visitors receive a pat down, a search of my files, date and address book. These are all done in front of a camera connected to a TV in the Warden's office. Because of my training with the Correctional Officers I am comfortable with this practice since contraband has to be kept out.

What about Jewish inmates? Each week I get a list of all those who told the admitting social workers they were Jewish. Still, I come across Jewish men and women who aren't on that list. They tell me they were afraid to say they are Jews for fear of retaliation from inmates and staff.

The Jewish population is spread out in six different facilities, which makes it difficult for me to see them all. Why are they there? One man I work with closely is a charming, competent person who has been arrested twenty-eight times and found guilty fourteen times. His last crime was for motor vehicle theft and violation of parole. As the Judge said to him, he does "jail well." It's life outside he does not do well. While he is incarcerated we talk about those triggers that cause him to recommit crimes over and over again. He is fifty-eight. Some of the men with whom I worked closely are charged with sex offenses. In the inmate hierarchy of people who are most disliked and have the highest risk of attacks by others are sex offenders and "baby killers." When one adds anti-Semitism, I follow these individuals especially closely since I am their advocate.

Many of the Jewish women I work with suffer from drug addiction and mental illness. They have sold drugs, distributed them, and often prostituted themselves to support their addiction. One woman told me she had spent fifteen years of her life in county, state, and federal facilities. We got to know each other very well. We said Kaddish together for her parents—she was so strung out on drugs she never attended their funerals.

I met her only child, a daughter who also had addictive disease. Soon after the woman's release her daughter was arrested. Two days after the daughter was released, the police found her dead body in a vacant lot. I presided at her funeral, one of the most difficult services I ever performed. Now, I keep looking for the mother since she is using drugs again. Because I believe that each person is loved and loveable and because I never give up on anyone, I will welcome her back when she is rearrested.

In Philadelphia's prisons I am the one who approves kosher meals, plans special Passover meals, and pays attention to the major holidays. I am unable to bring all the Jewish men and women together for religious services because their custody security levels vary and people of different custody levels cannot be in the same location. This inability to have services troubles me and the Jewish prisoners as well; there are many Christian and Muslim services. In the state and federal system this is not a problem since all the inmates are at the same custody level in their respective prisons and are not spread out into different jails.

I see my Chaplaincy role as caring for the spiritual needs of the inmates and also their families. I frequently get calls from family members worried about their loved ones. Since I work as an advocate, I go to the authorities if I get a worried call from a family member. For example, when one of the men from an Orthodox family was called "Jew boy" I worked with the shift commanders to make sure he was not harmed and also spoke weekly with his parents. When a Hasidic man was arrested I worked closely with him to get him kosher meals, access to a *tallit* and prayer books, which had to be x-rayed since they were large hardback books. I met his family, including his elderly mother who came up from Florida to see him. He received a 12–22 year sentence, which is a virtual death sentence since he is in his sixties and has chronic medical conditions. We correspond, as I do with the many of the Jewish inmates and non-Jews who are now serving state time.

Do I pray with inmates and staff? Yes. When they request prayer I'll ask what they want to pray about and incorporate that in our prayer together. Do I speak up when I feel that there is an injustice? Yes. Does it make my job harder at times? It does indeed, but I know that Micah tells us we are to "Seek justice, love mercy and walk humbly with our God."

One of the biggest needs many inmates have is financial. Some of the Jewish men and women do not have supportive families who can send them money periodically so they can buy supplemental food, cosmetics, and clothes from the commissary. (The average wage of a state inmate after expenses for restitution is taken out is $17 per month. The workers I have get $1.50 per day.) I applied to a small Jewish fund for money so I could use it to help the men and women get phone time to call their families. One man is originally from Israel and is serving a life sentence for murder. He has two children about whom he cares deeply.

The Jewish fund's money has been used to get a phone card so he can talk to his daughter once every month or two. He just became a grandfather for the first time and I am in touch with his daughter to see if the fund could finance a bus ticket for her and the baby. Another young man is in his twenties and is not due to get out until 2017. He needed a pair of sneakers that I was able to finance. He has no family still in touch with him. I am grateful for the availability of the fund that I've named the Jewish Indigent Fund, but I wish there was more response from the Jewish community. As one man wrote, "I do wish more Jews would reach out to Jewish inmates. We seem to be swept under the rug because we are an embarrassment, which I am sure we are. Yet, for a people commanded to be compassionate, who will give tremendously to Israel, Holocaust remembrance, non-Jewish victims of tsunamis and hurricanes, we do so little for needy Jews in our own backyard. The same people who think nothing of writing a $50 check to the Red Cross for Katrina victims or an Israeli fundraiser won't, with that amount, buy a *chumash* and *siddur* for an inmate in need."

In the Detention Center where I am the Chaplain we have a medical and psychiatric unit so I continue my work and ministry with those who are physically and mentally ill. I teach new correctional officers about grief and end-of-life care. As I talk about hospice care I explain that hospice is a philosophy of caring for people when the illness can no longer be controlled. It is applied wherever that person lives. That might be in their home, a nursing home, assisted living facility, or a prison or jail. As a Chaplain I address issues related to concerns about dying and death as well as remorse and forgiveness. I counsel inmates, correctional officers, and other staff. In a prison or jail, each day is potentially one of new beginnings (Rosh Hashanah) or atonement (Yom Kippur).

What is the impact of all this on me? I have learned that the power of the human spirit is awesome. As I learn the life stories of many of the people to whom I minister, I hear about lives filled with pain and suffering arising from physical, emotional, and sexual abuse. Amazingly, many have the will to live and make something better of their lives. But some people frighten me—people who don't see that their actions hurt others. They make me more cautious and a little less trusting. I have learned to ask hard questions when the men and women talk about what they did. I ask them what got them arrested and what would they do differently. One young man who is facing a very long sentence said what he would do differently is his whole life.

I have learned never to give up on anyone regardless of what they have done in the past. In a state prison I am working with people who have committed murder

done by Hakol Chai's staff is no different from mine. Attorney Tali Lavie, spokesperson and lobbyist of Hakol Chai, wrote:

> "Growing up in the suburbs, I saw animal suffering every day.
> Dogs were constantly abandoned near my house and my family was
> always taking in strays. When I was about twelve, I became aware
> that the municipal veterinarian of my city, Yavne, was destroying
> the dogs and cats, even those with families, on the pretext of
> preventing rabies. My dog, who is now fifteen and a half years old,
> survived only because we smuggled him out of the area. There were
> demonstrations and articles in the paper, but I felt so helpless. I
> dreamt that one day I would become a lawyer who protects animals.
> I would be the voice of the animals and shout out their cry."

Israel's evacuation of the West Bank and Gaza in August 2005 presented a new challenge, and CHAI/Hakol Chai converted its mobile spay/neuter clinic to a rescue vehicle and played a major role in rescuing animals abandoned by departing settlers. Every species, from cats and dogs to chickens, turkeys, parakeets, guinea pigs, and an iguana were transported to safety and efforts were made to relocate them with their former owners or else place them in new homes.

One of the dogs rescued and placed in a new home was a small brown and white terrier named Milo. Tali Lavie said:

> "When I held Milo in my arms and he clung to me," Tali said,
> "I couldn't stop crying inside. I dreamt about him at night. I saw
> him looking at me, putting his faith in me, and I was so scared to
> disappoint him.
>
> "When we tamed animals and made them totally dependent on
> us, we assumed responsibility for them, but instead of acting as
> compassionate guardians, we imprison them in cages, experiment
> on them, eat them, wear their fur and skin, and exploit them for our
> entertainment. I feel, in a visceral way, that this is morally wrong.
> Helping animals is in my veins because I cannot tolerate the exploitation and betrayal that is a large part of our interaction with animals. They are innocent creatures just trying to survive, and we take
> advantage of them."

In 2006, during the war against Hezbollah, CHAI/Hakol Chai sent truck-loads of food, each carrying four tons of dog and cat food, plastic water bowels, containers for volunteers to carry water to the bowls, tick repellant, leashes, medicine, and more to the north of Israel, saving hundreds of lives. CHAI/Hakol Chai voluhteers set food out on the streets in areas that had been evacuated. We then rescued animals left behind at the request of residents who fled to bomb shelters and also housed and found homes for animals roaming the streets.

Still, some persist in asking: Given Israel's current security and economic problems, why should we care about animals? Hakol Chai's director, attorney Yadin Elam, explained it this way: "I don't believe you can limit your compassion to only one part of the world around you—to Jews, or whites, or women and children, or humans." An ethical vegetarian while pursuing his LLB and LLM, Yadin chose courses that focused on the issue of rights and previously worked for a charity that assisted migrant workers:

> "A lawyer is someone you hire to represent you, to be your voice
> before those who have the power to make decisions that affect you,"
> he said. "Who is in greater need of a lawyer than those who
> cannot speak for themselves? I became an advocate for animals not
> because I love animals—I do, though I love humans no less—but
> because animals need a lawyer more than anyone else. This is where
> a dramatic change needs to be made and I want to help bring about
> this change."

The importance of proper care of animals for a healthy society is an integral part of Judaism. It is forbidden to cause suffering to an animal and we may violate the Sabbath and Rabbinical commandments to help an animal in distress, according to the Code of Jewish Law. Animals are to be fed and watered before we sit down to eat, and we are even supposed to help our enemies' animals if they are in distress. On CHAI's first video, Rav Shear Yashuv Cohen, Chief Rabbi of Haifa, pointed out that Jewish teachings about animals are *deoraita,* which means they have the force of the Torah, and are no less important than keeping kosher, observing the Sabbath, or any other Jewish tenets.

Despite Judaism's beautiful teachings about animals, many still do not yet understand their importance and how beneficial it is to incorporate these values in our daily lives. Our current environmental crisis shows that we are all interconnected strands in a web. If one strand suffers, the whole web is weakened. We recognize that we need trees for the oxygen, valuable medicines, and other benefits they provide. Recently, we learned that living with animals lowers our blood pressure, helps us recover faster after surgery, and reduces the likelihood that our children will have allergies. Author Alice Walker writes that if trees provide us with oxygen, animals provide us with spiritual oxygen. We are only on the threshold of understanding the benefits animals provide, without which we humans would not survive. For a happy, healthy world, we need animals as much, if not more, as than they need us.

Helping animals is helping people. Where there is abuse of animals there is likely to be violence against women and children, scholarly studies have shown while offering scientific backing for the writings of ancient Jewish scholars from Maimonides onward. Other studies have shown that teaching humane values to and fostering empathy in children as a regular part of the curriculum inoculates them against future violent behavior, and the attitudes they learn toward animals are transferred to people. As nineteenth-century scholar, Rabbi Samson Rafael Hirsch, wrote: "Above all, those to whom the care of young minds has been entrusted should see to it that they respect both the smallest and the largest animals as beings, which, like people, have been summoned to the joy of life." CHAI's extensive humane education curriculum for Jewish and secular schools will shortly be made available to the public.

When asked to envision the ideal world they would like to live in, teachers at CHAI's conferences told us what they wanted was a peaceful, caring world. Nonviolence goes beyond the absence of war and strife. It is the daily choices we make at each moment—to waste or conserve water and paper, to drive an SUV or a hybrid, to select or eschew food, clothing, and products that are the result of suffering, human or animal, and choosing to find entertainment in cruelty or kindness. Only when we extend the peace we seek to all living beings, regardless of race, color, creed, ethnic origin, sex, or species will we have it for ourselves. Only then will Isaiah's prophecy where "none shall hurt or destroy in all my holy mountain" become reality.

Maintaining peace requires vigilance. CHAI's Supreme Court case to block the government's decision to bring gambling on horse racing to Israel is an example. In reaching its decision, the government failed to consider the animal welfare implications, in violation of the Animal Protection Law. The cruelties inherent in horse racing violate the Jewish tenets of "*tsa'ar ba'alei chayyim* and *bal taschit*, the prohibitions against causing suffering to animals and against wonton destruction. Gambling, too, is prohibited in Judaism, because it enriches one at the expense of another.

In every country where this cruel industry exists, thousands of horses are bred annually, the few fastest chosen to race, the rest typically sent to slaughter. Catastrophic injuries, bleeding in the lungs, chronic ulcers, and heart attacks are an inherent part of the life of a race horse. When they are no longer fast enough, usually by the time they are six years old—though some thoroughbreds can live to twenty-five—even former champions are usually sent to slaughter or are sold from hand to hand in a downward spiral of abuse. CHAI believes the Israeli government can find other ways to boost the economy than by inflicting cruelty on animals and adding to the country's social welfare burdens.

Recently, CHAI/Hakol Chai was offered land to construct in Israel a Campus for Compassionate Living, including a horse/donkey sanctuary, education center, and veterinary clinic. The Campus CHAI is now raising funds for the construction of a place where other animals who share Shabbat the cart horse's unfortunate fate can be brought to live out the remainder of their lives, free from pain and abuse, and where children and adults can be educated to live humanely and peacefully with all other living beings. Where else but Israel should a model of humane values be most evident, and from where else is it more appropriate that they be taught?

Compassionate Listening: a Radical Approach to Conflict

Leah Green

In November 2004, our delegation of twenty-four Compassionate Listeners crossed into Hebron, in the heart of Palestine, to meet one of the founders of Hamas, Sheikh Talal Sidr. We sat in his living room sipping Arabic coffee, and listened to his story. He told us that he had been imprisoned three times by the Israeli military and in 1991 he was deported with 400 other Palestinian men from the Islamic movements, to a snow-covered hillside in southern Lebanon.

Sheikh Sidr spent a lot of time that year in his Red Cross tent reading his Qur'an. There, he found the inspiration to break the chain of violence—the endless cycle of vengeance and revenge that he had been caught up in. Since his return to Hebron in 1992, he's been an outspoken leader for dialogue and reconciliation—"Jihad for Peace" he calls it. We asked him, "How do you engage now with Hamas members who still promote violence?" And he answered, "How do you take anger and hatred out of the hearts of people? You must love them; you must rally around them and become their family."

This is the essence of what The Compassionate Listening Project has been doing since 1990—rallying around and becoming "family" to Israelis and Palestinians on all sides of the conflict, and bringing them together to discover their common humanity. Our training curriculum has grown organically from our years of work on the ground. It has been road-tested in what may be the most protracted conflict on the planet. In 1999, our work moved beyond the Middle East, as we began teaching Compassionate Listening worldwide. We now offer advanced training and a facilitator certification program in North America.

Compassionate Listening is a foundational skill set for everyday peacemaking in our families, communities, and in social change work locally and globally. I call it a spiritual practice, because we are truly learning "to be the change we want to see in the world," as Gandhi so eloquently put it.

How this work began for me is very much connected to my family. My grandparents told harrowing stories about escaping from persecution and pogroms in Eastern Europe. My grandfather Ben lost half his siblings in the Holocaust. As with many Jews, war and peace have always felt like personal issues for me.

I first lived in Israel at age nineteen. Two years later I returned to attend the Hebrew University in Jerusalem, and became involved with Jewish-Palestinian peacemaking. That year, I sought out people from every perspective I could find and listened to them. An eternal optimist, I wanted to understand what it was that made this conflict so intractable.

People were more than willing to talk. It was 1982 and the Israeli army had invaded Lebanon one week before my arrival. The country was at war, and by October we were all consumed by its intensity. On campus, young Israeli students did not return from the front. Palestinian students were in shock over Israel's collusion with the massacres at Sabra and Shatila camps in Beirut. Israeli Jews were becoming increasingly polarized over the legitimacy of the war. In February 1983, at a Peace Now rally, a right-wing Israeli lobbed a grenade into the crowd, killing a left-wing Israeli.

My previous life in placid Northern California had not prepared me for life in a war zone. When a friend invited me to take a course in Jewish-Palestinian reconciliation, I eagerly began making trips to Neve Shalom/Wahat as Salaam to participate in programs run by their fledgling School for Peace. In addition to our own training, I also observed weekend encounter seminars for Israeli Jewish and Palestinian high-school students.

At a typical seminar, busloads of students would arrive with their chaperones. Jewish-Israelis came in their buses, and Israeli-Palestinians arrived in separate buses from their towns and villages. The students were awkward and uneasy with one another. Even though some of them lived minutes apart from one another, the seminars provided them with their first opportunity to meet "the other" face to face. Their lives had been completely segregated.

During the seminars, I witnessed anger, defensiveness, and many tears. I also learned a critical ingredient for reconciliation. When one person empathized with another or acknowledged their suffering, without defensiveness, argument, or blame, the result was connection and healing, and allowed deeper dialogue to ensue.

By the end of the seminars, parting was often traumatic: tears, a frenetic exchange of phone numbers, and promises to stay in touch. Grateful to have been a witness, the sessions helped me to demystify the mechanics of peace building.

That year I also visited many West Bank villages and towns and befriended Palestinians living under Israeli military rule. This was not a common experience for an American Jewish woman. Most Jews could not understand what led me to "cross over" and make friends with the "enemy." (In 1982 it was illegal for an Israeli Jew to meet with members of the Palestine Liberation Organization (PLO), and almost every Palestinian adult living in the West Bank and Gaza considered the PLO their government in exile.)

I genuinely loved both Israelis and Palestinians, and one question continued to burn in my soul: How can enemies make peace when their narratives of shared historical events are so completely different, when they lead such segregated lives, and when there are so few opportunities to come together and discover their common humanity? How could anyone hold hope for this situation when it was not considered acceptable to meet or speak with people from the other side?

These questions continued to haunt me until 1990, when I was invited to lead citizen diplomacy trips to Israel, the West Bank and Gaza for an American organization. My goal was to provide Americans with an opportunity to enter both worlds, experience the conflict firsthand, and support reconciliation efforts.

Without a specific framework for reconciliation, however, the early delegations seemed to amplify the conflict. Participants came with their own strong opinions of who was right and who was wrong, and looked for experiences to validate them. I decided after several years of leading the delegations that I did not want my work to add to the polarization of this conflict. I began to actively seek a way to work for reconciliation.

I found what I was looking for in the writings of Gene Knudsen Hoffman, who became a mentor to me. Gene was a Quaker, poet, actress, and peacemaker. She related an experience she had in 1980 in London at a Quaker conference when she saw a notice posted that read, "1:00 P.M. WORSHIP FOR THE TORTURED, AND THE TORTURER." Previously she had only thought about the oppressed—never the oppressor. Now she began to explore the idea that the oppressor in any given situation was wounded and was worthy of and in need of compassion. Gene wondered if "perhaps every act of violence comes from an unhealed wound."

Gene and I decided it would be a good experiment to begin practicing compassionate listening in my delegations, especially since the participants had such varying ideas about who was the oppressed and who was the oppressor within the context of Israeli-Palestinian conflict. We asked our participants to agree to make an attempt to reach the humanity of every person with whom we come in contact. We defined our role as hearing the grievances on all sides and finding ways to tell each side about the humanity and suffering of the other.

We called our experiment Compassionate Listening. Our mission was to build trust and respect with Israelis and Palestinians on all sides, not just those we felt sympathetic to but also with extremists on both sides. Educator Carol Hwoschinsky joined our team and began training our participants.

People began to feel our sincere desire to understand them at the human level. Because of the trust that began to build up, after a couple of years we began to bring opposing sides together, and our public events and workshops began to attract Israelis and Palestinians from all political and religious sides.

Compassionate Listening has not been an easy sell to the Israeli public. One memorable night in Jerusalem our eighteen-member delegation presented our work at a public forum at the prestigious Van Leer Institute. There were about 150 Israelis present—from the far right to the far left. Immediately after our presentation we came under verbal attack: "What right did we have as outsiders to get involved in the conflict?" "How could we possibly understand?" "You can't believe what Palestinians tell you—you can't trust them. They're lying to you!"

For ten minutes we practiced Compassionate Listening: we did not interrupt; we did not contradict; we honored people's rights to their perceptions. Slowly, as everyone calmed down, Israelis began to speak up on our behalf. An Israeli woman stood up and said, "You know, we Israelis have to admit that listening is a very radical concept for us, but I think these people are onto something," and everyone burst into laughter.

The dialogue continued and there was a palpable shift in the audience that night—there was softness and tenderness. People looked dazed outside the conference room afterward. I heard several people ask one another, "What just happened in there?" This is the magic that comes with Compassionate Listening. The science of Neurocardiology confirms our ability to shift from fear to compassion when we learn to "listen with our hearts" in the heat of conflict.

My own personal journey with Compassionate Listening has held many surprises. I have an Israeli friend, Ester, who is a Holocaust survivor from Germany. Ester's parents were murdered in the death camps, but Ester has made peace with

Germany and now returns each year to dialogue with friends and tells her story to German schoolchildren. She's one of the most courageous people I know.

In 2001, Ester discovered I was afraid to go to Germany and told me it was time to face this pain. I realized what a strange contradiction I was living. I had devoted my entire adult life to helping Jews and Palestinians re-humanize the other, but I held a secret belief that Jewish reconciliation with Germany was impossible. Three months later I was invited to a conference in Germany and I knew it was time. When I arrived at the airport in Hamburg, I was terrified. While waiting for a friend to meet me, I calmed myself by looking at the innocent faces of children.

Much to my surprise, I found enormous emotional suffering among Germans from WWII, especially the children and grandchildren who inherited the unresolved guilt and shame of their Nazi-era elders. My friend Beate Ronnefeldt and I decided it would be worthwhile to bring Jews and Germans together to explore our collective wound, and we co-founded the Jewish-German Compassionate Listening Project. Since then, dozens have come together in Germany to listen to each other, to listen to "witnesses"—Jews and Germans who experienced the war firsthand—to tour Berlin, and visit a concentration camp together.

The first year of the project we listened to a former SS soldier named Otto. He was not able to face his past until at age sixty he began having nightmares, at which time he began to talk openly with his men's group at church. We listened to Otto one evening in Berlin, and his story was so painful to hear.

Afterward, a Jewish woman in our group, whose parents are both survivors of Auschwitz, began to wail. A group of us gathered around her. Otto remained across the room, a respectful distance away. But gradually he moved closer and finally into the circle, where he knelt on the floor in front of her with great humility. They looked at one another. Otto lowered his forehead to the ground, and said to her, very quietly, and with tears in his eyes, "I bow to your pain."

The next day the Jewish woman seemed transformed, light-hearted even. She told the group she had been to Auschwitz twice in an effort to heal the pain she had carried her whole life. On a note of particularly black humor, she told us that this experience with Jewish-German Compassionate Listening was "better than Auschwitz." This speaks to the critical ingredient in healing: The very people we believe are our enemies are the very ones who can help us the most in our own healing. She had gone to Auschwitz, but she did not find Otto there. Doing this work with a former member of the Nazi SS was the missing ingredient.

Before this, I had cast Germans outside the framework of "humanity." But as I listened to more and more stories told by the Germans, about the gradual erosion of their civil liberties that came with the Nazi regime, and the horrible consequences for speaking out—how you could be arrested and lose your children or be sent to a concentration camp or even executed—I realized that had I been in their shoes, I probably would not have done anything heroic. In fact I'm quite convinced I would have done anything to protect my family and my children.

My experience with the Germans gave me a sense of humility. I now understand that the potential for human insanity is present within all of us, and is something we must continually be watchful for and inoculate against. We recently convened a Jewish-German project in Washington, DC, and the German delegation had great difficulty in coming to America. They knew about the Patriot Act and the erosion of civil liberties in the US, and seemed much more attuned to the danger signals than Americans.

The level of dehumanization that many Jews still hold for contemporary Germany is what is going on now between Israeli Jews and Palestinians—many on each side want to cast the other outside of the framework of "humanity." It's amazing to hear exactly the same language from each side. "They are so evil." "How can you make peace with them?" "They are not human beings." "They are terrorists!"

In September of 2003, I had the honor of meeting Father Shufani—a heroic figure of our time. Father Emile Shufani, a Melkite Christian priest in Nazareth, Israel, is the principal of St. Joseph's school. An eminent humanitarian, he's worked to strengthen Christian-Muslim relations and is very proud that his school is 45% Muslim. For the past fifteen years he has also maintained a sister-school relationship with an Israeli-Jewish school in Jerusalem, involving a dialogue program for teachers and students. As a part of their program, the kids live for a few days each summer in each other's homes. Several summers ago, during the second Intifada, the teachers gathered in Jerusalem. One of the Jewish teachers said she was afraid to send her kids to Nazareth in light of the ongoing Palestinian uprising and violence. In that moment, Father Shoufani felt something like a bomb go off in his head. He said, "I understood that we Palestinians still don't understand Jewish fear and Jewish suffering, most of which occurred in recent history in Christian Europe." Shortly thereafter, he conceived of the idea to take a large group of Israelis (Palestinians and Jews), to Auschwitz.

In May 2003, 300 Israeli Jews and Palestinians traveled with Father Shufani to Auschwitz. The trip was to be a communion, with no political agenda. He said, "We discovered we were not Jewish, Arab, Christian, or Muslim, but simply human beings taking care of one another. That one can be my 'enemy' and at the same time take my hand and cry with me . . . It was like spiritual heaven—we felt we touched the image of God. What we touched was our own humanity in the humanity of the other."

Father Shufani told us what a profound liberation it was for both the Palestinians and the Jews. The Palestinians asked for nothing in return. It was an unconditional act. They did not ask the Jews to listen to their pain—they completely let go of what he called the ping-pong approach. This beautiful embodiment of compassionate listening sent large ripples through Israeli society and beyond. For this, Father Shufani received UNESCO's peace prize.

The scale of global conflict at this moment of our lives is overwhelming and yes, disheartening. Even so, when we look at the grassroots level, in the heart of these terrible conflicts, we find remarkable stories of healing and reconciliation— local projects and initiatives that are showing us our human and humane potential. The way I see it, conflict is our teacher. It is not something to be avoided, or escalated, but entered into with skill and compassion. Do we humanize people on all sides of conflict or do we feed polarization? How do we perpetuate conflict in our own families and communities? When we see ourselves only as victims, our actions create more damage and more pain for all. When we are able to hold compassion for everyone involved, then our actions are likely to result in connection and healing.

I've now led more than 450 Americans into the heart of conflict in Israel and Palestine. We've also practiced Compassionate Listening in Jordan, Syria, and Lebanon. Every person has a unique perspective that has developed logically from his or her life experience. Every person we've listened to has a story, every person has grievances, and everyone wants peace, dignity, and security for themselves and for their children. Perhaps, when we discover how to "rally around and become family" to those we consider our enemies, peace will be possible.

Khirkha: A Poem

Khirkha: Palestinian woman's veil, silk cross-stitch on handspun linen, Museum for Textiles, Toronto

Dorothy Field

I cross the gallery, feel my breath catch
seeing these *khirkas* blooming
like walled gardens on the stark white wall, stitched designs
remembered from childhood: a vase of leaves
like an outstretched palm, a bird on a rose, a border edging the desert
of unbleached linen. It might have been

                My grandmother
who wove this linen, stitched silk gloss—red, sienna, burnt umber,
like the soil of the Galilee—my grandmother
who worked me a crewel purse, cerulean, cherry, rose.

            In 1890 her parents filled a wagon
with their kids, their candlesticks, a brass mortar and pestle,
left a Polish shtetl for the Lower East Side.
Semitic hands, Semitic cross-stitch.
They might just as well have gone east

To Palestine.
Is this appropriation, this blurring of boundaries?
Would they care, those women who made these veils sixty years ago
their grandchildren now in Nablus, Hebron
throwing rocks at Israeli tanks that shell their houses,
their schools?

Would they care
that I am a weaver, know the grab as the spindle's twist
runs up the thread, the spring of yarn reeling
from the shuttle?

I remember Ramallah,
Palestinian women gathering olives
their skirts hiked, scarves pushed back
sun coppering their foreheads.

Forgive me
this lack of separation.
The whole world is a narrow bridge.
For thinking our divisions might be set in softer stone.
The important thing is not to be afraid.
That the lay of bright silk on linen web could be a bridge

That I cross,
hands, feet, heart, into that dusty grove,
look up at the faces of the women in the olive trees,
hold out a basket to receive the fruit.

Kol ha'olam kulo gesher tsarme'od. Veha'ekar lo lehifached.
The whole world is a narrow bridge. The important thing is not to be afraid.
—Rabbi Nachman of Bratslav

Kitchen Politics

Roberta Kalechofsky

I am frequently asked how I became a vegetarian and involved in the animal rights movement. My spiritual convulsion began twenty-four years ago when Richard Schwartz sent me a manuscript, "Judaism and Vegetarianism" for publication with Micah Publications, the publishing house my husband and I run. Surprised that anyone would send me something on that subject—I was a confirmed pastrami, salami, hot dogs Brooklyn gourmet. Kosher, of course. Still, my editorial responsibility obliged me to read at least the first chapter.

I did and my fate was sealed: I read a description of factory farming, of the battery hen, of the crated veal—terms unknown to me then, and experienced what the Jewish philosopher Leon Kass has incisively called "the ethics of revulsion" in a wave of nausea and incredulity. Surely the author couldn't mean "kosher meat!"

I called the supervisor of my kosher meat market and read the fateful passages to him, expecting that he would deny what Schwartz wrote. His response changed my life, instantly and precipitously, "Mrs. Kalechofsky, all meat prepared for the commercial meat market comes from animals raised the same way. We just kill the animal differently." I read the pages to my husband. Astonished—we were both carnivores, and the idea of never eating meat again was strange to us, but I could not eat the meat of a tortured animal. And neither could he. Where would we find the meat of animals that weren't tortured?

I published Richard Schwartz' book, and went on to answer the question of what to eat when you refuse to eat the meat of tortured animals. I learned enough about the subject to write several books and many articles of my own, and to give dozens of talks. Everywhere I met with the same incredulity from Jewish audiences that I first experienced.

"Surely this is not kosher meat!" Most Jewish children believe that *kashrut* (Jewish dietary laws) is the sign of purity and mercy. If we confused the meaning of ritual purity with mercy, there were the stories of how Rabbi Judah the Prince wept at the thought of having to kill a calf, and at how *shochets* (ritual slaughterers) were chastised when their knives were not sharp enough to cut through the trachea of a cow very quickly.

Tsa'ar ba'alei chaim, do no harm to any creature, is a biblical exhortation which has been affirmed by rabbis in every century for two and half millennia. Embedded in Jewish texts, in proverbs, in legends, in biblical stories for Jewish children, it has almost no application in the modern world.

I will accept as axiomatic that this piety was operative in a lost world where Jews, and everyone else, were closer to nature, where animal life, their birth pangs, the love of cow for calf, the insatiable anxiety of mother bird for newborn, could be observed and felt by anyone who had eyes in his head to see and ears to hear the moaning of a cow who had lost her calf. Maimonides wrote that the emotions of the mother animal for her young are no different from the emotions of the human mother for her young.

How had this piety been eroded? What killed off this Jewish sensibility? How had this knowledge disappeared, so that Jewish butchers could accept the meat of animals who are shackled and hoisted, who have their back legs tied in the slaughterhouse in spite of *halakhic* (religious law) prohibitions against such treatment, or could accept the meat of calves that had been taken from their mothers within forty-eight hours of birth, in violation of the *halakhic* stipulation that no animal should be taken from its mother in less than eight days, which is little enough time for maternal nurturing, but still better than two days, and in some cases one day, so that a calf can be born into this world barely knowing the milk of his mother, barely knowing the smell of grass or the warmth of sun, and be put almost from birth into a dark crate the size of a large desk and be buried there for the next sixteen weeks of his life until he is led to slaughter. Was the world mad?

Did we no longer know what animal life was, so that every moving creature on the face of the earth could become an object of scientific experimentation or industrialized farming?

What began as revulsion set me on a course of education for the next twenty years. Dr. Dallas Pratt's book *Alternative Experiments to Painful Experiments on Animals,* opened another abyss of animal cruelty. Single lines can pierce the heart like a bullet. In his book, Dr. Pratt wrote such a line that again, like Schwartz' book, sealed my fate: "To accept the pain of the animal without knowing what the animal endures is moral sloth." I stood accused. I had not thought of myself as a "moral sloth." But the knowledge of animal pain requires a descent into the demonic, into the fury of bureaucracies and lobbyists, the quagmire of statistics, while the public resists knowing because the material is unimaginably painful.

Against my better judgment—I am a novelist used to working independently, averse to organizational work—I founded Jews for Animal Rights (JAR). No sooner had I "opened shop" than mail began arriving accusing me of misanthropy, of protecting the reputation of ritual slaughter, of being a front for *shechitah* ("Kosher slaughter"), asking me how I could be in favor of abortion as an animal rights person, and finally, a letter from a Palestinian asking how I could care more about dogs than about the Palestinian refugees.

I told the "pro-lifer" that animal rights was pro-life and that I am not "in favor of abortion" anymore than I am "in favor" of any operation that might be necessary. I told the Palestinian that "victim" was not a blanket category, that "victims" come in all kinds of degrees especially degrees of self-responsibility and that the Palestinians had power, whether they recognized it or not: Yasser Arafat had been welcome in more countries of the world than Israel had embassies in, his voice was welcome at the UN when Israel's was not and, most important, they had the power of the press and of world opinion, and the power to negotiate terms out of their powerlessness. The animals never do.

Mary Midgley, the British philosopher, in *Animals and Why They Matter,* wrote that we are confronted by the real difference between power and powerlessness in the child battered by an adult and the animal hunted, caged, experimented on by a human, and we know it by our instant revulsion, unmitigated by history or arguments of cause and effect. Charles Patterson, in *Eternal Treblinka,* argues that the model for fascism is originally seen in the relationship between animal and human. The argument goes back to Aristotle who accepted the model of the hierarchy of dominion and power in nature as a suitable basis for human morality.

The insidious evil that attends animal cruelty is the secretiveness that shrouds it in the laboratories and on the farms, which prevents public discussion of the issues. There are laws that regulate what happens in a slaughterhouse (inadequate laws often inadequately enforced), but *none* that applies to farm animals. A farmer can kick his cow to death, and is beyond the law because animals are considered his property. Science *protects* the horrors of what happens in the experimental laboratories with a halo over the head of scientists.

Our fast food habit, our lust for fast-cooked processed meat and chicken has transformed American culture, our working conditions, our eating conditions, our deteriorating health, our increasing health care costs. In 1970, Americans spent $6 billion on fast food. In 2000 they spent more than $110 billion. Our deteriorating health and health care costs keep pace with this statistic. The situation, as Steve Shriffler, writes, could be the plot of a Stephen King thriller:

All the ingredients for a devilish tale are there: epidemics of Salmonella stalking unsuspecting consumers; slaughterhouse workers toiling in ghoulish conditions; stomach-wrenching mountains of manure and chicken carcasses; and brutally overcrowded factory farms. Trouble is—none of this is fictional.

Yet it is devilishly easy to end this nightmare: just close your mouth and say no to meat.

Bibliography

Davis, Karen. *Prisoned Chickens, Poisoned Eggs.* Summerton, TN: Book Publishing Co., 1997.

Kalechofsky, Roberta. *Vegetarian Judaism: A Guide for Everyone.* Marblehead, MA: Micah Publications, 1998, 2006.

Schlosser, Eric. *Fast Food Nation: The Dark Side of the All-American Meal.* Boston: Houghton, Mifflin, 2001.

Singer, Peter and Mason, Jim. *The Way We Eat: Why Our Food Choices Matter.* Emmaus, PA: Rodale, 2006.

Striffler, Steve. *Chicken: The Dangerous Transformation of America's Favorite Food.* New Haven: Yale University Press, 2005.

African Americans and Jews

Stefan Merken

As a grassroots organizer let me tell you about a success story in Seattle

In spite of some mythmaking there has rarely been a "golden moment" of harmonious relationships between African Americans and Jews, one that was completely free of friction and tension. Some Jews and African Americans speak fondly of a time when "our two communities got along much better." But the reality is, there has never been a time when there were not significant class, political, or social differences and disagreements.

Of course there are also many instances where individuals or small groups of African Americans and Jews have become close friends or worked together towards common goals, such as in the labor movement of the 1920s and 1930s, and the civil rights and anti-war movements of the 1960s. There have also been national organizations in both communities that have maintained close working relationships over the years.

Since the 1970s, however, the relationships between our two communities have grown more distant. There have been voices on both sides that have stoked the fires of suspicion, and there have been those who responded with fear and resentment.

As a long-time social-justice activist, I have often heard misconceptions and fabrications voiced with conviction in various circles, as if there were "correct" answers to the problem of why African Americans and Jews do not always coexist in a friendlier, more cooperative fashion. Some examples of these distortions: Jews owned slave ships and brought and sold slaves from Africa; Jews, like whites, see African Americans as inferior; Jews make money from the Black community and do not want the situation to change; Jews have been at the forefront of the push to undo affirmative action. Conversely, African Americans see Israeli Jews mistreating Palestinians (darker Semitic people) and identify with their cause; the Jews are all rich and African Americans all poor; Jews, like whites, don't want Black kids living in their neighborhoods or attending their local schools. Each of these is either exaggerated or simply untrue.

Still, changes of mind and attitude are possible

This is what happened in Seattle when a group of us set out to correct any misjudgments both communities held about each other. Our mutual goal was to improve the economic situation of the African-American community and help them on the road to economic self-sufficiency. We also wanted to try developing friendships between individuals. This, we hoped, would improve the health of the inner city and the larger community and improve the overall relationships between our communities.

This premise led to the birth of the African-American/Jewish Coalition for Justice (AA/JCJ). Before we formed the AA/JCJ no one had analyzed the problem existing between our two communities (Jewish population of Seattle: some 30,000; African Americans: about 70,000). While each of us separately recognized reasons why we did not get along better, there had been no dialogue. It was the AA/JCJ that sought to bridge the abyss that kept us apart.

What we discovered was that the similarities between our two communities are striking and can be the basis for friendship. There are no two segments of our nation (Jews are fewer than 3% and African Americans comprise less than 12% of the total population) that have more in common and historically suffered more at the hands of "white" society than African Americans and Jews. We share a history of slavery and degradation; we put a great deal of stock in family; and we have enriched each other's music and poetry. African Americans and Jews are deeply committed to religious and social institutions. Both establish fraternities of peers, value education, and generally—though not always—support policies of equity, justice and equal opportunity.

The Seattle model

In the AA/JCJ, the African American and Jewish communities are working together to build economic strength and community life.

We began meeting in November 1992 with two ideas: bridge the abyss between the African American and Jewish communities, while ending the wrong ideas each had about the other. A half-dozen Seattle Jews, members of the Jewish Peace Fellowship's Seattle chapter, met and began working with Reverend Robert Jeffrey, executive director of The Black Dollar Days Task Force. Together we set our agenda to include ways of furthering economic justice and stopping hate crimes, while building a closer relationship. Simple in concept, but not easy to put into effect.

At our first public event we invited Rabbi Michael Robinson of Sebastopol, California, who had a long history of social justice activism, to visit Seattle for a series of joint speaking engagements with Reverend Jeffrey. It was these two dynamic, intensely committed individuals, speaking in churches, synagogues, schools, and open meetings, who kicked off the process.

As we moved forward, we invited others to join us. We set up meetings in synagogues and churches. Many of those who initially came were ministers, rabbis and community activists. The first few meetings were spent getting to know one another so as to develop the confidence and trust to talk openly and candidly, even while disagreeing. As Reverend Jeffrey, a charismatic Baptist minister and activist whose leadership and personality was crucial to the success of many of the early meetings put it, "We need to become friends before beginning any work."

Being allies and friends is critical in social-justice work. It requires lots of meetings. It means having lunches together. It means being comfortable enough to discuss crucial, often sensitive issues. Most important, we needed to begin listening to one another more carefully. At one meeting, a member of a synagogue social action committee came up to me afterwards and told me she could not get a word in. I realized then that African Americans must often feel the same way, especially in the company of whites.

From the start we invited young people so they might meet and form friendships. That has been crucial from Day One. When "Daniel's Story" (a traveling exhibition from the US Holocaust Memorial Museum in Washington, DC) came to Seattle, we arranged for fifty youngsters from a local church youth group and a local temple youth group, to visit the exhibit as a group and talk about their feelings afterwards.

In Seattle, we placed tremendous value on building strong personal relationships. A group give-and-take session was a great way to begin the process. Working together, we came to realize, is where *real change* takes place.

Our first project was the Pairing Project. To develop better understanding and closer communication, we paired a Jewish individual (and in some cases entire families) with a Black individual or a family. We distributed forms for asking some basic questions so we might bring people together on the basis of interests, age, or family composition. Each member of a pair was given the other's phone number. Our instructions: meet for lunch. And try to eat in the African-American neighborhood to support a local restaurant. Talk about anything and everything that interests you. Meet at least once a month, more often if convenient. Try to attend AA/JCJ meetings together and sit alongside each other. We never had a format defining what "should" happen or a desire to "accomplish" something. Our aim was simply to introduce people to one another. We hoped that they would realize that they could talk to one another as fellow human beings.

Pairs working together on social action projects at least four times a year was something that both Jews and African Americans were excited about. *Tikkun Olam* (repairing the world) is a central focus of Judaism. Church-going African Americans are also regularly involved in social justice projects. Our pairs have cleaned a group home for AIDS victims; worked at food banks, including a food kitchen run by teenagers; and painted and cleaned a therapeutic child center. The result: African Americans and Jews worked together to improve local conditions while developing personal bonds.

Addressing racial and religious crimes that affect both communities is a critical challenge for the AA/JCJ. We found that African Americans are surprised that others outside their own community are concerned about the rate at which Black youths are being killed. Our Focus on Youth, an outreach program in which synagogue and church youth attend programs at museums, theaters, and other cultural events, seeks to widen their horizons. Bringing together ministers and rabbis has also been a rewarding project. Our first meeting of ten African-American clergy and ten rabbis was a tremendous success. They shared a kosher dinner, got to know one another, and set an agenda for future meetings.

The AA/JCJ publishes six newsletters a year, and holds four events attended by 100–150 or more people. Together we've celebrated Kwanzaa, Hanukkah, Christmas, and a Freedom Seder (before Easter and Passover)—recounting our journeys from slavery to freedom. Our event committees are always comprised of, and chaired by, African Americans and Jews. We've also sponsored a summer picnic and a Rev. Dr. Martin Luther King, Jr. breakfast celebrating what his life and work has meant for all of us.

Helping African-American entrepreneurs

All too often many large and successful businesses lure the hard-earned African-American dollar out of the African-American community without reinvesting a penny back into their community. When African Americans own and operate their own businesses they can fold their dollars back into their own community. When that investment happens, the economic situation can begin to change dramatically.

A major concern for Black communities today is economic self-sufficiency, namely building businesses owned by African Americans and hiring African Americans. These are concrete ways to create an economic base for long lasting, self-sufficiency. Helping African Americans attain economic security and financial independence is a critical issue for all of us. If one segment of a community suffers, the whole community suffers. If one part of the community is economically depressed, with their young having little or nothing to work or hope for, then everyone suffers. The cost is immeasurable.

We learned rather quickly of the desperate need for low-interest loans for small, new and existing minority-owned businesses, as well as the need for training for better-paid jobs. What we planned to do was create a mentor program of experienced businesspeople willing and able to assist new African-American business owners.

The creation of Campaign 5000 Endowment Fund was an important step in building economic self-sufficiency in the African-American community. The brainchild of Reverend Jeffrey, Campaign 5000 was launched in 1998. He was painfully aware of the lack of money available to young African-American entrepreneurs who had concrete, often creative ideas for starting businesses but were turned away from standard banking loans because of a lack of collateral or co-signers. Aware of the Hebrew Free Loan Society model from which Jewish immigrants borrowed seed money to begin businesses when they arrived in this country, he created Campaign 5000.

The AA/JCJ was helpful in getting Campaign 5000 off the ground. A $1.5 million endowment loan fund consisted of 5,000 stakeholders each donating $200 which, Reverend Jeffrey believed, would be augmented by half-million dollars from corporate sponsors. Campaign 5000 has thus far made several small business loans from the Endowment's interest, about $400,000, and the program is growing. Many men and women from Seattle's Jewish community saw the importance of supporting the Campaign and gave generously.

Looking to the future

African Americans and Jews can certainly replicate what we accomplished in Seattle. It takes only three things: a commitment for concerned people in both communities willing to sit down and talk about change and the future; integrity and determination to meet in social situations while working together for the common good; and above all, a willingness to look beyond one's own group.

OUR HERITAGE

The ultimate basis for understanding of any system of ethics, public or private, is the answer to the question, 'What is humanity?' One answer is given in the account of Creation from Jewish mystical tradition (Kabbalah).

—Rabbi Philip J. Bentley, "Fixing the World"

Violence and Nonviolence in Jewish Thought and Practice

Rabbi Arthur Waskow

Since Jewish thought has always proceeded in a spiral where the future and the past are intertwined, it is hardly possible to think about a future of assertive nonviolent Jewish action without unfolding the meaning of our memories.

For Jewish wisdom is neither the endless circle of tradition nor the abrupt progression of a straight line forward. Always it does *midrash*— takes an ancient tradition, gives it a twirl, and comes out somewhere new. Spiraling.

Faced with the earthquake of the Roman-Hellenistic conquest of the Mediterranean basin, the Jewish people created a macro-midrash: Rabbinic Judaism, with an outlook on violence and nonviolence very different from that of Biblical Israel.

Today we are in the midst of a similar transformation, sparked by the Jewish encounter with modernity, with external violence in the form of the Holocaust, with the complexities of power involved in controlling a modern nation-state, and with the complexities involved in having a share of power in governing great modern super-states.

I. Biblical Israel: Ultra-violence and Civil Disobedience

In Biblical Israel, there is a strand of willingness to use violence—sometimes hyper-violence—to advance the Jewish vision of a decent society; and there is a strand of constant willingness to challenge and disobey arrogant power, whether it's located in a foreign Pharaoh or in a Jewish king. One example of the first, from Deuteronomy 20: 10-18:

> When you draw near to a town, to wage war against it, you are to call out to it terms of peace.
>
> And it shall be: if peace is what it answers you, and it opens (its gates) to you, then it shall be that all the people that are found in it shall belong to you as forced laborers, and they shall serve you.
>
> But if they do not make peace with you, and make war against you, you may besiege it. And when YHWH your God gives it into your hand, you are to strike down all its males with the edge of the sword. Only: The women and the infants and the animals, everything that is within the town, all its booty, you may take-as-plunder for yourself; you may consume the booty of your enemies that YHWH your God gives you.
>
> Thus you are to do to all the towns, those exceedingly far from you, that are not of the towns of those nations. Only: in the towns of those peoples that YHWH your God is giving you as an inheritance, you are not to leave alive any breath; but: you are to devote them to destruction, yes, destruction, the Hittite, the Amorite, the Canaanite, the Perizzite, the Hivvite and the Yevusite, as YHWH your God has commanded you. In order that they not teach you to do according to all their abominations that they do with their gods, and you sin against YHWH your God.

Even within this approach, however, the Biblical model of Jewish life pre-served some limits on war. Even in wartime, the Israelite army was forbidden to cut down fruit trees, unless they were actually needed for bulwarks to carry out a siege. And the Torah provided for individual exemptions from the army for young people in the earliest journey of making a family, building a house, creating a vineyard—indeed, even for people who feared being killed in battle, or feared that they might become killers. The Maccabean revolt against the Seleucid Empire ac-tually applied these rules, even in the midst of a war to resist an occupying power that had desecrated the Temple and was forcing people to worship idols.

The Israelite tradition not only put limits on the exercise of military force, it also described the use of nonviolent resistance against unaccountable power.

There is another important strand of biblical teaching. The story of Shifra and Puah—the midwives who refused to obey Pharaoh's order to murder Hebrew boy babies—perhaps the first tale of nonviolent civil disobedience in world literature.

The Hebrew Bible also describes nonviolent resistance to Babylonian and Persian power. For example, Jeremiah warns against using violence and military alliances to oppose the Babylonian conquest, and argues instead that God will protect the people if Judah acts in accord with the ethical demands of Torah—freeing slaves, letting the land rest. Daniel and his friends famously are cast into the lions' den for nonviolently refusing to obey the king's command to worship foreign gods. And, although the Book of Esther ends in violence, Esther herself demonstrates nonviolent civil disobedience when, in fear and trembling, she approaches the Persian king without having been invited so that she can carry out her mission to save the Jewish people from a murderous tyrant.

We might say it is not surprising that Israelite culture would celebrate resistance to foreign potentates. What about Israel's own kings?

Here, too, there are tales of nonviolent resistance. There is a powerful story of an Israelite king, Saul, who had to deal with an underground guerilla whom he thought of as a terrorist, named David. And David, with a very small band of underground guerillas, went off, hungry and desperate, and found food and protection at a sacred shrine, where they asked the priests to let them eat the show-bread, the lehem panim, the sacred bread placed before God, because they were desperately hungry. And the priests fed them from the sacred bread.

When Saul heard about this, he said (more or less), "Anybody who harbors a terrorist is a terrorist!" And so King Saul ordered his own bodyguards to kill the priests of Nov. But the bodyguards refused.

Torah also bears descriptions of how it would look to have power made accountable to the public and to the guardians of Torah. In Deuteronomy there is the description of a constitutional monarch who must write, day by day, those passages of Torah that restrict his own power. He must not multiply horses—cavalry, the tanks and Apache helicopters of that day. He must not pile up money for his treasury. He must not send the people back into *Mitzrayim*, which didn't mean sending them back to geographical Egypt, it meant sending them back to slavery. And he had to read the Torah, in public.

II. Rabbinic Judaism: Internal Tikkun and Passive Nonviolence

But the Jewish people faced both an outside practical challenge to that set of assumptions about military power, and an internal ethical challenge to it.

The external challenge came from the Hellenists and the Romans who swept over the Mediterranean basin, conquering the Jewish state. Jews revolted, most famously under the Maccabees and under Bar Kochba, until the Romans finally proved military revolt against their empire impossible by decimating Israel's Jewish population. After this Diaspora, the Rabbis refused to make heroes of Bar Kochba or even of the Maccabees. Rabbinic Judaism essentially said, "No longer can military power create a decent society in this sliver of land. Can't be done. Shouldn't be tried."

Internally, the Rabbis also decreed that military power should no longer be used. They did this by evading, nullifying, and otherwise interpreting away the Torah's genocidal commands against the Canaanites and other idolatrous people. Instead of extrapolating from these commands that it would be all right—even obligatory—to wipe out any people that rejected the Jewish God, the rabbis went in the opposite direction, ruling that the Canaanite example was a limited one— by the time of the rabbis, a nullity—because the Assyrians had scattered and shattered them as well as the "ten lost tribes" of Israelites themselves.

The Rabbis who were so creative in applying ancient Torah in a new situation could certainly, had they wished, have understood the Jebusites, Hivites, Amalekites, and so on as symbols for ongoing threats and dangers to be dealt with militarily. They chose instead to nullify the genocidal meaning of the text. And they even dismissed the Torah's commands to execute a rebellious Israelite child or wipe out a rebellious Israelite city, saying, "This never happened and it never will." Perhaps "this never happened" was a historical claim, but "it never will" expressed an ethical decision never to carry out the seeming command of Torah.

While some may say the rabbis were merely being pragmatic, given the power of the Roman and Byzantine empires these rulings on matters internal to the Jewish people certainly point to a real ethical revulsion against the use of violence,

Indeed, the rabbis, who continued to shape a court system within Jewish society, mostly rejected the violent punishments prescribed in Torah. "A court that sentences even one person to death in seventy years," they said, "is a court of murderers."

But most basic transformation of all was that the Rabbis constructed a nonviolent way for the Jewish people to live in the world. Living in the nooks and crannies of Roman, Christian, and Muslim civilizations, Jewish communities in the Rabbinic period created decent societies of their own and gave up on the vision of toppling the Great Powers and transforming the world as a whole.

Only within ourselves, said the rabbis, can we make a decent world. Someday, if we do a good job, then somehow a transcendent God will come and bring *Mashiach*, bring the Messiah, and so transform the world. But as for us? For our own action being able to mend the clearly broken broader world beyond our boundaries? Forget it.

People sometimes call Gandhian nonviolence "passive resistance" even though Gandhi's form of nonviolence is in fact highly assertive. But in the case of Rabbinic Judaism, the phrase "passive resistance," or "nonassertive nonviolence," is fairly accurate. For almost two thousand years, Rabbinic Jews accepted that they would suffer expulsions, they would suffer pogroms, but believed that the Jewish people could live beyond expulsions and pogroms.

III. Reviving a Military Model

Rabbinic Judaism's model of nonassertive nonviolence worked well until the last century or so of modernity, when sadism became industrialized, when we experienced not only pogroms and expulsions, but the *Shoah*, the Holocaust, the death of one-third of the Jewish people. It then became clear to almost all of us that we could no longer live with the Rabbinic model.

What to do?

The first response to industrial sadism and arrogance was to revert to the military model of the biblical period (though without its acceptance of imposing genocide). Jews thought: "We need to protect ourselves from the modernized hatreds of other peoples with military force. And we can do this once more on the eastern edge of the Mediterranean."

This was the response of what became the major forces in the Zionist movement, the Zionism of Herzl (who chose the music of Wagner to be played at the first Zionist Congress), of Ben Gurion as well as Jabotinsky, of the left-wing Palmach and the right-wing Irgun. (There was another Zionism: that of Ahad Ha'am and Martin Buber and Henrietta Szold; but their vision and version of Zionism were almost drowned out, especially by the flood of bloodshed in the Holocaust.)

When military force was first applied by the Zionist *yishuv*, some elements of the Jewish military forces tried to apply the concept of "self-restraint" and "purity of arms." Perhaps this was a throwback to the ethics of the Rabbis. The idea behind the "purity of arms" was that civilians should not be attacked, that Jewish settlements established by purchase should be defended whenever necessary, but that Palestinian Arab towns should never be attacked.

Never was this purity quite pure, and some branches of the Zionist movement did not honor such strictures. Yet the effort to secure and defend Palestinian territory on which to build a Jewish society was originally prepared for compromise, partition, and self-restraint.

But it is clear that more and more, this decision to use military force sparingly has changed into an addiction to use military force and violence, aggressively as well as defensively, for conquest as well as for self-defense.

Successive governments of Israel have chosen the path of competing with the Great Powers of the world. Tanks, planes, even H-bombs, till as I write, the State is in the midst of a massive repression of a rebellious people, and the rebellion as well as the repression is taking crueler and crueler forms.

It is already becoming clear that a small people cannot maintain "purity of arms," cannot wage an ethical military effort, cannot compete with the Great Powers—and carry on a decent society at the same time. Not even the Soviet Union, a continental super-state, could shoulder this burden. It is not altogether clear that even the richest society in the history of the world, the United States, can for generations wage continuous war—even "a pure war"—and remain or create a decent society at home.

The chances that Israel can do so are very small. Pursued to its logical fulfillment, this reversion to the biblical path leads to a dead end. And I do mean a dead end.

IV. A New Tikkun Olam

What is a decent alternative to military action?

The advantage of the Biblical vision was that it was assertive, rather than passive. The advantage of the Rabbinic vision was that it avoided violence. Is there a way to synthesize these virtues in the new era of Jewish peoplehood into which we have entered? Is there a way to create a Jewish path of assertive nonviolence?

Let's look at what may have been the most successful single use of nonviolent civil disobedience by the Jewish people since the midwives Shifra and Puah, even though we have almost never put the tag "nonviolent movement" on it.

That was the Soviet Jewry movement. With only one or two exceptions, it avoided the use of violence and used assertive nonviolence to win freedom for Jews in the Soviet Union.

Dancing in the streets of Moscow on the night of Simchat Torah. Marches, demonstrations, boycotts. Sit-ins in the Supreme Soviet. I can remember when people thought, "Hey, a sit-in in the Supreme Soviet? All those folks will be dead in a week!"

But they weren't. Indeed, they won allies. Jews around the world, and members of other communities as well. We did not need to stand alone. Through years of struggle, this movement made some cracks in what to many had seemed a monolithic Soviet totalitarian state. Even before those cracks and many others brought the whole system down, millions of Soviet Jews either became free to leave or free to begin recreating a Jewish community and culture.

Why did we not think of this movement as Gandhian or Kingian? I think it was because we were deeply puzzled as to how to cope with such a way of understanding ourselves alongside the State of Israel during that same period. But the movement to free Soviet Jews was an assertive nonviolent movement. We should with joyful pride name this nonviolent victory as what it was, lift it up to our own awareness, and celebrate it.

This effort was the strongest, but not the only, use of assertive nonviolence by Jewishly conscious Jews during the past generation.

There were the Freedom Seders of the early 1970s, aimed against racism and the Vietnam War, all of them rooted in affirming the liberation struggle of the Jewish people alongside the liberation struggles of Black Americans, Vietnamese, women, Nicaraguans. One of those Freedom Seders actually poured blood, frogs, and cockroaches—the symbolic plagues—on the fence around the White House. Another brought together 4,000 people in the Cornell University field house, where Daniel Berrigan actually came out from the underground to which he had fled from the government's prosecution of his anti-war activities. Assertive nonviolence, with allies. Both a new approach in Jewish life.

And there was the Jewish Campaign for Trees for Vietnam, with Rabbi Abraham Joshua Heschel as its Honorary Chairman, which challenged the actions of the US government in deliberately destroying the forests of Vietnam to deny tree cover to Vietnamese guerrillas. The Trees for Vietnam campaign drew on both the Torah's prohibition of destroying trees in time of war, and the Jewish practice of planting trees in Israel. Raising money for these purposes was an act of civil disobedience. More recently, that environmental activism has continued with a Tu B'Shvat Seder in the redwood forest, concluding with a "plant-in" on the very property owned by a corporation that was logging the ancient redwoods.

The movement toward a Jewish nonviolent civil disobedience has helped invigorate and renew Judaism. For example, *Hoshanah Rabbah,* the seventh day of *Sukkot,* was originally a ceremony that happened at river banks. Since ancient times, Jews beat willows on the river bank, dancing seven circles with the Torah and calling out to God to save the earth from drought and locusts, famine and plague. But in modern times, Hoshanah Rabbah has mostly been limited to beating willow branches on the rugs in the small chapel at the back of a few traditional synagogues, having no way of connecting with the festival prayers for healing the earth.

In 1998, a small group of Jews changed all that by beating willows on the earth on the banks of the Hudson River—aimed against General Electric's refusal to clean up the river after poisoning it with PCB's. That fused the ancient meaning of this festival with an act of assertive nonviolence against one of the Great Powers of the planet.

Today, as the State of Israel pursues the older, biblical path, using military action to push its policies, Jewish nonviolence sadly must be used against Jewish military action. So we see Israeli Jews and Jews from the Diaspora, along with international supporters from many countries, sitting down against the Israeli bulldozers destroying Palestinian homes. With their own bare hands, pushing aside the concrete blocks that cut off Palestinian villages in blockades, in sieges. Coming on *Tu B'Shvat* to replant olive trees destroyed (despite the prohibitions of Torah) by Israeli soldiers and settlers in Palestine as well as replanting palm trees and pine trees destroyed by Palestinian arsonists in Israel. Being arrested, even beaten, for their nonviolent resistance.

And we have seen Israelis, soldiers and reservists, who have refused to serve in the Army of Occupation, citing God, ethics, Torah, and the true security of Israel as their reasons. And going to jail for refusing. In these brave nonviolent protesters we see the hope and the promise of an assertive, yet nonviolent means to secure Jewish life and culture.

Most of these campaigns and struggles have drawn explicitly on Jewish ceremony and Jewish practices. For that reason, they did not have to choose between being "Jewish" and being "universal," they did not even have to "balance" being "Jewish" and being "universal."

In the very depth of their being, they were simultaneously and organically both Jewish and universal. Putting energy into them did not draw Jews away from their Jewish heritage in order to heal the wounded world; it actually deepened their Jewish knowledge and experience.

Nor did these actions pull people into Jewish tribalism at the expense of lost concern for the others endangered on this planet. Like a hologram, like the presence of DNA in every cell of the body, they taught that the whole is fully present in each part. The highest good of each community and the highest good of the planet as a whole are enwrapped within each other. That is why we call this new Jewish form of assertive nonviolent civil disobedience *tikkun olam,* the healing of the world.

V. Creating the Future in the Present

Surely the development of Jewish assertive nonviolence has owed much to the experience of the movements we connect with Gandhi and with King. Yet there are differences. Not only does Jewish nonviolence draw on Torah to embody as action-forms, it also draws on the Jewish tradition for counsel on when violence itself may be necessary, even for the committed nonviolent activist.

Just after World War I, in his essay "Recollection of a Death" (published in *Pointing the Way*), Martin Buber thought deeply about whether the means might justify the ends. He wrote about the Leninist "Red Terror" of the period—"I cannot conceive of anything real corresponding to the saying that 'the end sanctifies the means;' " but I mean something which is real in the highest sense of the term when I say that the means profane, actually make meaningless, the end, that is, its realization!"

He continued, "The more out of accord with the goal is the method by which it is realized, the farther will be the goal that is actually realized from the one that was set."

At first glance, this may seem not different from Gandhi's teaching that "You must be the end that you seek," or A. J. Muste's teaching, "There is no way to peace; peace is the way."

It is surely closely connected with those teachings, but a close reading of the way Buber puts his point suggests a different possibility: that Buber is not so absolutist about the avoidance of all violence. All his thought and writing leans away from enshrining rules of behavior and toward experiencing the unique need in the unique moment.

In one such specific situation, during a dialogue/debate with Gandhi over how the Jews of Europe should respond to Nazism, Buber actually did distinguish his own views from absolutist pacifism. In the passage above, Buber is not necessarily saying you must choose a means that matches your end. He sternly warns you should realize that if you want, for example, peace in the end, it will be far harder to achieve if the means you use is war.

The point is that Buber is, in a sense, describing a "sliding scale" of social change. The more violence in the means, the more violence will remain in the goal achieved. In the Soviet Union of Lenin and Stalin, the "means" of the Red Terror became the (perhaps unintended) "end" of a totalitarian dictatorship. Buber makes clear in the essay that he was strongly opposed to that means and prophetically understood what end would be achieved. In 1949, when he published *Paths in Utopia*, he unfolded in great clarity his critique of what had happened in Soviet reality.

But implicit in Buber's dread of the unfolding of violence into more and more violence, there is also the possibility that an activist may use certain limited forms of violence in extreme necessity, while being fully aware that this is likely to corrupt the society that s/he is trying to bring to birth. This awareness might make it possible to take steps to reduce the corruption that results.

This willingness to consider violence makes Jewish civil disobedience different from the Gandhian or Buddhist model. After the passiveness of the Rabbinic model, with its acceptance of pogroms and massacres, Jewish nonviolence must be robust, and perhaps even willing to consider the possibility of violence in the last resort.

The main thrust of Buber's point, however, is that the best way to bring about the future you desire is to actually build a miniature or microcosm of that future in the present. No longer a passive nonviolent protest against the world we disdain, Jewish nonviolence today stresses that we must actively and positively create the world we want.

There is an ancient Jewish teaching that encodes this wisdom: According to the ancient Rabbis, if the entire Jewish people were to observe *Shabbat* twice in a row, the Messiah would come. Since Shabbat was understood as a foretaste of the Messianic Age, this teaching meant: "Bring it by doing it."

Indeed, I suggest that this "law" of social action (in the sense of the law of gravity—a description of empirical reality) is so basic that it applies whether the activist's vision and practice are nonviolent, or not.

One of the clearest cases of the power of this form of social action was the sit-in movement in the United States. The sit-inners did not begin by trying to change the laws that mandated or permitted segregation. They did not attack the restaurant owners. They envisioned a future of integrated public places, and in the present they integrated them. They put on the society at large the burden of deciding what to do about them.

By disobeying the law, they changed the law. And since they tapped into a latent value system among the majority of Americans that supported racial equality and opposed segregation, they initiated a great wave of social change that echoed and intensified what they were doing, carrying their basic values into areas they had not addressed.

Let us look at a movement that ideologically, in values and worldview, was quite different—but that structurally had much the same effect. That is the ideologically motivated settler movement that began in the 1970s to set up Israeli enclaves in the West Bank, when to do so in the places they chose was not legal. (I call them "ideologically motivated" to distinguish them from Israelis who later bought homes in West Bank settlements because government subsidies made them much cheaper than houses inside the 1967 Israeli borders.)

These settlers were not committed to the universalist values that imbued the sit-in movement. They were nationalists who had no compunction about using violence against Palestinians, or threatening to use it even against Jews in a "civil war" if a Jewish government were to try to force them to leave their settlements. So from a values standpoint, they were quite different from the American sit-in movement.

But they were very much like the sit-inners in that they enacted in the present the future they envisioned. They imagined a West Bank populated by Jews, and they acted to make it so right away. They confronted the Israeli government and public and the Palestinians with their *faits accomplis*— and challenged them to respond.

Like the sit-in movement, through the boldness and clarity of their action they created waves of political energy that moved in their direction. For an entire generation, they have had a profound effect on Israeli politics and culture. For like the sit-in movement, they tapped into latent support for their values among the society around them: in their case, among Israelis who were drawn to the notion of a Jewish/Israeli West Bank, whether for religious, nationalist, territorial-security, or financial reasons.

Several of the recent actions by Israelis of a very different political persuasion have also begun to enact the future in the present: peace demonstrations jointly planned and held by Palestinian and Israeli women; joint Israeli-Palestinian actions to open roadblocks on Palestinian roads, replant trees in Palestinian villages, rebuild demolished Palestinian homes; Israeli reservists' refusing to serve in the Occupation army. It remains to be seen whether these actions also tap into a latent value-system among a sizeable number of Israelis.

Seeing the issues of violence and nonviolence in social action through this lens of "enacting the future in the present" may offer a new way to understand and to choose a course of action for tikkun olam.

VI. Finding Allies

To act in this way, the Jewish community must see ourselves as no longer utterly engulfed by enemies. For the assertive nonviolence of a small and lonely people challenging Great Powers will simply bring catastrophe the sooner, if there are no allies for the challenge.

The mindset that felt we stood alone imbued both biblical and Rabbinic Judaism. It grew up in the effort to conquer Canaan against what we thought was an ocean of idolaters and the effort to survive the Roman Empire. That mindset was reinforced by Inquisitions and pogroms and even by the gentler Muslim habit of treating the Jews like tolerated pets.

Whether we were making a decent society with military means in the ancient land of Israel, or making a decent society in the nooks and crannies of other civilizations all over the world, both Biblical and Rabbinic Judaism said, "We are on our own. Nobody else cares. Nobody shares our vision. They're all enemies and only we carry the vision."

For centuries, this may well have reflected considerable truth.

But one thing that modernity has brought with it has been the discovery that there are other communities in the world with which we can in fact share a vision of a decent society. It is possible to find allies.

Now we have to behave in a certain way to be able to find allies. But it is no longer impossible to find them. And the question is whether, in response to the smashing of Rabbinic Judaism by modernity, we can connect with Christians who are responding to modernity's shattering of the Christianity that has till now existed, and with Buddhists who are struggling with a Buddhism similarly shattered by modernity, and with Muslims struggling with a shattered traditional Islam.

Within each of these traditions—within the Jewish people, within Christian communities, within Islam, within Buddhism, within Hinduism, there are some who say, "Then let's go back two centuries, three centuries, and vomit out this disgusting, destructive modernity.

"Let's put women back in their place, the earth back in its place and especially the other communities back in their places."

All of those places were, of course, underneath, below, subordinate. From that standpoint, these efforts to restore pre-modern religious cultures cannot make allies with each other, because each denies the others' legitimacy. (They may become de facto brothers in blood, each fuelling the other's violence.)

Indeed, these restorationist versions of Judaism, Christianity, Islam, Buddhism must be far more coercive, more violent, than the traditional communities they are hoping to restore. For it always takes more force, more coercion, to force a genie back in the bottle than it did to keep it there in the first place. Two centuries ago, no one had to beat up women to keep them from vocally, audibly *davvening*—praying—at the Western Wall. They just didn't try. Now—throw chairs at them to "restore" the past. Use State power. All new, in the name of restoration.

From this restorationist energy have stemmed the terror attacks of 9/11, the Christian anti-abortion bombings, Baruch/Aror Goldstein's murder of twenty-nine Muslims at prayer in the Tomb of Abraham, the Hindu burning of the Golden Temple, the Buddhist-Hindu violence of Sri Lanka.

But these restorationist forces are not the only response to modernity's shattering of traditional religious life. There are also energies that say, "Let's make distinctions between what is holy and what is destructive. Surely the modernity that made possible the Holocaust, the H-bomb, and even the burning of the Amazon Basin is not wholly good. But some of modernity is sacred, and that part we can absorb into our traditional religious teachings and go forward. Let's renew our communities rather than restoring them as they were three or four centuries ago.

"Let's renew the sacred teaching of the sacred earth, for which indeed we have ancient warrant. And the sacred teaching of the sacredness of the full equality of women, for which neither we nor any of the old traditions has warrant. And the sacred tradition of the sacredness of other strivings for truth from which we can learn and with which we can make allies.

"We can no longer hide alone in nooks and crannies, we can no longer conquer or even defend alone our own decency, and we must try to mend the whole world after all.

"So let's reach out for allies—and let's bring assertive nonviolence, not passive but assertive, to bear on transforming or even toppling the Great Powers of the earth, so as to heal what now needs to be a planetary community."

VII. Seeing Ourselves Mirrored in the Other

To heal the world, we cannot see ourselves as utterly pure and the world as utterly polluted. Just as we must be able to see the good in others if we are to find allies, so we must be able to see the violence we hide within ourselves.

Rabbi Abraham Joshua Heschel reminded us of this wisdom in an essay on "The Meaning of This War [World War II]," in *Moral Grandeur and Spiritual Audacity,* edited by Susannah Heschel.

The date of this remarkable essay is crucial to understanding its depth. It was written in 1943 and first published in February 1944. Heschel asks the question: "Who is responsible [that the war has soaked the earth in blood]?" And he—the Polish Hassid just transplanted to America—answers as a Hassid might, by quoting the Baal Shem Tov: "If a man has beheld evil, he may know that it was shown to him in order that he learn his own guilt and repent; for what was shown to him is also within him."

When the Baal Shem Tov said this, he almost certainly was focusing on the spiritual situation of an individual who in order to grow must take the world not as an external object but as a moral mirror—one who must treat the discovery of evil as a spur to look inward, to examine what evil lurks in his/ her own heart.

But Heschel takes this insight in a new direction. He applies it to a whole society, a whole people, when it sees political evil at a national level. Heschel writes:

> "We have failed to offer sacrifices on the altar of peace; now we must
> offer sacrifices on the altar of war.... Let Fascism not serve as an alibi
> for our conscience.... Where were we when men learned to hate in
> the days of starvation? When raving madmen were sowing wrath in
> the hearts of the unemployed?
>
> "Good and evil, which were once as real as day and night, have be-
> come a blurred mist. In our everyday life we worshipped force,
> despised compassion, and obeyed no law but our unappeasable
> appetite. The vision of the sacred has all but died in the soul of man."

By 1943, Heschel knew that members of his own family and already more than a million other Jews had already been savagely murdered. Yet he could draw on the depths of Hasidism to call Jews themselves, along with all of Western civilization and culture, to face their own share of responsibility for letting the disaster happen. And he could fuse questions that were conventionally seen as distinct—

issues of economics and issues of religious and spiritual experience. For, he said, "the vision of the sacred" had been killed by "greed, envy, and the reckless will to power," by not addressing such economic problems as unemployment.

Heschel, we should be clear, did not back away from a radical condemnation of Nazism. He did not oppose the war on which the Allies were then engaged. Yet he could in the very midst of that war write, "Tanks and planes cannot redeem humanity. . . . The killing of snakes will save us for the moment but not forever."

He could look deep into that war, beyond it and within it and beneath it, to ask not merely what were its causes, but what was its meaning? And he found spiritual meaning in taking responsibility upon himself, ourselves, for having helped create the world in which "the mark of Cain in the face of man has come to overshadow the likeness of God."

What is the significance of this teaching, as we search toward a theory and practice of *tikkun olam* that can help support an assertive nonviolent transformation of the Great Powers of the earth?

Perhaps it would be instructive to imagine this teaching placed in the context of American life after the terror attacks of 9/11/01. If Heschel could write in this way in 1943, what would it have meant for an American to write this way in 2002?

It would have challenged both the single Greatest Power in the world, the United States, to have reflected on its own responsibility for creating the world in which terrorists chose to wear the mark of Cain. And it would have challenged us all at the level of our everyday lives—emotional, economic, political. As Heschel says later in the essay, "God will return to us when we are willing to let Him in—into our banks and factories, into our Congress and clubs, into our homes and theaters."

It would have called on us to make the sacrifices of peace lest we need forever to make the sacrifices of war, the war against terrorism that has already been proclaimed endless and that indeed is likely to be endless because every act of war is likely to create new terrorists.

What are these sacrifices of peace? In Jewish language these are *korbanot,* "near-bringings," bringing near to the Unity of All what is nearest to our own selves.

The first such "near-bringing" would be to do as the Baal Shem Tov and Heschel teach, bringing near the evil behavior we see in others as a mirror to look within our selves. Looking at Al Qaeda, to see the CIA that trained them. Hearing Bin Laden's call for jihad, hearing our own President's call for "crusade."

The second would be taking time to reflect, to bring our own life-experience and our own consciousness—often so divorced from each other—near to each other. Time out—time not used to multiply the military, imprison immigrants, name more countries for devastation or embargo, but time simply to reflect. To pray, to learn, to listen, to explore new possibilities.

Such a time out—setting aside, for example, time to reflect on our experience and the meaning of the 9/11 terror attacks and on America's place in the world—would carry into public space the Jewish wisdom of the Ten Days of Awe and Transformation between *Rosh Hashanah* and *Yom Kippur*.

Indeed, it would tune in to Heschel's teaching after the essay I have just quoted, encoded in the well-known book *The Sabbath* he wrote soon after World War II, while the blood of the Holocaust and Hiroshima was barely dry—his teaching that the Sabbath, taking time to restfully reflect, is the deepest challenge to a civilization of techno-idolatry.

And the third "near-bringing" would be creating in the present the institutions and practices that we dream of for the future. Making near in reality what seems far from possibility.

And finally, let us bring near our wholeness as a community: that we do this not only in addressing specific wounds in the body politic with specific acts of tik-kun, but also at the level of the meaning of Jewish peoplehood: That we see the Jewish people in our era as a transgenerational "movement" to heal the wounded world. Not through violence, and not through passive nonviolence. Not walking alone to conquer, not walking alone to cower.

Rather, as a carrier of assertive nonviolence to open up and transform the Great Powers of the world, working with allies who share many aspects of our vision.

Will There Ever Be Another Holocaust?

Edward Feder

The answer is yes. Unless the weapons frenzy stops, our time may come again. Since the time of Egypt, there have been wars, pogroms, and expulsion orders against the Jews. Hitler's Holocaust was unique, because it occurred in a civilized country, against a literate people who occupied high positions in government, education, and the sciences.

Yet Jews have not been the only victims. Ethnic cleansing and mass murders have been going on for a long time, and it is still going on in our time. Weapons of destruction have become more sophisticated and deadly. Pictures of dead Tutsis or Bosnians resemble dead Jews in the concentration camps. If we recall Picasso's *Guernica*, we can visualize the same pictures of horror and death, a vivid foreshadowing of the war to come and its deadly camps.

In truth, we can only eliminate future holocausts for the Jews by eliminating them for all people. To eliminate holocausts, we must eliminate or sharply reduce the sale of weapons. There are plenty of pseudo-Hitlers and Stalins and other tyrants around, but they are powerless without guns. And that is the problem. All over the world there are men in jackets and ties selling the latest weapons. Some of these are the most deadly devices ever made: F-22 fighter planes, Stinger shoulder-fired missiles, Apache attack helicopters, Abrams battle tanks, Strike Eagle fighter bombers. The list is endless.

The post–Cold War era was supposed to be a period of weapons reduction. The opposite has occurred. There has been a frenzy of selling, with the US far ahead of all other countries. In fact, our shipments total more than all other countries combined. Attempts were made for conversion (having our defense plants manufacture other items, and retraining workers for other jobs), but this has largely failed. The Cold War mentality still prevails, and our defense contractors are still devising more deadly weapons. And what are we doing with our stock in hand? It is being given away. I have a list before me of more than 20 items being offered, including 130 Sea Sparrow missiles to Turkey, 4,562 M164A1 rifles to Uruguay, 10 TA-7C attack aircraft to Greece, and 6 Bell Cobra attack helicopters to Bahrain. The price tags? Nothing. And other large nations are following the American example. . . .*

Today there are many grassroots organizations in Washington working to push through a Code of Conduct Act, which, if it ever passed, would eliminate up to 90% of our arms shipments. This proposed act forbids any shipments to non-democratic countries, to countries which deny human rights to their own people, or are at war with their neighbors. This act would make a tremendous difference in the availability of weapons. All American Jewish organizations should participate in this effort.

The horror of Hitler's Holocaust against the Jews is not diminished if we recognize the existence of other holocausts past and present. Stalin's killing and imprisonment of millions of Ukrainians, Russians, and others was a "holocaust." So were the nuclear bombings of Hiroshima and Nagasaki, as well as the fire-bombing of Dresden. If we turn the pages of history, we can find many more instances of such catastrophes. We now read that former Defense Secretary Robert McNamara says the war in Vietnam was a mistake. 58,000 Americans were killed (and more wounded in body and mind), and more than a million Vietnamese and Southeast Asians were killed or wounded. Chalk up another "holocaust."

Defense contractors will surely fight the proposed legislation to limit arms production and sales. They have powerful lobbies. The thousands of workers they employ will be against it too—though they can't be blamed. Their jobs are at stake. Our government should spend billions of dollars to help these companies convert to peaceful production. And if an army base is closed, efforts should be made to replace military employment with other non-military opportunities.

Where will the money come from? From the many billions of dollars that can be saved by keeping our defense costs to a sensible minimum. Even more billions could be saved, too, by our not promulgating or intervening in unnecessary wars. In the meantime, US taxpayers pay for all this.

Our main priority, then, is to do something about the pervasiveness of weapons. We must stop making and selling them. We can't change human nature quickly. There will always be killing, pseudo-Hitlers, and heartless leaders ready to foment mini-holocausts. But without weapons, they cannot function. And that will mean fewer holocausts for everybody, including Jews.

Note

* Essay excerpted and updated. See Polner, Murray and Goodman, Naomi, eds. *Nonviolent Activist: The Heart & Mind of Edward Feder* (Nyack, NY: Jewish Peace Fellowship, 2022), pp. 34–35.

Berlin Stories

Claudia Dreifus

On a burnished autumn afternoon some years ago, the very first day of my first trip ever to Germany, I bought a map, attended a political rally in the former West Berlin, and after it, dragged my friend Jorgen, a Berlin-based political consultant to an apartment house in the Charlottenburg district of town. I had to see a certain building at 89 Kantstrasse. Yes, Kantstrasse, as in Immanuel Kant, the nineteenth-century German philosopher who wrote that God, freedom, and immortality had to be presupposed—even though they could not be proved.

I am an American political journalist who was born in New York in 1944. For all of my Manhattan childhood, I imagined this building in Charlottenburg. 89 Kantstrasse was where my grandparents, the late Emmy Oppenheimer Willdorff and Benno Willdorff lived between 1912 and 1939. This was where my late mother, Marianne, and her older sisters, Lony and Inge, were born. This is where my family lived until they fled for America with five hundred dollars and their Jewish lives in October 1939.

The Willdorffs made their escape through Sweden and then on to New York by way of a complicated miracle that they could not share with the rest of their relatives. Fourteen of my Oma's relations—sisters, brothers-in-law, nieces and nephews were subsequently murdered because they could not find a similar way out.

And all this—the immigration, the genocide—happened in the years immediately preceding my birth. Think about how traumatized families are where there has been one murder. In mine, there were *fourteen*. I grew up among people in a kind of hyper-mourning, full of guilt about their survival, measuring every day whether life had any value at all. My grandmother always voted for life. My mother, on the other hand, spent her small lifetime cruising around death. In the spring of 1977, at fifty-five, she killed herself. She'd been flirting with suicide for decades.

The building that Jorgen and I found at 89 Kantstrasse proved a rather ordinary pre-War Berlin apartment bloc: four stories of gray-brown stucco facing out on a tree-lined street. Yet, it was so moving to see it. I could hardly believe that I was looking at the very courtyard my mother had played in as a child. I kept touching the front door, this huge ox of a wood and glass door, which had to be the last thing the Willdorffs saw of their home as they set out for America. "Isn't it amazing," I kept repeating. "They actually came from somewhere!"

Eventually, a man came along and unlocked the front door, I thoughtlessly flew inside and quickly ran up the staircase to a first floor apartment, where I found a doorbell that my Aunt Inge Brenner—my only living relative with any memory of Berlin—promised would be marked, "Blumenstein."

Without hesitation, I rang it. "I'm sorry to disturb you madam," I called to the apparently elderly woman on the other side of the door. "Before the war, my family lived in this apartment and it would mean so much to me I could see it."

Fear seeped out from the behind the bolted door. "No. Absolutely not. Certainly not."

"But Frau Blumenstein," Jorgen broke in. "Ms. Dreifus here is an American journalist. You wouldn't want her to come away with a bad impression of Germany."

"Go away," the woman said, nastily.

Realizing that I might have upset an elderly person by arriving unannounced, I tried to calm her. "Well, perhaps we could come back at more convenient moment?" I said while slipping my calling card under the door. "I'm staying at the home of Karsten Voigt—he's a member of your Parliament, the Bundesdag. Surely, you know his name? You could phone him and he will vouch me."

"My husband is dead," was Blumenstein's strange response. "Now, go away."

In the coming weeks, I would make two more attempts to see the flat. Once, I took flowers and a hand-written letter explaining my motives. I left messages on a voice-mail.

Jorgen believed that Blumenstein probably thought I was a *verbrecher*—a mugger. Brigitta Voigt, Karsten's wife, had grown up in East Germany and she had a more material theory: "Maybe she's afraid that you've come to reclaim the apartment."

"Sixty years later?" I said, incredulously.

"Sure, why not?"

* * *

When I was a child living in my grandmother's two-room apartment on Amsterdam Avenue and West 100th Street—89 Kantstrasse was an address that loomed huge in my imagination, tremendous. It represented the alternate life, the other existence, we might have had.

In the early 1950s, we were the most poor and isolated of families. While I watched the wholesome nuclear family of the Lassie's television clan, my family was really just my "Omi" and me.

My father was an unemployed union organizer, caught in the Red Scare of McCarthyism; my mother was mostly off in Greenwich Village playing at being a painter. Occasionally, my parents would get enraged at my closeness to Oma and drag me off to live with them.

That would last for a month or two until they tired with the demands of a child. In the end, I was always returned to my grandmother—where I was happy. Somehow, my Oma found ways to scrape together some income to support me. She took in sewing, did tailoring, and dressmaking.

Most days, my Oma and I would sit at her sewing machine—me with my dolls, she with her alterations—and she'd tell me stories of another more glamorous world. At Kantstrasse, there had been seven rooms full of Persian carpets and good art and huge dinner parties where all manner of Oppenheimers and Willdorffs gathered in warm celebration of each other.

I pictured Kantstrasse as a semi-palace, with marble carvings and baroque fixtures, a dream from an operetta.

Of course, I knew the other side of this Old World fantasy. In many families of Holocaust survivors, the children are shielded from what the previous generation suffered. In my family, partly because I was born so close to the trauma, it was topic number one. I was very young when I understood that my rococo dreams of Kantstrasse were death dreams.

One of my first childhood memories—something that would come up again later in a long psychoanalysis—is of my grandmother going to the mailbox, taking out a packet of letters marked "addressee unknown," and crying inconsolably. "What is it, Omi?" I must have asked her.

But Oma couldn't speak.

The letters—I was to learn later—were her missives, sent over the years to her sisters in Berlin. That they were being returned in this fashion meant the women were certainly dead. She'd feared this since 1942, when she stopped getting mail from them. But here, in her hands, was the irrefutable confirmation of . . . the worst.

My childhood was spent in fractured time. There was the past, which I hadn't known, but which everyone around me seemed to be still living in. And then, there was the present, which as best I could tell, was odd. Early on, I realized that I had to protect myself from my mother's death-rapture. I never liked, for instance, the implications of a story my grandmother told about the family's immigration.

"Your mother wouldn't leave Germany," Oma said. "After we got the immigration number to come to the United States, she wanted to stay behind with her teenage boyfriend, a nice young man named Fritz Brill. Poor thing. His parents were already in concentration camps. Your grandfather had to tell her, 'You're a minor and you'll come with us.' She was my husband's favorite, but she never forgave him."

Once in America, Marianne sulked and wrote letters to her Fritzie. Until Pearl Harbor, it was still possible to get mail to Germany. And Fritz would send her desperate messages: "Marianne, please save me. Get me a visa so I can come to America."

Of course, the Willdorffs weren't even able to help their own. Oma's sisters were trapped in Germany. My grandmother's only brother, Joseph Oppenheimer, had managed to get to Australia and was killed by a hit-and-run driver in 1940. In the middle of this all, Marianne began a romance with my father, Henry Dreifus, an organizer with a strange Trotskyite group that was developing, astonishingly enough, GI resistance to World War II. The Willdorffs loathed my father instantly, which made him irresistible to my mother. "Let's hope that Marianne gets over this crazy communist, and soon too," my grandmother kept praying.

Instead, my mother eloped with him.

A year after the wedding, my grandfather was dead from what everyone dubbed "the strain of the immigration," and mother was pregnant. By then, all she wanted was a divorce and an illegal abortion. But my grandmother wouldn't hear of it. "You can't. You could die from the operation," she pleaded. "There's been enough death already. I'll raise the child."

And so I became my grandmother's fourth, and most adored, daughter. I've often thought I was born because she needed an answer to the Holocaust. My grandmother was so deeply lonely at that moment. She'd lost her sisters, brother, husband, language, and culture. A child at sixty reconnected her to the living. And she desperately wanted a reason to go on.

I'd come to Berlin, originally, to observe the September 1998 Chancellorship election. For years I'd avoided any travel to Germany—not an easy thing to do considering my profession and the fact that the country sits at the absolute heart of Europe. But now that I was actually spending three weeks in this mythic land of wurst and Bach and terror, it felt right to investigate my own pre-history.

In my childhood, the very word *Germany* had the power to frighten. Now I had the opportunity to free myself of what essentially was my mother's fear. I could do it by facing it.

"You should go over to the Jewish Community Center at 80 Fasanenstrasse and take a look at their archives," my hostess Brigitta Voigt, suggested one morning. "They have documents there. You can find out what happened to your aunts and uncles. The Nazis, you know, they kept such good records."

And indeed at the Fasanenstrasse archive, I found books—huge volumes the size of a Manhattan telephone book: compilations of the Nazi's deportation records. Slowly, while reading the names and facts surrounding these souls, I located the names of fourteen murdered Oppenheimers and Willldorffs I was related to. There were also postings for five Dreifuses from the small West German town of "Permisens"—my father's people.

But there on paper was the story of my family—and all the Jews of Berlin. A typical entry, for my grandmother's sister Rosa, the first Oppenheimer to be deported, said that she was born on October, 3, 1877, in Ratibor, Silesia. She lived, according to the record, in Charlottenburg at 15 Windscheidstrasse, and was transported to "the East" on March 10, 1942. The place of death is "Reval." Her fate is, "*vershollen.*"

"Excuse me, my German is not that good," I asked the librarian. "What does 'vershollen' mean?"

"Disappeared," she answered.

"And where is this Reval? Is it a concentration camp?'

"No," she answered. "They deported them to Estonia, to the capitol, Tallinn. It was terrible. They buried them alive there."

Nineteen murdered relatives. NINETEEN. One can know the facts and I always have, but seeing it listed in this cold way, made it all quite real. This was different from reading impossible numbers that one can never quite concretize—six million Jews, 1.7 million Cambodians, a half million Hutus, a million Tutsies. These people were *my kin*. If they'd lived, they would have been figures in my childhood.

This was not the Hollywood Holocaust of a Stephen Speilberg movie: full of drama and easy catharsis. This is what genocide looked like: middle-class people with impeccable manners who one day they found themselves herded onto a train, sent to a strange land and buried alive in a pit.

Glancing through these documents, I could see that the pattern my family suffered was typical of the Holocaust. Women were killed first, particularly the older, single women. The poorer relatives, or at least the ones who lived in poorer districts, appeared to have been taken earliest.

In one of the first deportations of Jews from Berlin, my grandfather's two older sisters, Lotte Willdorff, 67, Theresa Willdorff Fischel, 66, were taken and shipped together to Riga, in Latvia, where they were, apparently, shot in pits.

A week later, Betty Willdorff, 64, another great-aunt, was arrested and sent to Riga. And then, two months later, Rosa Oppenheimer, my grandmother's eldest sister, was deported to Estonia.

According to historians, the Nazis were uncomfortable with the mass killings in Estonia and Latvia. Too messy. Too unpredictable. By the spring of 1942, the more efficient death factory at Auschwitz was on line and it was there that the rest of the family story, as that of most of the Jews of Berlin, ends.

My grandfather's sister, Selma Willdorf Freund, 62, my mother's cousin Walter Willdorf and his wife, Augusta Friedeman Willdorf, my grandmother's sister, Anna Oppenheimer, my grandfather's brother Georg Willdorff, 70, his son Botho, 36, all die in Auschwitz.

In my family, we'd always known something of the deportation of my great Aunt Paula Oppenheimer Becker and her husband, a disabled Captain from World War I, Solly Becker. My grandmother's friend, a Christian woman named Mrs. Ripine who lived in the rear house at 89 Kantstrasse, came regularly to the Beckers' 15 Windsheidstrasse flat and brought them food. It was a dangerous thing to do. But in Germany, as many Nazis as there were, there were decent people as well.

One day, while on one of her mercy-calls, she witnessed the Gestapo arresting Solly Becker. Without saying a word, Mrs. Ripine kept walking. According to what she wrote my Oma after the war, my great-Aunt Paula, whose name was not on the deportation list, insisted that the Gestapo take her too. "My husband won't survive the trip East without me," she reportedly said.

And so the Nazis arrested Aunt Paula. The last recollection Mrs. Ripine had of them was of the crippled Solly Becker hobbling down the stairs at Windsheidstrasse, with Paula helping him negotiate the steps.

Family legend had it that the Beckers died together. Their story had always been told to me as a parable about loyalty. Yet as I sifted through the documentation, I discerned something particularly horrible. Pauline Becker was sent to Auschwitz on March 1, 1943.

She died two days later—very likely on the train. However, the records on Solly Becker, suggest that he was held in Berlin until March 3, and then sent off to Auschwitz, where he was murdered on March 15. Her sacrifice had been for nothing.

As a final step, I looked for the name Fritz Brill—my mother's teen love—on the deportation lists. Amazingly, he wasn't there. I looked twice. Perhaps he'd survived the war, hidden somewhere? That happened occasionally. Perhaps Brill had even gotten out? One thing was sure: he hadn't been deported from Berlin. How ironic that mother was torturing herself all those years for a boy who may have lived.

After my day at the library, it seemed terribly important to see 15 Windsheidstrasse, clearly the second most important station on this family's cross. Paula and Solly Becker had lived there for all their married life. Rosa and Anna Oppenheimer moved in with them in 1938, after they were turfed out of their own flat for the sin of Jewishness. Thus one Sunday, I hailed a taxi and headed back to Charlottenburg. Twenty minutes later the cabby deposited me at a spot that looked oddly familiar. Though I hadn't yet seen much of Berlin, I'd already been at this place. And then I looked about and discerned something touching. My grandmother's sisters had lived directly around the corner from 89 Kantstrasse, something I hadn't known before.

These people, they'd really been a family; their daily lives had been completely intertwined—a hard thing for an American, with our sense of mobility and privacy, to imagine.

The block itself had charm. There were trees everywhere, and small shops and cafés. I looked at the mailbox at 15 Windsheidstrasse. This is where my grandmother had sent those terrible letters. This the place to which they were never delivered. This was the scene she was visualizing the day I witnessed her cry so uncontrollably. And the infamous stairs that Paula and Solly Becker climbed down in March of 1943, jutted out from the building; they were steep, steep steps.

It wasn't difficult to imagine how terrified the disabled war veteran, Solly Becker, must have been, as he tried to negotiate them. Mrs. Ripine said she'd never seen him stand, let alone walk, before.

I closed my eyes and sought to imagine what this pleasant street had looked like on that awful day. I wondered what Solly Becker's Windseidstrasse neighbors thought of what they'd witnessed. Did the really believe—as the official story went—that this frightened cripple was being sent to "non-parasitic work" in the East?

* * *

After the Beckers were arrested, they were very likely transported to the site of the First Jewish Old Age Home at 26 Grosse Hamburgerstrasse. This was the walled building that the Gestapo used from 1942 on as a kind of way-station to Auschwitz; 55,000 of Berlin's Jews were held there before being sent to their deaths.

The building doesn't stand anymore. Late in the war it was destroyed by Allied bombers. Only the high containment wall, which kept people from freedom, remains. And also a small monument, piled high with stones—left, according to Jewish tradition, by visitors mourning the dead.

So there I stood, on this warm September afternoon, lighting candles I'd brought with me, when amazingly I spied two sweaty young men in jogging clothes—and they were urinating against the wall of this sad, sad place!

I froze. Should I say something? No, I'd only be creating a scene and embarrassing Brigitta, who was standing with her baby not far away. Besides, I wasn't sure my German was good enough to make myself understood. On the other hand, why be polite about these things? "Excuse me," I stammered, "how would you feel if I pissed on your church?"

The joggers looked at me as if I were a madwoman. "I didn't pee on the monument, I peed on the wall," one of them declared.

"The whole place is a monument, you dumkopf," I ranted. "55,000 of your neighbors went to their deaths from here."

"But I *needed* to go," this man said, as if his body's urges explained everything.

"Try a toilet," I snapped.

These guys weren't anti-Semitic; they were unconscious—which is something else. But still, it was ugly. Genocide could occur in Nazi Germany because a part of the population was enthusiastic about it and an even bigger part didn't really care about their neighbors. Here, in this moment, with these joggers, I was confronting the stuff the Holocaust was made of. *The basic ingredient hadn't been just the banality of evil, but also indifference.*

On a spring morning in 1977, I received a phone call from a hospital in Nevada. "We have someone here named Marianne. She's in a coma. I don't think she'll last very long."

By the time my Aunt Inge and I flew to Reno—the wild-west town my mother inexplicably had moved to—she was dead.

At first, we thought she'd had a stroke or had died of malnutrition. My mother was always starving herself down to concentration camp size; when she died, she was no more than ninety pounds. However, when Inge and I entered her two-room studio, there were signs everywhere of suicide. On tables, chairs, and in the kitchen, we discovered an amazing number of open pill bottles—medicines that should never be mixed. At her desk, were farewell letters to me and her sisters. There were also funeral instructions.

The most horrifying thing was the studio itself. My mother had turned her home into a kind of concept art-Auschwitz piece. On the wall, were these gruesome paintings of concentration camps—with herself drawn in as an internee. In one corner of the room was a stack of eyeglasses; in another, a pile of gold dental fillings. Where on earth had she gotten them? "This is the most terrible sight I've seen in my entire life," Inge kept repeating.

My aunt wept for the entire three days we spent taking apart the studio. Now and then, she spoke of Berlin. "When we were young girls," Inge recalled, "we would walk in fear of Storm Troopers who beat up Jewish children. Marianne looked very Jewish. She was always darting into shops and buildings in Charlottenburg trying to avoid attack. And then there was the trauma of Kristallnacht on November 9, 1938. The Nazis burned our shop and Marianne and I were summoned to go with father to sweep up the ashes while Nazi mobs menaced us. She was never right after that."

At the funeral, I found it hard to cry. My mother and I, we'd never had a normal closeness. Like many children of survivors, I often had to function as her mother and resented it. Throughout the service, I kept thinking of Antigone's speech to her sister Ismene in the Sophocles play: "Be of good cheer—thou livest. But my life hath long been given to death so that I may serve the dead."

My grandmother went back to Germany. Once. The year was 1971. The Mayor of then West Berlin was putting on some sort of a freebie tour for persecuted former citizens. She was invited for a week's worth of goodwill meetings, trips to the opera, and walks through museums. Oma accepted the junket for reasons of her own: she wanted to go to East Berlin to visit the grave of her father buried in the Jewish Cemetery in Weissensee.

Samuel Oppenheimer, a slender six-foot-tall Rabbinic scholar from an old Sephardic family, was the last Oppenheimer to die in Germany of natural causes. He'd contracted pneumonia in 1933. Oma always said that she was glad he didn't live to see too much of the Nazi era.

The little he saw, however, he fought with wonderful dignity. According to family legend, the old man used to spend his afternoons caring for my mother and Inge.

Late in the day, Inge would walk him home.

Once the Nazis came to power, however, the ritual became dangerous. The streets were full of SA men, who found it great sport to attack anyone who might be Jewish. As it happened, at the corner of Windsheidstrasse one day in 1933, Inge and her grandfather were set upon by two SA men who began threatening them, screaming, "Filthy Jews! You Swine. You dirty old pig."

To which, the very formal Samuel Oppenheimer, raised his walking stick and began beating at one of them. "How dare you speak so disrespectfully to an old man," he reportedly shouted. "You should have better manners."

Inge claims she nearly died of fright. But they were even more astonished to watch these Nazis retreat. "You're great-grandfather was fearless," Inge claims, with fond pride.

What Oma wanted to do in 1971 was go to the cemetery and clean his grave. However, when the tour group made its trip into East Berlin, they left my grandmother behind—they felt she was too fragile, too old for an arduous day of border crossings and cemetery walkings

Undaunted, my Omi went alone and presented herself at Checkpoint Charlie where the East German border guards refused to let her pass. Till the day she died in New York at the age of ninety-two, it troubled her that she hadn't been able to finish up this last bit of family business. Well, now that I was in Berlin, I could do that for her. I loathe cemeteries; never visit them, but this felt like an obligation.

Thus on a damp Berlin afternoon, Brigitta and I packed up little Gunnar, put on work clothes, and drove out to the gloomy East Berlin suburb of Weissensee to the largest Jewish cemetery in all of Europe.

This vast cemetery had been opened in 1880—and was a repository of much of Berlin's Jewish history. The huge marble tombs and statues were signs of the prosperity of the community. It was fascinating to see how many Jewish women of the nineteenth century had the words "Doctor" and "Professor" inscribed on their tombstones.

But it was equally saddening to see recently erected stones—put in place of graves—with markings that said things such as, "Unforgotten—our martyrs to the Nazi regime, murdered in the years 1942–1943, Family Zadek, Wilhelm, 53, Erna, 51, Sigfried, 54, Hulda, 47, Hanna, 19, Ruth, 19.

As for my great-grandfather, he was nowhere to be found. A clerk at the cemetery offices insisted that he was buried in Section K, Part II, Row 7. Brigitta and I checked through every grave in Section K, Part II. I counted them forwards, backwards—wading through mud in my overpriced shoes . . . and no sign of Samuel Oppenheimer, nothing, anywhere. When the baby started to get cranky, we gave up.

Two days later, I put on some junky rubber boots, borrowed a set of gardening shears from Brigitta—and returned to Weissensee. For an entire afternoon, I marched through Section K, Part II, doing the most unpleasant of gardening work, pulling up shrubbery, detaching ivy from stones, digging now and then at a buried tablet—to see if it might be grandfather.

I'd brought with me a plant I'd intended to plant at Samuel's grave. At the end of the afternoon, I put it down over a spot where he might be. "Even if this isn't grandfather," I thought to myself, "it's someone who hasn't had a visitor in sixty years and they deserve remembrance too."

For my third visit to Weissensee, I did some preparation. Through a friend, I got the name of the cemetery's caretaker, a Frau Borgamann, and phoned her.

By the time I arrived at her office later that day, Borgamann had indeed located my ancestor. Samuel Oppenheimer turned out to actually be quite near to the spot where I'd left the flowers—three graves over, in fact. His tombstone had fallen over years earlier and was completely buried. A jungle of shrubbery covered it.

Frau Borgamann and I pulled and dug—and eventually excavated a tablet with extremely weathered writing on it. For clarity, she covered the stone with white chalk and finally, we read, "SAMUEL OPPENHEIMER," beloved father and grandfather, born 1851, died, 1933."

It was so moving. This was the normal way people died—these were the normal epitaphs put to stone. Gently, I moved the azaleas to his spot—and wept just a bit for this ancestor I'd never met. The stories I'd heard about him had always been wonderful. By finding his grave, cleaning it, paying the cemetery to re-erect the memorial stone, I felt I was in gaining a measure of control over events that had always imposed themselves on me. One can't really change history. But one can stare it down.

Before I left great-grandfather's grave, I went to my purse and took out a silver and turquoise Jewish star that my mother, the suicide, had willed me. It seemed fitting to return the piece to this spot. This is where Marianne would have ended up if history hadn't gone haywire.

On one of my last days in Berlin, Brigitta, little Gunnar, and I made one more try at 89 Kantstrasse. Our hope was that the baby might melt Mrs. Blumenstein's heart and show her that I wasn't really a *verbrecher*. I mean, how many *verbrechers* do their mugging while loaded down with babies, diapers, and bottles?

We rang the front bell. We rang it several times. Again, we snuck inside the building and then went up to the first floor landing. But all we got for our efforts was a studied silence. Either, Blumenstein was out—or not answering. Once, from downstairs, I thought I saw a shadow at the window, then nothing.

The only thing I could think to do was take the flowers and a memorial candle that I had brought with me and leave them at the front door. If this bothered Mrs. Blumenstein and her neighbors, well, too bad. It could hardly hurt them to learn that Jewish people named Willdorff had once lived here, and that unlike so many other Holocaust victims, there was a descendent. Who insisted on remembrance.

Postscript

I've recently found my grandmother's only surviving relatives and their descendents, lost for more than sixty years in Australia. My grandmother's brother, Joseph Oppenheimer, emigrated to Australia in 1938. He died in a car accident in 1940. Well, thanks to the Internet, I found his grandchildren—and my Aunt Inge was able to speak to her first cousin, Rosemarie, for the first time since their Berlin childhood. Rosemarie's children were stunned to discover that they had relatives. As my second cousin, Lynn, said, "We always felt like people from a sperm bank." She also wanted to know if I spent my childhood afraid of Nazis—because they spent their youths hiding in trees—fearful that Nazis would come to get them.

A True Story

Rabbi Abraham Joshua Heschel

During the spring of 1921, the Grand Mufti of Jerusalem, Haj Muhammed Amin el-Husseini, instigated one of his organized pogroms against the Jewish population in Palestine. When a group of Arabs threatened to attack Jewish homes between Jaffa and Tel Aviv, Jewish defenders went forth to meet them. An exchange of fire ensued, which threatened to escalate into full-scale warfare.

At this moment, a remarkable man intervened, Rabbi Ben Zion Uziel, then the Sephardi Rabbi in Tel Aviv (and later Sephardi Chief Rabbi of Palestine), donned his Rabbinic robes and turban and went out to the battlefield. He asked the Jewish fighters to hold their fire and proceeded alone toward the Arab positions, calling out to them to also hold their fire. The sheikh in command of the Arabs instructed his men to stop firing in order to hear what the rabbi had to say. Rabbi Uziel delivered an impassioned appeal to the Arab fighters, which included these words:

> "We candidly stretch out our hand to you with true peace in our hearts and say: We have the entire land in front of us, let us work shoulder to shoulder to cultivate her, uncover her treasures, and live together in brotherhood. . . . Make your peace with us and we shall make peace with you and together we shall enjoy God's blessings on this holy land.

"Our dear cousins! Our common father Abraham, the father of Isaac and of Ishmael, when he saw that his nephew Lot was causing him trouble claiming there was not enough room for both his flocks and Abraham's flocks to live together, said to him: 'Let there be no quarrel between me and you, and between your shepherds and my shepherds, for we are people like brothers.' We also say to you, this land can sustain all of us and provide for us in plenty. Let us, then, stop fighting each other, for we too are people like brothers."

The Arabs who had listened to Rabbi Uziel's words in silence then dispersed quietly.

—1968

Fixing the World

Rabbi Philip J. Bentley

Jewish activists on all parts of the political spectrum claim Jewish tradition for their own ideology. The truth is that Judaism is a living tradition almost 4000 years old while Western political philosophies are a few centuries old at most. Jewish tradition is on a completely different track from the spectrum that includes "left" and "right." Nonetheless it is true that the Jewish vote and Jewish activism generally tend towards the left. Why is that? The purpose of this essay is to explore briefly some aspects of Judaism that may help explain this undeniable fact.

Fixing the World

The ultimate basis for understanding of any system of ethics, public or private, is the answer to the question, "What is humanity?" One answer is given in the account of Creation from the Jewish mystical tradition (Kabbalah):

> Before Creation God was infinite and, for reasons we cannot conceive of, withdrew to create space-time. Into space-time God sent emanations of ten divine attributes, which were to take shape in vessels. A cosmic accident occurred and the vessels for the emanations were shattered causing the divine sparks to be mixed up and hidden among the shards that became shells around the sparks. It was then that Heaven and Earth were created and humanity placed on earth in order to retrieve the sparks from the shells. This process of is called

Fixing the World (*Tikkun Olam*). The role of humanity is to re-establish this world as it was supposed to be by releasing the divine spark hidden in everything in the world and restoring it to its source.

Judaism is a this-world religion, even in its mystical expression. The relationship between a human being and God includes not only that individual's faith and observance of religious precepts and laws, but in the way an individual treats other human beings. Most of the 613 Commandments (Mitzvot) in Judaism are concerned with social relationships. All of the piety and religious observance in the world means nothing if a person does not use life to make the world better.

The Most Important Verse

A group of rabbis, many centuries ago, argued about which was the most important passage in the Bible—the one that sums up the purpose of all of the Scriptures. The "winner" was "This is the record of Adam's line—when God created man he was made in the image of God." (Genesis 5:1) That verse is followed by a series of "begats" telling the genealogy of ten generations of Adam and Eve's descendants. The Rabbis however read this verse as affirming that all of humanity has one ancestor and that every human being is made in the divine image.

Why, the Talmud asks, was all of humanity descended from one couple? There are several answers given including one that says no one should be able to say, "My Adam and Eve were superior to your Adam and Eve." Another says that this establishes the life of every human being as equal to an entire world. Thus we have the famous dictum, "One who destroys a single human life destroys an entire world; and one who saves a single human life saves an entire world. Human life in this world is considered the highest ethical imperative in Judaism.

Every single human being who has ever lived or who will ever live must be thought of as made in the divine image and worth the life of the entire world. Anyone who takes this doctrine seriously must see in every human being a face of God. It then becomes impossible to intentionally harm or degrade any person.

Who Would Believe It?

The Jewish religion cannot be understood without knowing the unique historical experience of the Jewish people. Our very existence defies the rules of history. Deutero-Isaiah commented twenty-five centuries ago, "Who can believe what we have heard?" (Isaiah 53:1) is an expression of amazement at our survival.

The Land of Israel is situated between two ancient powerful rivals: Egypt and Mesopotamia (modern Syria and Iraq). For more than 4000 years and down to the present day these two giants fought over the small territory that divided them. We suffered from the passage of huge armies through our land and sometimes we were pawns in international rivalry. In Jeremiah's day Pharaoh convinced the King of Judah to rebel against Babylonia with a promise of support. The rebellion took place, no help was forthcoming and, as a result Jerusalem and the Temple were burned to the ground and those people who did not escape to Egypt were exiled to Babylonia.

Thus throughout our Scriptures there is distrust of great cities, kingdoms and empires. The powers of the Jewish king were always limited because the king was to be subject to the law and to the ethics that ruled everyone else. In the Bible the person who is a great warrior or athlete or who has great political power or wealth is not regarded as a hero. The great person is the one who is just, kind and learned. Our peculiar historical situation gave us a view of the world different from that of other peoples.

Now We Are Slaves

Most nations tell of their glorious, heroic origins. Every year on Passover Jews sit down at a table and tell how we began our history as slaves in Egypt. But we do not stop there. we affirm that if we had not been taken out of Egypt we would still be there. In the course of the Passover Seder ritual we try our best to relive the experience of slavery and liberation. "In every generation it is incumbent on each person to see him/herself as having personally experienced the Exodus from Egypt." We do not even credit Moses as our liberator. He is barely mentioned in the traditional text. God took us out from Egypt. Furthermore we state, "Now we are slaves; next year may we be free." We see liberation as an ongoing process rather than as a static ancient event.

The Torah (The five books of Moses) tells us thirty-six times: *You shall not oppress the stranger for you know the heart of the stranger having yourselves been strangers in the land of Egypt.* The purpose of constantly reminding ourselves of our humble origins is to remind ourselves that we must have compassion towards others, including those who are not like us.

Among The Nations

When Solomon's Temple was destroyed by the Babylonians (586 BCE) we began an aspect of our history that makes us truly unique. More of our people have lived outside of our ancestral homeland than within it. Since the Second Temple was destroyed by the Romans (70 CE) we have been scattered to every corner of the globe and have survived as a vulnerable minority under all kinds of conditions.

We have therefore had to learn to survive every imaginable kind of situation without resort to force of arms. Our situation has often been precarious. As outsiders we were forced to perform social and economic functions, which those in power preferred to give to outsiders. We were not allowed to own or even work land, join craft guilds, or participate in the military. We were forced to become moneylenders, tax and rent collectors, and do other services for the local sovereign who, in return, was supposed to protect us. Sometimes Jews were even given such powerful or sensitive positions as royal financier, physician, or even chief minister of government. The reason for this was that no Jew could possibly be a threat to the throne and therefore no Jew would be likely to use power against the king. Of course when times became bad the Jews were typically blamed and were made to suffer persecution or even expulsion.

In a sense we were like a canary placed in a mineshaft. When poisonous gases are released the canary will stop singing and die before the miners are in danger. Often the first victims of social and economic unrest have been the Jews. We have had to learn to be sensitive to changing conditions. Jews almost always fare better when the national mood is positive and when human rights and dignity are widely respected. An eighteenth-century Polish rabbi commented on the verse "Proclaim liberty throughout the land unto all of its inhabitants." (Leviticus 25:10). Why "all" of its inhabitants? Because if anyone in a nation is not free then no one in that nation is free. Over the centuries Jews have learned that only if everyone's rights and dignity are protected can we feel safe. It should therefore come as no surprise that Jews are often in the vanguard of human rights activities.

The Hardest Lesson

There are two ways to respond to the lessons taught us by the Holocaust. We can say, "No one is our true ally, therefore we must concern ourselves only with ourselves." Or we can say, "The Nazis were able to demonize the Jews and then murder millions of us because we did not do enough to bring others to our cause. We must therefore fight every kind of bigotry and tyranny from the outset lest we become victims." A national trauma like the Holocaust brings out the best and the worst in people.

Our history in modern times does not, in itself, give us reason to go rightward or leftward politically. We have been scapegoated, persecuted, and murdered under communists, fascists, and nationalists of every kind. Even in the United States it wasn't until the post–WWII decades to guarantee that Jews could live, work, and study wherever we wanted. We still suffer demonization by extremist groups ranging from the Aryan Nations to the Nation of Islam. The State of Israel is a favorite whipping boy in international political rhetoric by demagogues of both the right and the left.

The hard lesson of the Holocaust is that we must be quick to respond to every threat to ourselves, but also to every kind of racism and bigotry no matter whom its victims are. We must rely on ourselves but we must also take part in the efforts of others towards social justice.

In the End of Days

Judaism teaches that Creation has purpose. It had a beginning and will have an end. Since the days of the Biblical prophets we have had a vision when all wrongs will be righted and humanity will know a time of universal justice, security, prosperity and peace. That vision is not attached to any political ideology but is reflected in many of them. Our vision of the Messianic Age, whether or not embodied in a single messianic figure, is one that requires us to do more than wait. We are required in our individual lives to try to make the world around us better for everyone. The traditional Jewish community cared for the poor, the disadvantaged and the stranger. We are therefore inspired to strive to make this world like the world-to-come in every way possible. One tradition says that the messiah will only arrive when we have succeeded in this effort. As Franz Kafka expressed it, "The messiah will arrive only when he is no longer needed."

Therefore . . .

Our theology, our ethics, our history, and our vision of the world's purpose all bind us to the belief that we must make the world a better place. Is it any wonder, then, that American Jews not only vote for the more liberal candidate but also actively pursue justice and peace in the world?

Reading the Second Text:
Meaning and Misuses of the Holocaust

Helen Fein

Note to the reader: *This article was first written twenty-six years ago in 1981, before the Israeli war in Lebanon and two years after the completion of my book, Accounting for Genocide: National Responses and Jewish Victimization During the Holocaust. I wanted to consider what I had learned, to unveil the mystifications and misuse of the Holocaust and consider its political and ethical implications.*

We have recently witnessed another Israeli war in Lebanon (2006) with sad results, not achieving its professed end of greater safety for Israel and leading to the death and displacement of thousands of Israeli and Lebanese citizens. Its long-range consequences are unclear at the moment. There is again a proposal for "transfer" in order "'to expel the great majority of the Arabs' from the West Bank and 'sweep the Israeli Arabs from the political system,'" reportedly by "a leader of the joint Knesset faction aligned with Orthodox Zionists worldwide" (Forward, September 15, 2006).

Iran, the sponsor of Hezbollah (whose missiles were among the precipitating causes of the war), is headed by a president who has denied the Holocaust and flaunted his denial in the area for his own political purposes. At this writing, it is not clear what his long-range aims are or how these are related to Iran's nuclear ambitions.

Iran is currently sponsoring an exhibit of anti-Semitic propaganda (a"Holocaust International Cartoon Contest"or"Holocust") depicting Israelis as aggressors and Muslims and Palestinians as victims.

The Holocaust continues to be misused by all sides. Analogies drawn from such misuses provide little guidance to Jews and Israelis as to how to achieve security and resolve realistic conflicts with their neighbors.

* * *

During the past decade, scholarly and popular interest in the Holocaust has grown along with awareness of genocide and mass slaughter in modern history. Because the Holocaust is so central to modern and Israeli consciousness, it has become embedded in the imagery, allegories, and ideology of all parties to the Middle East conflict.

At its most fundamental level the Holocaust is a set of historical events, whose record comprises a singular text. But for Jews, recollecting the Holocaust exposes a second text that is often not made explicit. This text, written over the historical text of our collective memories and taken-for-granted conventional wisdom, is the background that ignites our latent fears.

How true is this conventional wisdom? How are the supposed "facts" and paradigms based on the Holocaust embedded in myths, ideologies, and judgments in Israel and concerning Israel? And finally, what can we learn from the Holocaust about social solidarity and interdependence, and about the Holocaust's contemporary implications for morally grounded Jewish political evaluation and action?

The Articles of Faith

Article I*: The Jew as everywhere alone, deserted by others. In the camps, each looked after him or herself; those who survived eluded the gas chambers by individual cunning, daring, and luck.*

The fact is that over half of the Jews survived in eight of the twenty-one states of Central and Eastern Europe, where pre-war anti-Semitism was highest and where the majority of European Jews outside the USSR lived. But where Jews had been integrated as citizens and anti-Semitic movements had not made significant political advances, other citizens and state officials were more likely to resist the steps—registering, stripping of roles, segregation—that made Jews vulnerable to being seized.

In every case where the majority of a nation's Jews were saved, the authorities of the dominant church had protested promptly, justifying non-cooperation with and subversion of German orders. Germany's allies and satellites were sovereign and could refuse to deport their Jews (as did Finland and Italy before its occupation by the Germans in 1943) and could refuse to honor agreements to do so (as did Bulgaria, France, and Rumania). In German-occupied states where Germany could authorize and execute raids—such as Belgium and Norway (1942) and Denmark, southern Greece and Italy (1943)—native social defense movements emerged in time to help Jews avoid the German net when native authorities repudiated Jewish persecution swiftly. In all of these states, except Greece and Rumania, the majority of Jews was saved. (For more on this aspect of the Holocaust, see my *Accounting for Genocide: National Response and Jewish Victimization During the Holocaust*, published in 1979).

Solidarity among friends and kin also helped in camps. Many survived not just by cunning but because of bonds to others who both protected them and sustained their desire to live, as memoirs of survivors and Terence Des Pres's study, *The Survivor* (1976), show.

Implicit in the first article is:

Article 2: *"We" cannot trust "them." The world is a dangerous place; our existence is always in peril.*

This is, indeed, too often the case, but it is a half-truth that may become a self-fulfilling prophecy if acted on literally. Virtually every instance in which a Jew was saved in a German-occupied state involved trust, trust that linked a network of strangers. When we compare accounts of evaders who depend on bribery with those who depended on social defense movements, we discover how unreliable dependence on money was. Bribes were often accepted and then doubled by betraying the "client" in instances in which relationships had not produced a sense of mutual obligation. We must understand why in some nations it was normal to betray Jews, in other nations normal to save them.

The ring of distrust includes other Jews. The next article is less often publicly stated:

Article 3: *We can't trust Gentiles, but neither can we trust Jews. We have been betrayed, undermined from within.*

By whom? Pick any of the following (a) the *Judenrat* and other Jewish leaders, (b) the Zionists, (c) the American Jewish establishment, (d) the rabbis, (e) the Jewish

Communists, or (f) all of the above.

In viewing this folk belief with skepticism, I do not mean to imply that there should be a communal taboo against making such judgment. But what is implied by this article of faith is the existence of a "we"—a collectivity that shares values, expectations and moral obligations—that knew what had to be done.

However, there was no "we"—no collectivity with a leadership concerned with the interests of all Jews. Jews in Palestine and North America and Zionists and non-Zionists had different agendas. Sadly, even among the potential victims, the most commonly shared view was the misperception that some other type of Jew was destined to be the victim.

In 1941 virtually no Jews or other citizens of German-occupied or -allied states understood the German aim. Most Jewish as well as Allied leaders failed to grasp the true meaning of "the Final Solution of the Jewish Question" until it had been in operations for over a year. No Jewish prewar party or ideology anticipated or provided a guide for coping with an enemy intent on total murder. Recognition by both the victims and the citizens of the Allied states that the German intended to annihilate all Jews was belated, because the idea of collective punishment runs counter to all our paradigms of crime and punishment: In a just world, people are not punished just for being.

Article 4: *The majority of Jewish victims went dumbly and submissively to their deaths, "like sheep to the slaughter."*

Blaming victims for their fate is still widespread. Shame and embarrassment, and denials of the charge of passivity, reveal our discomfort over Jewish responses at the time. Contempt for Jewish helplessness is often balanced by admiration of Jewish resistance—equated with fighting and direct action. It is no wonder that the commemoration of the 1943 Warsaw ghetto uprising has become a central event of Holocaust—week observances. As the triumph of Easter, celebrating the Resurrection, redeems the tragedy of Good Friday among Christians, commemoration of the ghetto uprising redeems the stigma of impotence and suffering among Jews.

Before we examine how Jews became victims, we must become aware of and reject the intuitive notion that becoming a victim is shameful. When we observe that in some states the great majority of Jews who reported for "resettlement" were women, children and the elderly, we ought to ask what social meaning can be imputed to reporting (or failing to report). The late Abba Kovner, author in 1941 of

majority will have to be excluded from citizenship and remain a subject class.

Three positions on this issue emerge among the messianic Zionists. Some would limit or deny the rights of Palestinians. Kahane, who had been criticized by some on the right for talking too soon and too loudly about what should be done, had proposed legislation similar to the Nuremberg Laws to regulate the status of Jews and Arabs and to segregate them. He had also called for the expulsion of all Arabs from Israel. Rabbi Israel Hess of Israel's Bar-Illan University compared the Arabs to the Amalekites, whose extermination was mandated by the Torah, in an article, "The Genocide Ruling of Torah," in that university's official magazine. The late Professor Uriel Tal considered this a justification of future genocide ("The Foundations of Political Messianism in Israel,") *Ha'aretz*, September 26, 1984). Although Hess's "position is an isolated one," wrote Ehud Sprinzak in his 1986 study of Gush Emunim for the American Jewish Committee, "none of these three approaches to the problem of the non-Jewish inhabitants of Israel is considered il-legitimate or abhorrent [by the messianic right]. More important, none has thus far been ruled out as erroneous by Israel's Chief Rabbinate, the highest official re-ligious authority in the land. It is not clear whether the silence . . . is evidence of disapproval or of political prudence."

Genocide and forced emigration are strategic options—sometimes alterna-tives, sometimes complements—for states that deny minorities the right either to assimilate or to participate in power sharing. Both depend on the governing class to limit its qualms of conscience to its own class. Once the "others" are excluded from the universe of obligation, they can be driven out or murdered without guilt. he "Final Solution" itself only became German state policy after the Jews had been segregated and stripped of citizenship, rights, roles and property, and the possibil-ity of emigration—in 1938 the German goal—foreclosed.

A contrasting misuse of the Holocaust is the abstracting of the roles of Jews and Nazis as a paradigm of victims and oppressors. This is most likely to be used by socialists, pacifists, and the left. Louis Schneider of the American Friends Ser-vice Committee, quoted by Marvin Maurer in *Midstream* in 1977, casts the Jews as the universal victim: "Now Israelis are making Jews out of the Palestinians. In the Palestinians I recognize the Jew." In a related vein, Father Daniel Berrigan, writing in *Liberation* in 1974, castigated the Jews for becoming "like the goyim, the idolaters," rejecting the role of prophet or suffering servant. While criticizing the acts of Israel, he declared, "I am a Jew, in resistance against Israel."

Here the label of Jew has become not a stigma, as the Nazis' yellow star in-tended it to be, but a symbol prized by all victims. To complete the role reversal, some go on to identify the Israelis as the new Nazis.

The 1982 war in Lebanon evoked a parallel rhetorical combat between Prime Minister Menachem Begin and European, American, and Israeli critics of Israel's invasion; both sides misused the Holocaust for justification. Begin identified Israel's enemies with the Nazi enemy, while some critics cloaked the Israelis in Nazi uniforms, calling urban bombing "genocide" and excoriating Israel's "Judeo-Nazi" policies. Jacobo Timmerman, a prominent critic of the war in Israel, argued without any apparent effect against such "truculent comparisons," observing that they "will move no one."

Jews and Nazis were on the same side in the former Soviet Union's singularly malign reinterpretation of the Holocaust. This was apparently designed to reconcile Soviet antagonism to Israel with the fact that the Nazis murdered millions of Soviet Jews because they were Jews. During World War II, the Soviet Union publicized the Nazi extermination drive against Jews, but in the postwar era it obliterated the Jewish identity of the victims. This was symbolized in the official Soviet memorial at Babi Yar, dedicated in 1976 to "100,000 citizens of the city of Kiev and prisoners of war"—a memorial erected only after a decade of protest against the filling-in of the ravine in which the victims were shot.

Soviet ideologists explained Nazism as an instrument or outcome of monopoly capitalism, and either denied that Jews were a special object of Nazi racism or claimed that only work class Jews were persecuted. Moreover, they accused the Zionists and the Jewish bourgeoisie of collaborating in the annihilation of the Jewish masses. Soviet propaganda credited the Nazi leaders with using the Zionists to "create a pro-fascist Jewish state in the Middle East," and it claimed that Adolf Eichmann was an agent of the state's creation who had to be captured "to ensure secrecy over the number of Zionists' deals and the collaboration of their secret services with the Hitlerites during the World War II." (See *Soviet Anti-Semitic Propaganda*, published in London in 1978 by the Institute for Jewish Affairs).

The object of this campaign was the delegitimization of Israel through the charge that Zionism is Nazism, a libel that emerged after the 1975 United Nations "Zionism is racism" resolution. According to *Soviet Anti-Semitic Propaganda*, the Soviets claimed the "Democratic strata of the Israeli population realize that the persecution of the Jews by the Nazis, which was justified by racial theories, can be identified with the genocide applied by the Israelis to the Arab people of Palestine." Note the further reversal: Jews were merely persecuted, but the Arabs are subjected to applied genocide.

Others who seek to delegitimize Israel deny categorically, as did the delegate from Saudi Arabia in the United Nations General Assembly in 1976, that the Germans murdered the Jews of Europe. Throughout the world, such "revisionists"—usually neo-Nazis and their collaborators—collude in this lie, denying that Nazi Germany organized the murder of five to six million Jews between 1941 and 1945.

* * *

The text with which I begin is Hillel's injunction: If I am not for myself, who will be for me? And if I am for myself only, what am I?

The first part implies that we must accept responsibility for protecting the rights of Jews elsewhere—in Eastern Europe, Ethiopia, Iran, Syria, the former Soviet Union—whether they are victims of anti-Semitism or of generalized violations of human rights as a result of state terrorism. While both anti-Semitism and state terrorism—indeed, all terrorism—menace Jews—Jews at least initially—are not the first or primary victims. State terrorism and genocide are functionally related. Thus I believe that Jews should have a special commitment to human rights everywhere and should reject ideologies, whether of the left or the right that rationalize invasions of such rights.

To protect the rights of Jews today also means to assert their right to exist in a Jewish state as well as in Diaspora. But unfortunately there are many Jews in Israel and in the Diaspora who have not grasped—or wish to deny—the responsibilities that accompany that right. Surely, the right to statehood does not include the right to deny minorities the same rights granted to Jews or to limit their participation as Israeli citizens, for we have not the right to do to others what we rejected as unjust when we were similarly victimized. Indeed, because the Holocaust testifies to human dependence on reciprocal solidarity for survival and because of the historical experiences of Jews, we have a special obligation to recognize and protect the rights of minorities in all states of which we are citizens.

Ruling over another people who claim not merely minority rights but the right to self-determination as a people should be as abhorrent to Jews as was our powerlessness. Governing without consent demands the use of repression. No more than the Americans, or the British, or the French do Jews have the capacity to rule over another people without becoming captive to their rule, without playing the role of the oppressor. This endangers the moral integrity of the Jewish state from within and makes it prone to disorder and terrorism.

In divided societies, each side, by excluding the other from a common universe of obligation, tends to punish "them" collectively or randomly—by beating, murder, or massacre—for their crimes against "us." This may lead to a crime-punishment-crime cycle. The random murders of Jews by Arabs and of Arabs by Jews in Jerusalem and the West Bank in recent years illustrate this. Some Zionist maximalists apparently intended to provoke intergroup violence with their plot—thwarted by Israeli police—to blow up Jerusalem's Dome of the Rock mosque, hoping to trigger Moslem rioting and Israeli retaliation.

Further, the response to terrorism (on both sides in recent years, although Israel only began prosecuting Jewish vigilantism and terrorism by settlers in 1984) has led to sanctioned violations of human rights in Israel—e.g., the beating to death in 1984 of two Arab bus hijackers in custody. Thus, the definition of the Palestinian as outside the Jewish universe of obligation has undermined the rule of law within Israel. Justification of double standards in the name of *raison d'etat* overlooks the subversion of state institutions that follows.

The hostile exclusionary attitude toward Arabs in Israel among Jewish Israeli youth (as demonstrated in polls) is unlikely to be changed by programs to change attitudes. To try to teach them respect for democracy and tolerance of Arab Israelis will prove futile if the situation that causes them to see Arabs as the inferior class and as enemies is not changed. The choice is to rule and repress, reinforcing contempt for the group oppressed, or to create a new situation in which neither group dominates the other. The options, Israeli West Bank expert Meron Benvenisti asserts in *Conflicts and Contradictions* (1986), are partition (ceding the occupied territories), power sharing or majority tyranny (the Likud vision)—a "*Herrenvolk* democracy where the minority is disenfranchised and deprived of basic civil rights."

The challenge facing Israel is to be neither oppressed nor oppressor—"neither victim nor executioner," as Albert Camus expressed the challenge of our time in 1946. We, too, should say "No" and refuse to justify the killing of the innocent, whether as a means toward liberation or for reasons of state. It is not enough to say "Never again!" unless one refuses to create new victims and throws out a lifeline when boat people are sighted on the horizon.

This is not a utopian program. Rather, I believe it is an authentically Jewish agenda after the Holocaust.

Justice, Not "Just Us"

Rabbi Michael Rothbaum

Scarcely one-third of the way through the book of Genesis, we encounter an event that has the power to move even the most hardened of skeptics, a brief exchange whose implications beckon to us from across the centuries. Abraham and Sarah are in the midst of an arduous physical and spiritual journey. They pursue a truth that, though shared with almost no one else on the planet, has led them to make innumerable sacrifices. The couple, childless despite their resolve, welcome and then feed a trio of strangers—men, messengers, angels perhaps—who subsequently inform Sarah that she is pregnant. The dedication of the world's first Jews, it seems, may be paying dividends. A confirmation of the physical survival of, well, us. The Jewish people. But are we concerned with *just* us?

It is not long before Abraham makes a discovery that literally stops him in his tracks. G-d, it seems, is poised to destroy the cities of Sodom and Gomorrah with a tactical air strike of fire and brimstone. The sins of these two cities are apparently *so* grave that none of their inhabitants are worth saving.

What might we expect of Abraham in this situation? Perhaps he would be indifferent to this news, preoccupied with his pending fatherhood. Maybe a little uneasy, disturbed by the proximity of the carpet-bombing? Instead, what follows is an incendiary monologue. Perhaps, suggests Abraham, there are fifty innocent people in the cities. Remarkably, Abraham defies G-d to take note of those fifty, rather than allow them to perish with the guilty. "Far be it from You to do such a thing, thunders Abraham, "to bring death upon the innocent as well as the guilty, so that the innocent and the guilty fare alike." And with a damning finality, Abraham inquires, "Shall not the Judge of all the Earth deal justly?"

G-d's response? "You're right. If I find fifty innocent people in the cities, I'll save them." But Abraham is far from satisfied. "What if the fifty should lack five? Really G-d . . . fifty, forty-five? What's the difference?" G-d consents: "I will not destroy for the sake of the forty-five." Abraham presses on. "What about forty?" G-d agrees to save for the sake of the forty. And so forth and so on, Abraham and G-d methodically hammering out a deal in which the cities will remain intact if but ten righteous individuals can be found within their borders.

Throughout our short story, there is one common theme: Justice. In seventeen verses, the words for justice, "*tzedek*" and "*mishpat*," appear in some form no less than eleven times.

Of course, what makes Abraham's obsessive pursuit of justice so remarkable are the folks on whose behalf he argues. The residents of Sodom and Gomorrah are not only unrelated to him—non-Jews at that—but they further embody the grievous sins of inhospitality, and disdain for the poor. The *Zohar* tells us that there was a stream in Sodom that divided to swallow any stranger who dared enter the city. Were such a stranger somehow able to evade this murderous stream, the *Zohar* continues, the people of Sodom would cast into the deepest part of the river both the stranger, and anyone within the town who had offered food or drink. Abraham has no stake in such a town, no land-holdings, no commodities, no rental properties.

Stuck inside Sodom's borders, however, are Abraham's nephew Lot and his family. Abraham could have simply requested that G-d liberate his relatives, and to Hell (literally) with the rest of the people. Yet, in the course of our passage, not once does Abraham invoke the name of his nephew Lot.

Instead, he presents a universalist argument, addressing G-d in terms of *justice* and righteousness. Justice, not "just us." Abraham, fresh from establishing eternal covenant with G-d, still recuperating from a self-performed circumcision, and largely unaware of the scope of and capacity for vengeance, nonetheless chooses to challenge the judgment of the Earth's Judge. In choosing this path, not only challenging authority—and the Ultimate Authority at that—but also working out a manageable and just solution, Abraham has served as model for Jews throughout the ages.

A question: Would the residents of Sodom and Gomorrah have returned the favor? Would they have petitioned to save Abraham from some undetermined calamity? The question is, of course, absurd. The residents of Sodom and Gomorrah were so wicked that it was apparently too much to find even ten righteous citizens among them. Certainly they would have no special love for Abraham.

And this, friends, is precisely the point. Abraham does not argue for the people of Sodom and Gomorrah because it's a "shrewd move." He does not weigh personal costs and benefits, taking a "calculated risk." He has one concern, and one concern only: the saving of innocent lives. The pursuit of justice, the one sacred concept upon which his entire life—and, by extension, our religious tradition—is based. He does not do what is "good for the Jews," as it were. He does what's good for Judaism. Justice—not "just us."

Another question: Would today's Iraqis profess a particular love for us? Probably not. Is caring about *them* "good for the Jews?"

When presented with the possibility that US citizens might be troubled by televised images of the suffering of Iraqi civilians, an American general had this suggestion: "Change the channel." Could we at least know the number, how many Iraqi civilians have lost their lives in the course of the war? Replied yet another American general, "We don't do body counts."

The website www.iraqbodycount.net, as its name implies, does body counts. As of February 18, 2007, it estimates that between 56,574 and 62,296 Iraqis have lost their lives. There are some who may say these numbers are inflated, that they reflect a "political agenda." Perhaps those people are right. So if not sixty thousand dead civilians, then thirty thousand? Is that acceptable? What about fifteen thousand? One thousand? One hundred? Fifty? Forty? Ten?

There are those Jews who blithely shrug off such concerns. They argue that history presents us with a stark choice: concern for Jewish justice or concern for Jewish safety. The choice is a false one. We are right to be vigilant, to oppose Jew-hatred, to speak out against the ugly suspicions and vicious lies that once again rear their head in Europe, the Middle East, and even some of our own college campuses. But let us be clear. When we neglect our people's ancient call for justice, we are not "standing up for Judaism." It is, in fact, quite the opposite. Even in light of the brutal history of anti-Jewish violence, sacrificing Abraham's call for justice in the name of "survival" is self-defeating. We seek survival, yes, but of what? The survival of Jews without the survival of Jewish ethics? Moral relativism can be a comfort for only so long.

It is a frightening path to seek justice for others, to care for their fate, even when one's own are in danger. But it is the Jewish path. It requires courage, to be sure. But courage is needed and so desperately in these troubled days. The Jewish soul, born in our father Abraham, is nourished by a holy, precious structure of cherished values. We define ourselves by our fidelity to those values. If we ignore them in the name of expediency, if Jews cease to behave as ethical Jews, we accomplish the goals of all who have sought to destroy us.

Angels come to Abraham and Sarah. The promise of new life. The fulfillment of the promise of the covenant. Physically, Jewish continuity is assured. But the story is incomplete. G-d, it would seem, is not assured that the promise will be secure until Jewish ethical continuity is assured. Yes, Abraham has been good at being obedient, doing what G-d says. But in the twilight of a lonely desert encampment overlooking the cities of Sodom and Gomorrah, G-d is not looking for obedience. G-d seeks not a meek and fearful servant, or a dumbstruck submissive devotee. G-d seeks—no, G-d *demands*—a sacred relationship with an earthly partner. A partner who will be engaged in the common pursuit of righteousness. A figure resolute in the conviction that justice is *not* the sole possession of Heaven. A brave individual unafraid to demand that justice be brought to earth, here, today.

G-d finds that individual—that partner—in Abraham. "I know him," G-d says of his sacred partner Abraham. "He will command his children and his household after him, and they shall keep the way of *Ad-nai,*, to do justice, and righteousness." We are the children and the household of Abraham. He has indeed commanded us. The question remains: will we maintain his pursuit of justice?

If you listen closely, you can still hear that command of our Abraham, drifting this way and that slipping through the cracks and crevices of a broken world, waiting for his children to make good on its ancient yet timeless promise.

CHAI rescuing animals in
Israel during wartime in the
summer of 2006
(photo by Avi Hirshfield)

Hillel Cafe photo: This photo was
taken after a suicide bombing at the
Hillel Cafe in Jerusalem. People visit
the sites of suicide bombings to
remember the murdered and post
photos and leave behind poems,letters
and flowers. (photo by Leah Green)

Leah Green of Compassionate
Listening planting a tree in honor
of Rachel Corrie, who was killed
by an Israeli bulldozer as she was
protesting the demolition of a
Palestinian home.
(photo by Deborah Rohan
Schlueter)

Entering Gaza: A crossing gate between Gaza and Israel.
(photo by Linda Wolf)

Jews protesting Apartheid outside
the South African Embassy in 1985
(photo by Paul Tick)

"Another Grandpa for Peace."
Hundreds of thousands of Americans gathered September 24, 2005
in Washington, D.C. in support of
peace. (photo by Jesse Abrahams)

One of many marches in Tel Aviv for "Peace between Israelis and Palestinians (photo by Paul Tick)

Palestinian women expressing
their delight upon discovering
Jewish Israelis of Peace Now were
supporting their human rights.
(photo by Paul Tick)

Neve Shalom, a Jewish- Palestinian farming and peace center and cooperative, annually hosts young Jews and Palestinians so they may work and learn together. (photo by Paul Tick)

Idan Halili, Jewish and 19, was Israel's first female Conscientious Objector. "I as a feminist, feel I must avoid military service and act tolimit and reduce the influence of the army on civic society," she said. Her attorney added, "her ideology of feminism also means she was a pacifist, objecting to any military system." Idan was jailed for two weeks and later told she was "unsuitable" for military service. (photo by Tal Hayoun)

Giving Charity (*Tzedakah*)

To help the poor and hungry and to support communal purposes and institutions, Judaism places great stress on the giving of money as an act of righteousness (*tzedakah*). In the Jewish tradition, *tzedakah* is not an act of condescension from one person to another who is in need. It is the fulfillment of a *mitzvah*, a commandment, to a fellow human being, who has equal status before God. Although Jewish tradition recognizes that the sharing of our resources is also an act of love (as the Torah states, "Love your neighbor as yourself" [Leviticus 19:18]), it emphasizes that this act of sharing is an act of justice. This is to teach us that Jews are obligated to provide people who are in need with our love and concern. They are human beings created in the Divine image, who have a place and a purpose within God's creation.

In the Jewish tradition, failure to give charity is equivalent to idolatry.[4] Perhaps this is because a selfish person forgets the One Who created and provides for us all, and in becoming preoccupied with personal material needs, makes himself or herself into an idol. The giving of charity by Jews is so widespread that Maimonides was able to say: "Never have I seen or heard of a Jewish community that did not have a charity fund."[5]

Charity even takes priority over the building of the Temple. King Solomon was prohibited from using the silver and gold that David, his father, had accumulated for the building of the Temple, because that wealth should have been used to feed the poor during the three years of famine in King David's reign. (I Kings 7:51)

Judaism mandates lending to the needy, to help them become economically self-sufficient: "And if your brother becomes impoverished, and his means fail in your proximity; then you shall strengthen him; . . . Take no interest of him or increase . . . You shall not give him your money upon interest . . ."   (Leviticus 25:35-37)

Every third year of the sabbatical cycle, the needy are to receive the tithe for the poor (one tenth of one's income).   (Deuteronomy 14:28, 26:12)

The following Torah verse indicates the general Jewish view about helping the poor: "If there shall be among you a needy person, one of your brethren, within any of your gates, in your land which the Lord your God gives you, you shall not harden your heart, nor shut your hand from your needy brother; but you shall surely open your hand unto him, and shall surely lend him sufficient for his need in that which he wants."   (Deuteronomy 15:7-8)

Jewish tradition views *tzedakah* as not only an act of love, but also as an act of justice; in fact, the word "*tzedakah*" comes from the word "*tzedek*" (justice). According to the Torah, the governing institutions of the Jewish community are responsible to help needy people.

Maimonides writes in his code of Jewish law that the highest form of *tzedakah* is to help a needy individual through "a gift or a loan, or by forming a business partnership with him, or by providing him with a job, until he is no longer dependent on the generosity of others".[6] This concept is based on the following Talmudic teaching: "It is better to lend to a poor person than to give him alms, and best of all is to provide him with capital for business."[7]

Hence Jews should provide immediate help for poor people while also working for a just society in which there is no poverty. In Judaism, *tzedakah* is intertwined with the pursuit of social justice.

An entire lengthy section of the Code of Jewish Law (*Shulhan Arukh*), *Yoreh De'ah* 247–259, is devoted to the many aspects of giving charity. Some of the more important concepts are given below:

247:1. It is a positive religious obligation for a person to give as much charity as he can afford. (A tithe of ten percent of one's income is incumbent upon every Jew.)

247:33: God has compassion on whoever has compassion on the poor. A person should think that, just as he asks of God all the time to sustain him and as he entreats God to hear his cry, so he should hear the cry of the poor.

248: 1: Every person is obliged to give charity. Even a poor person who is supported by charity is obliged to give from that which he receives.

249:3: A man should give charity cheerfully and out of the goodness of his heart. He should anticipate the grief of the poor man and speak words of comfort to him. But if he gives in an angry and unwilling spirit, he loses any merit there is in giving.

250:1: How much should be given to a poor man? "Sufficient for his need in that which he requires." (Deuteronomy 15:8) This means that if he is hungry, he should be fed; if he has no clothes, he should be given clothes; if he has no furniture, furniture should be brought for him. (This is to be dispensed by the person in charge of community charity funds.)

According to the prophet Ezekiel, failure to help the needy led to the destruction of Sodom: "Behold this was the iniquity of thy sister Sodom; pride, fullness of bread, and careless ease . . . neither did she strengthen the hand of the poor and needy . . . therefore I removed them when I saw it. . . .   (Ezekiel 16:49, 50)

A relationship between personal misfortune and a failure to help the poor is indicated in Proverbs 17:5, 21:13, and 28:27. For example, Proverbs 21:13 states:

"The person who fails to hear the cry of the poor will later also cry, but will not be answered."

Acts of Loving Kindness

As important as *tzedakah* is, the Jewish tradition states that even greater is *gemilut chasadim* (acts of loving kindness): "One who gives a coin to a poor man is rewarded with six blessings, but he who encourages him with kind words is rewarded with eleven blessings."[8]

Of course, providing both charity and kind words is best of all.

The sages interpret "acts of loving kindness" to include many types of gracious action, such as hospitality to travelers, providing for poor brides, visiting the sick, welcoming guests, burying the dead, and comforting mourners. *Gemilut chasadim* is deemed superior to acts of charity in several ways: "No gift is needed for it but the giving of oneself; it may be done to the rich as well as to the poor; and it may be done not only to the living, but also to the dead (through burial)." 9

The purpose of the entire Torah is to teach *gemilut chasadim*. It starts and ends with an act of loving kindness.

For in the third chapter of Genesis, the verse reads: "The Lord God made for Adam and his wife garments of skin and clothed them." (Genesis 3:21), and the last book of the Torah reports: "and He buried him (Moses) in the valley." (Deuteronomy 34:6)[10]

Jewish Views on Poverty

Judaism places emphasis on justice and charity and kindness to the poor because of the great difficulties poor people face: "If all afflictions in the world were assembled on one side of the scale and poverty on the other, poverty would outweigh them all."[11]

Judaism believes that poverty is destructive to the human personality and negatively shapes a person's life experiences: "The ruin of the poor is their poverty." (Proverbs 10:15) "Where there is no sustenance, there is no learning."[12] "The world is darkened for him who has to look to others for sustenance."[13] "The sufferings of poverty cause a person to disregard his own sense (of right) and that of his Maker."[14]

Judaism generally does not encourage an ascetic life. Insufficiency of basic necessities does not ease the path toward holiness, except perhaps for very spiritual individuals. In many cases the opposite is true; poverty can lead to the breaking of a person's spirit. This is one reason that holiness is linked to justice.

Many Torah laws are designed to aid the poor: "the produce of corners of the field are to be left uncut for the poor to take" (Leviticus 19:9); "the gleanings of the wheat harvest and fallen fruit are to be left for the needy" (Leviticus 19:10); "during the sabbatical year, the land is to be left fallow so and the poor (as well as animals) may eat of whatever grows freely." (Leviticus 25:2-7)

Failure to treat the poor properly is a desecration of God: "The person who mocks the poor blasphemes his Maker." (Proverbs 17:5) Abraham, the founder of Judaism, always went out of his way to aid the poor. He set up inns that were open in all four directions on the highways so that the poor and the wayfarer would have access to food and drink when in need.[15]

The Jewish tradition sees God as siding with the poor and oppressed. He intervened in Egypt on behalf of poor, oppressed slaves. His prophets constantly castigated those who oppressed the needy. Two proverbs reinforce this message. A negative formulation is in Proverbs 14:31: "He who oppresses a poor man insults his Maker." Proverbs 19:17 puts it more positively: "He who is kind to the poor lends to the Lord." Hence helping a needy person is like providing a loan to the Creator of the universe.

Compassion

The Talmud teaches that "Jews are *rachmanim b'nei rachmanim* (compassionate children of compassionate parents), and one who shows no pity for fellow creatures is assuredly not of the seed of Abraham, our father."[16] The rabbis considered Jews to be distinguished by three characteristics: compassion, modesty, and benevolence.[17] As indicated previously, we are instructed to feel empathy for strangers, "for you were strangers in the land of Egypt." (Deuteronomy 10:19) The *birkat ha-mazon* (grace recited after meals) speaks of God compassionately feeding the whole world.

We are not only to have compassion for Jews, but for all who are in need.

Have we not all one Father?
Has not one God created us? (Malachi 2:10)

Rabbi Samson Raphael Hirsch writes very eloquently about the importance of compassion:

> Do not suppress this compassion, this sympathy especially with the sufferings of your fellowman. It is the warning voice of duty, which points out to you your brother in every sufferer, and your own sufferings in his, and awakens the love, which tells you that you belong to him and his sufferings with all the powers that you have. Do not suppress it! . . . See in it the admonition of God that you are to have no joy so long as a brother suffers by your side.[18]

Rabbi Samuel Dresner states "Compassion is the way God enters our life in terms of man's relation to his fellowman."[19]

The Jewish stress on compassion finds expression in many groups and activities. Jewish communities generally have most if not all of the following: a *Bikur Cholim* Society to provide medical expenses for the sick, and to visit them and bring them comfort and cheer; a *Malbish Arumim* Society to provide clothing for the poor; a *Hachnasat Kalah* Society to provide for needy brides; a *Bet Yetomin* Society to aid orphans; a *Talmud Torah* Organization to support a free school for poor children; a *Gemilat Chesed* Society to lend money at no interest to those in need; an *Ozer Dalim* Society to dispense charity to the poor; a *Hachnasat Orchim* Society to provide shelter for homeless travelers; a *Chevrah Kaddishah* Society to attend to the proper burial of the dead; and *Essen Teg* Institutions to provide food and shelter for poor students who attend schools in the community.[20]

Judaism also stresses compassion for animals. There are many laws in the Torah which mandate kindness to animals. A farmer is commanded not to muzzle his ox when he threshes corn (Deuteronomy 25:4) and not to plow with an ox and an ass together (Deuteronomy 22:10), since the weaker animal would not be able to keep up with the stronger one. Animals must be allowed to rest on the Sabbath Day (Exodus 20:10, 23:12), a teaching so important that it is part of the Ten Commandments. A person is commanded to feed his animals before sitting down to his own meal.[21] These concepts are summarized in the Hebrew phrase *tsa'ar ba'alei chayim*—the mandate not to cause "pain to any living creature."

The Psalmist emphasizes God's concern for animals, for "His tender mercies are over all His creatures." (Psalm 145:9) He pictures God as "satisfying the desire of every living creature (Psalm 145:16) and "providing food for the beasts and birds." (Psalm 147:9) Perhaps the Jewish attitude toward animals is epitomized by the statement in Proverbs "The righteous person regards the life of his or her animal." (Proverb 12:10) In Judaism, one who does not treat animals with compassion cannot be considered a righteous individual.[22]

Rabbi Moshe Cordovero (1522–1570) indicates the importance Judaism places on the proper treatment of animals, as well as people:

> [One should] respect all creatures, recognizing in them the greatness of the Creator who formed man with wisdom, and whose wisdom is contained in all creatures. He should realize that they greatly deserve to be honored, since the One Who Forms All Things, the Wise One Who is exalted above all, cared to create them. If one despises them, God forbid, it reflects on the honor of their Creator...
> ...It is evil in the sight of the Holy One, Blessed be He, if any of His creatures are despised.[23]

Consistent with this precept, the Jewish sages teach, "Whoever shows mercy to God's creatures is granted mercy from Heaven."[24]

Judaism and Business Ethics

The Torah provides instruction in honest business practices: "You shall do no wrong in judgment, in measures of length, of weight, or in quantity. Just balances, just weights, a just *ephah* [the standard dry measure] and a just *hin* [a measure for liquids], shall you have. I am the Lord your God, who brought you out of the land of Egypt. (Leviticus 19:35, 36)

The rabbis of the Talmud give concrete expression to the many Torah and prophetic teachings regarding justice and righteousness. They indicate in detail what is proper when conducting business. Rabbinic literature translates prophetic ideals into the language of the marketplace in terms of duties of employers to employees and of workers to their employers, fair prices, the avoidance of false weights and measures, proper business contracts, and fair methods of competition.

Rava, a fourth-century Babylonian teacher, taught the wealthy merchants of his town the importance of scrupulous honesty in business dealings. He stated that on Judgment Day the first question God asks a person is "Were you reliable in your business dealings?"[25] The rabbis stress that a person's word is a sacred bond that should not be broken. The Mishnah states that God will exact punishment for those who do not abide by their promises.[26] Cheating a Gentile is considered even worse than cheating a Jew, for "besides being a violation of the moral law, it brings Israel's religion into contempt, and desecrates the name of Israel's God."[27]

The sages are very critical of attempts to take away a person's livelihood by unfair competition.[28] Their overall view of business ethics can be summarized by the verses "And you shall do that which is right and good in the sight of the Lord" (Deuteronomy 6:18), and "better is a little with righteousness than great revenues with injustice." (Proverbs 16:8)

The very high ethical standards of the Talmudic sages are exemplified by the following story:

> "Reb Saphra had wine to sell. A certain customer came in to buy wine at a time when Reb Saphra was saying the *Sh'ma* prayer (which cannot be interrupted by speaking). The customer said, "Will you sell me the wine for such an amount?"[29] When Reb Saphra did not respond, the customer thought he was not satisfied with the price and raised his bid. When Reb Saphra had finished his prayer, he said, "I decided in my heart to sell the wine to you at the first price you mentioned; therefore I cannot accept your higher bid."[30]

It is essential that Jews work to establish systems and conditions consistent with the basic Jewish values of justice, compassion, kindness, the sacredness of every life, the imitation of God's attributes, love of neighbors, consideration of the stranger, compassion for animals, and the highest of business ethics.

Notes

[1] Quoted in J. H. Hertz, *The Pentateuch and Haftorahs*, London: Soncino, 1957, p. 820. Rabbi Hertz also offers a Chassidic rebbe's interpretation of this Biblical verse: "Do not use unjust means to secure the victory of justice." (p. 820)

[2] Rabbi Emanuel Rackman, "Torah Concept of Empathic Justice Can Bring Peace," *The Jewish Week*, April 3, 1977, p. 19.

[3] Rabbi Levi Yitzchak Horowitz, the Bostoner Rebbe, "And You Shall tell Your Son," *Young Israel Viewpoint*, Spring, 1997. Quoted by David Sears, *Compassion for Humanity in the Jewish Tradition*. Northvale, New Jersey/Jerusalem: Jason Aronson, 1998, p. 22.

[4] *Ketubot* 68a.

[5] Maimonides, *Mishneh Torah*, *Zeraim*, Gifts to the Poor, 10:7

[6] Maimonides, *Mishneh Torah*, Gifts to the Poor: 10:7.

[7] *Shabbat* 63a.

[8] *Baba Batra* 88b.

[9] Maimonides, *Mishneh Torah, Hilchot Avadim* 9:8.

[10] Sotah 14a.

[11] Midrash *Exodus Rabbah*, *Mishpatim* 31:14.

[12] *Pirke Avot* 3:21.

[13] *Betza* 32a.

[14] *Eruvin* 41.

[15] Genesis 18:2; *Abot de Rabbi Nathan* 7:17a,b.

[16] *Betzah* 32b.

[17] *Yebamot* 79a.

[18] Samson R. Hirsch, *Horeb*, trans. Dayan Dr. I Grunfeld, London: Soncino, 1962, vol. 1, chapter 17, 54-55.

[19] Samuel Dresner, *Prayer, Humility, Compassion*, Philadelphia: Jewish Publication Society, 1953, p. 183.

[20] In Judaism, there are just two limits to compassion. The first is that a judge must apply the law equally, without regard to whether a person is rich or poor. Only the strict rules of justice must apply. Second, one need not show compassion to those who lack compassion and practice cruelty. A Talmudic sage taught: "He who is compassionate to the cruel will, in the end, be cruel to the compassionate" (*Yalkut*, Samuel 121).

[21] *Gittin* 62a; *Berachot* 40a.

[22] For a detailed study of the Jewish tradition on compassion for animals, see Noah J. Cohen, *Tsaar Ba'alei Chayim: The Prevention of Cruelty to Animals, Its Basis, Development, and Legislation in Hebrew Literature* , New York: Feldheim, 1976; Also, see *The Vision of Eden*, an unpublished manuscript by Rabbi David Sears.

[23] Rabbi Moshe Cordovero, *Tomer Devorah*, Chapter 2, Quoted by David Sears, *Compassion for Humanity in the Jewish Tradition*, Northvale, New Jersey/ Jerusalem: Jason Aronson, 1998, 3.

[24] *Shabbat* 151b.

[25] *Shabbat* 31a.

[26] *Baba Metzia* 4:2.

[27] *Baba Kamma*, 113b.

[28] *Sanhedrin* 81a.

[29] *She'iltot, Parshat VaYechi*

[30] *She'iltot, Parshat VaYechi*.

Judaism, Feminism, and Peace in the Nuclear Age

Rabbi Sheila Peltz Weinberg

I am writing this on August 6, 2006, the 61st anniversary of Hiroshima; the first time in history an atomic bomb was used. Simply to say the word Hiroshima reminds us of horror and devastation. Among the many violent conflicts raging on the planet, my eyes are now especially drawn to the two that involve my people—the war in Iraq and the war between Israel and Lebanon. I smile when I read a phrase in the article below I wrote nearly twenty years ago: "In this time of danger and fear... ...."

I hearken back to the speech that Martin Luther King, Jr. gave at Riverside Church in April 1967, in the middle of the Vietnam War called "A Time to Break Silence." He said: "This kind of positive revolution of values [from the pursuit of war to the pursuit of peace] is our best defense against Communism. War is not the answer. Communism will never be defeated by the use of atomic bombs of nuclear weapons. . . . our greatest defense against Communism is to take offensive action in behalf of justice. We must with positive action seek to remove those conditions of poverty, insecurity and injustice which are the fertile soil in which the seed of communism grows and develops."

It is very easy to replace communism with terrorism in King's speech. Rather than new ways of thinking espoused by our spiritual sources, feminism and MLK, the great superpower, the United States, has found another enemy which it now objectifies as the root of all evil. Terrorism has replaced Communism as the cause for the pursuit of war. Despite the words of visionaries and the tears of mothers and fathers and orphans, violence and war prevail. It is as if there must be a reason found to pursue war because war is the force that energizes our economy, our national spirit, our very identity as people.

There are 150,000 Hiroshima-size bombs in the US arsenal. The $17.6 billion they cost the American taxpayer could rebuild all the schools in the country and provide Head Start and health care to every child (the true majority). History, however, keeps confirming again and again that violent action, destruction, bombing, aggression, do not end enmity. Our war in Iraq has vastly expanded terrorism in the Middle East, and sadly, it was Israel's first war in Lebanon that created Hezbollah and today's actions that have dramatically increased Hezbollah's worldwide support. Why is it so hard to see that there needs to be another way? This is still a "hard and frightening time" and we need an alternative vision more than ever—even if that vision seems ridiculous, impossible, idealistic, naïve. Despite all of that, because of all of that, those of us who can see even the smallest glimmer of a new way of thinking cannot keep silent. We must continue to advocate for justice, reconciliation, peace building, and deep inner reflection as alternatives to violence. Today as in 1987, as in 1967, "Judaism and feminism share a radical alternative vision of the world as well as a basic optimism that change is possible—not easy and not fast, but possible." Because it is so hard to hold onto this faith, it is even more important to do so.

I would like to share with you thoughts about how Judaism and feminism nourish and encourage working for disarmament, and how these seemingly disparate approaches to reality can stimulate and enhance the personal and collective pursuit of peace.

Historically, both women and Jews have lived the role of victim, of objectified "other." From that special vantage point as stereotyped and oppressed, we understand that true liberation consists in affirming ourselves without objectifying the opponent. The arms race feeds on a mentality of objectification. From earliest childhood we were reared on images of the Russian people and their leaders as warmongers and madmen. We are still being urged to believe in a win-lose model of international relations that mirrors interpersonal relations in traditional hierarchical societies. Feminism introduces a model of participation and empowerment as opposed to competition and absolute individualism. In the nuclear age, the winners versus the loser, the good guys versus bad guys, the wild-west macho cowboy mentality is totally obsolete. It never functioned very well. But in today's world, still encircled by fifty thousand nuclear warheads, the idea of "winning" a nuclear war is suicidal thinking.

It is true that not all people who experience oppression develop an ethic that is opposed to oppression. Such an ethic, however, is central to most feminist theory and practice, and I believe it is absolutely integral to Judaism. The central historic event in Jewish life is the Exodus from Egypt, the liberation of a ragtag horde of slaves who at the beginning of the story are quite unaware of their own oppression. Ultimately they become sufficiently empowered to be partners with the Creator of the Universe in a very demanding and ethical covenant. The eternal message of the Exodus is not to glory in the defeat of the oppressors or wait until they become the losers and we the victors. The essence of the teaching is a rejection of master-slave power relations. The main message is that whichever way you turn in a relationship of exploitation or objectification, you lose.

There is a metaphor in Jewish prayers that is difficult to relate to as a democrat, never mind as a feminist. Yet I have pondered it for a long while, and I believe that in its own dated language it expresses a fundamental truth about power relations. The metaphor is that of God as King. It means that the earthly power of kings and states must be limited. This metaphor is a cry against the assumption of absolute power, which is exactly what underlies bloated defense budgets and recycled cold war rhetoric. As we experience empowerment as women and Jews, we tap into the power of divine sovereignty, which forces us to challenge the assumptions of the nations who play god.

Judaism and feminism share a radical alternative vision of the world as well as a basic optimism that change is possible—not easy and not fast, but possible. Jewish images of the alternative future abound. We call it the Messiah. We mean world peace. The Hebrew prophets are the most articulate in expressing the vision. The *Sukkah* is an adumbration of the security to come, based on inner strength.

Rabbi Levi said: "Beloved is peace, for all the blessings end with 'peace.' In the recitation of the *Shema,* God spreads the tabernacle of peace; the *tefilah* ends with 'peace,' the priestly blessing ends with 'peace'—and give the peace." (*Deur. Riba* V, 15)

Rabbi Simeon b. Halafta said: "See how beloved is peace, when God sought to bless Israel He found no other vessel which could comprehend all the blessings wherewith [She] would bless them, save peace, How do we know it? For it is said, the Lord will give strength unto [Her] people, the Lord will bless His people with peace." (Psalm 30:11; Deur. Raba V, 15)

Awareness of the interconnections of life comes from the experience of women who feel life moving and pulsing within and know from inside the rhythms of creation and change. We also affirm the truth that the same life-denying violence that flees from its own insecurity is found in the rapist, in the wife-beater, and in the insatiable urge for security through more and more and more firepower.

Judaism's deepest insights concern the consciousness of the creation of the world by a purposeful and loving creator. All and everything is related by virtue of our common male/female parent. On Rosh Hashanah, the Jewish New Year, two themes predominate. First it is the birthday of the world—our sensitivity to creation is aroused. The second theme is a renewal of faith and commitment to growth on a personal and collective level. Our awareness of creation in all its wondrous reciprocity fills us with a sense of mutual responsibility. This leads us forward as individuals and groups to fulfill our unique and important part in the web of life.

Indeed, Judaism, like feminism, is a political theory and a path that holds life to be the highest value. Women and Jews are, we might say, obsessed with life, obsessed with survival. This passion is now desperately needed. Judaism and feminism see not only murder, but also hunger, poverty, ignorance, psychological manipulation and lack of meaningful work as forms of violence that destroy life and the human image. My own sense of God comes from this awareness. As Mordecai Kaplan taught, God is found in the emergent faith in the worth of human personality.

Our faith in God is democratic and human centered. We feel we are part of a process of raising the value of life. We search for God within ourselves, within the intricate patterns of life. Our commitment to work toward disarmament is a manifestation of that faith. Our God is not an external authority, but the energy that helps us to move out to one another, share out dreams and fears, encourage and validate ourselves beyond the temptations of despair, anxiety, and denial. As Jews and as women we know that denial makes us powerless and passive. The Jewish ritual of grief and mourning is an excellent example of moving through deep feelings into an affirmation of life. We recite a special mourner's prayer that begins *yitgadal viyitkadash sh'may raba* ("magnified and sanctified may the name of the Creator be").

So far we have described the value base that underlies our willingness to explore new ways of thinking and acting that can nourish life in all its fullness and remove from our world the specter of nuclear holocaust. In Judaism we speak of the Torah as the tree of life. The Torah is a term that cannot be translated into any other language. It has far too many connotations. It embodies the alternative vision that we spoke about earlier. But it is more than a vision. It is a blueprint, too. It suggests that one must translate visions through two fundamental methods, law and education. This, then, is what the peace movement, women's movement, and Judaism are seeking to do.

There is a relevant story related in the Talmud *Brachot* 10a). There were once some highwaymen in the neighborhood of Rabbi Meir who caused him a great deal of trouble. The rabbi accordingly prayed that they should die. His wife, B'ruriah, said to him:

How do you allow such a prayer to be permitted? It is written: "Let sins [*hataim*] cease." Is it written: "sinners" [*hot'im*]? No. It is written "sins" [hataim]. Further look at the end of the verse (Psalm 104:35), "and let the wicked men be no more." Since the sins will cease, there will be no more wicked men. Rather, pray for them that they repent, and there will be no more wicked.

He did pray for them, and they repented.

Perhaps it is no accident that it was a woman, surely one of the very few female sages whose words were recorded, who makes the distinction between one's being and one's behavior. This is a polemic against any and all oppression based on objectification and stereotyping. It is also a commitment to faith in the goodness of human life and the possibility of return and renewal. In this time of danger and fear, I find sources of courage and hope in being a Jewish woman. I pray that I can share this Torah with my sisters and brothers of all religions, so that together we can pursue peace.

Impossible Pacifism: Jews, the Holocaust, and Nonviolence

Evelyn Wilcock

Long before other people asked me how a Jew could be a pacifist after the Holocaust, I put that question to myself. Pacifism and Jewishness after Hitler seemed to defy logic. One story sticks in my mind. It was told to a teacher at my own school by a refugee boy newly arrived via the *Kindertransport* in December, 1938. He had been in Vienna; his mother had gone to Berlin to find out what had happened to his father, who had disappeared in Dachau: "[Adolph] was shut up with other Jewish boys in a cellar for two days without food, and then as they were made to ascend one by one, a shot rang out as each one reached the top, and the boys began to cry. 'And I was afraid too,' says Dolphy—but it was only the Nazis having a little game by firing over each boy's head as he emerged."[1]

There is a moment of outrage; it becomes imperative to intervene with a stronger man, a larger gun. Hannah Arendt explained her attachment to Zionism after 1933: "When one is attacked as a Jew, one must defend oneself *as a Jew*. Not as a German, not as a world citizen, not as an upholder of the Rights of Man."[2] The idea is that if the roles were reversed, if the gun were in Jewish hands that would be all right.

The propaganda image in the film *Triumph of the Will* is of a Nazi rally as a well-ordered camp, built by glowing, healthy young men and women. We have no comparable visual image to advertise the fortitude with which Jewish families withstood exclusion and disparagement. The view among many Israelis that Jews died without resistance during the Holocaust and that if we do something different next time around—fight, for instance—the outcome will be different, is widely prevalent.

Armed defense of Poland and France did not prevent the Holocaust. Jews participated fully in military operations during World War II, both in regular armies and armed resistance movements. A separate Jewish force would have been numerically insignificant. Soviet armies failed to prevent twenty million Soviet citizens dying in the war. Even after America entered the war, the Allies were not able to launch an immediate attack on Germany, which controlled the industry, raw materials, and manpower of all Europe. By 1945, foreign workers made up 30% of industrial labor in Germany, and 20% of the troops in German uniform were non-German.[3]

At some level we hanker after a Jewish community to match that image on the German film. On Purim, the children in Kraków Ghetto were allowed to dress up. Their teacher said, "Strangely, they want to play OD (Jewish Police) or SS men. They dressed for their parts as well as they could, using sticks for rubber truncheons. In their acting the little observers displayed all the cruelty the OD had inflicted on their siblings."[4] Yeshayahu Leibowitz argues that when Jews fight as Jews, for a Jewish nationalism, they cease to be Jews in a meaningful sense, and become like Nazis.[5] Few heeded Rabbi Weissmandel, rescuer of Jews in Slovakia, when he warned about the shrinking parameters of Judaism. "Because Rabbi Weissmandel was a religious man par excellence, he conceived Jewish nationalism as the great sin of assimilation in a national disguise, as a substitution for a universal religion, which, like all religions, has the purpose to give sense to one's life and solve the personal and collective dilemma of man in this world."[6]

Ever since biblical times, Jews have regarded defeat and natural disaster as God's punishment for their sins. It provided an explanation for suffering, and furnished hope that they could avert future catastrophe by mending their ways. We, too, want to feel we are in control and that it won't happen again. One is struck by the way the Holocaust literature—whether personal memoirs or academic analysis—is characterized by Jewish accusation and self-reproach.

We have internalized the German message that there was something deeply wrong with being a Jew at the time of the Holocaust. A distinguished therapist who grew up in Germany confessed that when her darker-haired sister was singled out as a Jew, she failed to own up to the relationship. Still, we Jews are not to blame for having normal reactions in situations that are altogether not of our devising. A strictly observant teacher from the Beit Yakov community in Kraków was gnawed by pangs of guilt because she let slip a meeting with a Polish policeman who might have negotiated freedom for her family. "Did you do everything possible to save them; did you?" is a question we all ask.

The absence of certainty in the Holocaust means that it was not possible to take meaningful decisions and be sure of the outcome. In some situations going to a work camp meant death, but in others a work permit saved one. Some Jews resisted the Nazis by acquiring papers that would keep their families from the transports as long as they possibly could. But sometimes Jewish resistance meant volunteering to die in place of a wanted man: A young man from Wlodawa gave his life, unsuccessfully claiming to be the Rabbi from Radzyn.[7] People blamed themselves for leaving their families, or for staying with them, for not giving their lunch bread to beggars in the ghetto, or for refusing the offer of food.

Historians blame Jews who failed to escape from Paris or parents who prevented their children escaping from transports.[8] But in her diary, Etty Hillesum described Jews successfully hunting down a terrified young boy whose running away meant fifty extra victims were piled on the train as a deterrent. She wondered how the boy could live with the guilt.[9] We cannot make free decisions for the future unless we get rid of the feeling that we did it wrong last time. Claude Lanzmann describes in *Shoah* how the victims were driven with unprecedented violence and beatings to the very door of the gas chambers, but without words, without any explanations.[10] We have no explanations either; we are not able to ensure that it will not happen again. Leibowitz says, "That may be the real horror of the Holocaust, that there is no lesson. . . . Atrocity is utterly senseless."[11]

In "Nonviolence in the Holocaust" in my book *Pacifism and the Jews*, I question the view that Jews complied with their own extermination and argued that, on the contrary, the prevailing Jewish nonviolence constituted a courageous assertion of Jewish difference that should be endorsed and admired.[12] I want to take the argument further and suggest that nonviolent minority dissent rescued Jews in the Holocaust and provides a model for effective practical resistance. The Final Solution was an emanation of state authority; the people most likely to challenge it were those who felt themselves governed by a higher authority than that of the state. For some this higher authority was a religious imperative; for others it was a question of individual conscience.

The Holocaust was not a military problem. It began with small difficulties in small towns and seemingly trivial relationships. Hannah Arendt described what *gleichschaltung* meant: "Cooperation (with the Nazis) meant that your friends co-operated. The problem, the personal problem, was not what our enemies might be doing, but what our friends were doing. This wave of cooperation—which was quite voluntary, or at least not compelled in the way it is during a reign of terror, made you feel surrounded by an empty space, isolated. "[13]

Individuals became significant when they refused to go along with the majority. On the day of the boycott of Jewish enterprises on April 1, 1933, one headmistress, Frau Heinzmann, sent flowers to the mothers of all the Jewish pupils who had been excluded from her school.[14] One should not naively suppose that a totalitarian society is established only as an armed camp, by arms; it recruits those whose cognition regulates society, those who engineer its physical, mental and spiritual health. The Holocaust began when you could no longer confide in your doctor, or your child's teacher. Historians have recorded how German theologians, doctors, and psychoanalysts cooperated with the Nazi regime. The implications of such cooperation have to be agonized over on the personal level. The safest professional and personal relationships were unsafe. Breakdown of social support could not be remedied with a gun.

Wolfgang Benz points out what nonviolent solidarity achieved when Jewish husbands in mixed marriages were arrested in the *FabrikAktion* of February and March, 1943: "When the non-Jewish spouses heard that their partners had been arrested and taken to the Assembly Point in Rosenstrasse, to be deported, they got together, besieged the Rosenstrasse and protested. 6,000 women shouted, screamed and howled for their husbands." It worked. The arrested were freed after a few days. [15] Conscientious objection to military service involves refusing to go along with majority demands. Ten of the writers included in Wolfgang Benz's anthology of German pacifism from 1890 to 1939 were either Jews or of Jewish descent.[16] It is perhaps still not safe to say so. It might substantiate the Nazi accusation that Jews, particularly Jewish women in peace movements, had undermined the fighting spirit of young Germans in World War I. The idea that Jewish pacifism caused the Holocaust comes from Nazi ideology.

On the Allied side, Jews themselves became suspicious of pacifism. Pacifists were occasionally suspected of Nazi sympathies or, at best, regarded as bystanders who did nothing to save Jews. Doing nothing during the Holocaust was the greatest reproach that Jews have leveled against themselves (and God). It was always the people of the next continent, the next country, or the next town, often helpless themselves, who were looked to for rescue. Polish Jews in Auschwitz accosted the newly arrived Hungarian Jews, asking how they could have gone on living normally while their brothers and sisters from Poland were dying.

Few pacifists continue to live normally through a war or other humanitarian crisis. It is not surprising that many of those who actively opposed the Holocaust were themselves objectors of conscience or linked to peace movements. The father of Hans and Sophie Scholl, the students who gave their lives for the nonviolent German resistance group the White Rose, had been a pacifist in World War I.

The Protestant minister at Le Chambon, in the Cévennes, André Trocmé, was a conscientious objector and his wife said: "The Protestant church was not happy about it, because at the time conscientious objectors were not admitted as ministers. But the parish wanted a man like my husband, not only because of his ideas about war and peace but on account of his general ideas about truth and justice."[17]

Trocmé was part of the Fellowship of Reconciliation. He was asked by Burns Chalmers, then working with Quaker Relief in camps in the south of France, to assist in rescuing Jews. Trocmé had warned his congregation about Nazism, preparing them for what might come to France; the village responded. Between 1942 and 1945 the five thousand people of the Le Chambon area sheltered between 2,500 and 5,000 Jews, at least one for every household. Trocmé narrowly escaped arrest when he refused to hand over a list of the Jews in his parish. His cousin Daniel was deported and died with the young Jews he had sheltered in the Youth Center.

In Le Chambon, Assistant Pastor Edouard Theis was also a pacifist. On the day of the French armistice with Nazi Germany, the two men preached that the responsibility of Christians was to resist through the weapons of the spirit the violence which is brought to bear on their consciences. Pierre Sauvage, whose parents were sheltered at Le Chambon, remarks that weapons of the spirit saved Jews, and so Jews should be interested in, them.[18] If Jews allow the Holocaust to dictate a withdrawal from peace movements, our absence may carry its own message about what Judaism means.

Weapons of the spirit had always belonged to Jews. "By encouraging Torah study, one saves our nation physically as well as spiritually. Anyone who remains indifferent to a program [of Torah] obviously transgresses the passage, 'Do not idly stand by the blood of your brother.'"[19] The words match those of the priest in Janowka, near Tarnopol, who could not openly tell the congregation to save the Jews but would say in church, "Not one of you should take the blood of your brother." The villagers understood and left food for Jews sheltering in the nearby forest.

Jewish nonviolence is voiced at the margins by the observant Hasidim or ultra-Orthodox, whose views are discounted by academic intellectuals, and by American Reform rabbis, who work closely with non-Jews in welfare movements and whose theology has been suspected by some of syncretism.

Orthodox pacifism has been ignored, tainted with the idea that undermined all belief namely, that the Holocaust was either God's punishment or God's negligence. Reb. Chasim dispensed with that argument. "My teachers, you heard, 'God destroys His people from off the face of the earth because of their sins.' Isn't it foolish to believe that? If this were a punishment from Heaven because of our sins, why did all the rabbis, the pure and holy Tzadikim who were full of Torah and good deeds, why did they die?"[20]

Pacifists felt strongly that the conflict was the result of human behavior, the failure of modernity; some rabbis held Jews themselves at fault if they had identified with modern society. After *Kristallnacht*, Rabbi Wasserman wrote:

The whole of mankind is seized with tension . . . One country against another, within the country one people against another, and finally in the people itself one faction against another. All are ready to tear each other to pieces. This appearance, too, was foreseen from the very beginning for the days of the Epoch of the Messiah: 'I will set each man against his fellow.' (Zechariah)[21]

Christian pacifist Evelyn Underhill wrote of pacifists as a tiny minority, strangers in a foreign land: "I think Hitler is a real 'scourge of God,' the permitted judgment on our civilization." Not a judgment on the Jews, one should notice; she held all responsible, including herself. By remaining pacifist, she abstained from the violence that marked the Nazi rise to power in so many German towns.[22] Rabbis did the same; like Underhill, they saw Hitler as a prelude to the messianic age, an Armageddon after which all would be judged. Only in that context should we understand those Orthodox believers who refused to participate in the war because it was a conflict belonging to God rather than to man. Orthodox Jews had long seen through the hollow attraction of keeping peace through force. Jewish teaching already explained that relying on military force to prevent persecution in the end carries the message that might is right.

Jews were never the stronger community. Fighting served no moral purpose. But renouncing war did not mean renouncing nonviolent defense. In his book on the Orthodox response to the Holocaust, David Kranzler dismisses the establishment view that the United States could do nothing to rescue the Jews beyond hastening the end of the war. He says that for Orthodox Jews it was a matter of morality and an urgent priority to prevent Jewish deaths.[23] Just as Quaker relief and service required action, so Torah also required that a "Jew should dedicate some of his time to fulfillment of the divine precepts and of good deeds to help others to the best of his ability. 'Be ye Holy'; the Jew must be Holy, his house must be Holy, and his whole heart must be holy."

"And I have separated you from the nations to be mine." [24]

It was that otherworldliness that sent the young Rabbi Solomon Schonfeld from London to the continent to gather Jewish children for the *Kindertransport* and that drove Rabbi Michoel Ber Weissmandel, son-in-law of Chief Rabbi Ungar, of the town of Nitra in Slovakia, to bargain for Jewish lives. When Weissmandel was at last arrested, he was persuaded by his followers to jump from the train on which his wife and children were being taken to their deaths.

One rabbi abandoned his family for the sake of the community; another died with them. Reb Yerahmiel Taub, a Hasidic rabbi in Warsaw, gave his followers permission to escape to the Russian forces even though it would involve eating forbidden food and not observing the Sabbath. But "he himself did not wish to leave the ghetto so he could remain with the other Jews. He was later sent to Treblinka (1942) where he died a martyr after his whole family had been exterminated by the Germans."[25] It was not the act itself which was specified by *halakhah* but the exercise of individual religious choice.

This was not a test in which there were right answers. One Jewish family deliberately ate on Yom Kippur to preserve their strength before a deportation. Other Orthodox Jews felt that their survival as Jews entailed conducting themselves as Jews even to the point of starvation—by observing dietary laws and fasts. Rabbi Wasserman was killed in Kovno while studying Tractate *Niddah*. If we think that it was his own fault, we do him an injustice. What he did determined only the character of his dying. Keeping religious law resisted Nazi law.

In the Holocaust, rigid ideas of what was legal and what was illegal could no longer be relied on. The food allowance for Jews in Warsaw was only 184 calories a day. The ghetto was kept alive illegally by child smugglers trading with peasants at subsistence level, or bringing gifts from the "Aryan" side. Sometimes the soldiers and Jewish police turned a blind eye, or unpredictably they shot to kill. One of the children says it was hard to smuggle. They had been brought up to know that was a bad thing to do.

Jews had a problem with law. It was the custom to safeguard the community through self-regulation and adherence to local law. Questions certainly arose about the persistence of this policy beyond the point when it could produce the hoped-for benefit. Particularly problematic is the role of the Jewish police who, hostages themselves, facilitated selections for transports. It is hardly necessary to point out that few pacifists serve in police forces, most of whom carry arms, or that refusals to serve might have obstructed the Nazis. Officials like Dr. Giuseppe Jona in Venice died rather than hand over Jewish records. The Hasidic rabbi from Radomsko refused to cooperate in the arrangements to transport Jews from the Warsaw Ghetto. Rabbi Eliyahu Laskowsky refused to work with the ghetto *Judenrat* in Davart.[26]

Odette Meyers observed that geniuses were people who broke rules. She was saved from the Germans by Madame Marie Chotel, the concierge at the building where they lived in France. "I would say that one of the things that saved me was the fact that in thought, in action, even in her life-style, this woman broke rules, yet she was a genius at humanity."[27]

When the Jews of the Netherlands or of Paris were ordered to register, most obeyed. But at the age of sixteen, Paulette Szlifke disobeyed her mother by refusing to wear a yellow star. She had fair hair, could pass as non-Jewish, and became part of a Jewish resistance movement that distributed leaflets and engaged in industrial sabotage. Rule-breaking was perhaps taken to extremes by Major Julius Schmahling, the German occupation governor of Haute Loire, who (we are told) was the opposite of an "orders are orders" personality. It was he who diverted the attention of the SS from the Jews hidden in the village of Le Chambon.[28]

Recalling her solitary survival in the Netherlands, Marga Minco describes being delivered to the door of a day laborer who had to vacate his own bed so that she might sleep alongside his wife. The extra bed promised for her by the rescue organization never materialized, and the laborer who left daily for work at crack of dawn was always too exhausted by Sunday to make further inquiries. Asking whether the rest of the girl's family had all gone, her hostess stolidly remarked, "Not one ever comes back from there, they say."[29] The knowledge and courage of these people have, sadly, been underestimated.

Pacifists had always mitigated their isolation by forming support groups. People who hid Jewish children were also individualistic, but not isolated. A loose, informal network located homes for Jews while providing information and support to the rescuers. Group conformity has been unduly blamed in the Holocaust but social institutions also facilitated rescue. Priests and nuns were already dedicated to nonviolent service and to an authority higher than the state. Moreover, they had institutional buildings, local and regional contacts, and no families to be held for ransom. Trapped in occupied France, the Little Sisters of St. Vincent de Paul provided refuge in their school at the Chateau de Prèlefort. Local villagers managed to delay a German inspection. So when the officers arrived, the children were on their daily walk, and none of the staff was available. On another occasion twenty-eight adult fugitives were warned in time to leave, and the Germans discovered nuns and children assembled for a mass.[30]

Knowledge of the effectiveness of Christian nonviolent intervention in the Holocaust should prompt honest appreciation of Jewish organizational nonviolence as well. Blanket charges of conventionality and assimilation raised against European Jewish leaders ignore the benefits. The Danish Jewish community identified fully as Danes, and its leaders persuaded their members to exercise restraint and rely on Danish resistance to Nazism. Cooperation and, for the most part, nonviolence saved the majority of Danish Jews.[31] It was the same in Bulgaria. In both places there were popular demonstrations against the Nazi Jewish policy.

The orderly and non-confrontational demeanor of Jewish groups working in other parts of Europe for rescue and relief was not as dramatic as the exploits of armed resistance but was the means of survival for many Jews. The Nazis deliberately deprived Jews of their social-support networks by uprooting families, ordering them to cities where they knew no one, or turning them into refugees. It has been suggested that Italian Jews survived because there was no centralized Jewish council, but the Committee to Assist Jewish Refugees (Comasebit) functioned throughout the Mussolini period and (reconstituted as Delasem) continued even after 1939, with the staunch involvement of senior clerics. Organizations became counterproductive only where they inculcated false confidence that the situation was under Jewish control, and thus stifled individual initiative. Part of the Nazi plan was to deflect criticism onto Jewish organizations. The Union Général des Israélites de France (UGIF) has been accused of compliance. Raymond-Raoul Lambert in Marseilles did conduct quasi-legal negotiations with the Vichy authorities over the fate of foreign-born Jews, but recent research points out that UGIF was not monolithic. Lambert did not call central meetings, and outlying groups were left free to take what action they could.[32]

The saving of lives depended on French Jewish organizational liaison with Quaker and Christian relief societies. The head of the Protestant youth movement was asked to find homes for 600 immigrant Jewish scouts. Partnership and the acceptance of shared objectives were worth more than militancy. Yvonne Nevejean, director of L'Oeuvre Nationale de l'Enfance, the Belgian child-welfare organization, responded to an approach by the Jewish Defense Committee and placed at least 3,000usand children in foster homes. In August 1944, Marie Blum, one of the Jewish activists, telephoned everywhere—to convents, to all kinds of hostels, to homes for war orphans and prisoners' children—doggedly pleading the Jewish cause before influential people, and finally obtained shelter for the children in

AGAINST WAR

Combat itself was the most unspeakably horrendous hell
I have ever known or could possibly imagine. . . .
How a single one of us left Iwo Jima alive is a miracle.

—Rabbi Roland B. Gittelsohn, Chaplain, Iwo Jima

A Matter of Conscience: Militarism and Conscientious Objection in Israel

Ruth Hiller and Sergeiy Sandler

Israel is a country where military service is mandatory. In most parts of Israeli society it is assumed that "everybody" enlists. But we know this assumption does not reflect reality. There are Israelis who raise the question of whether serving in the army is compatible with the call of their conscience. The Israeli military's actions in the Occupied Territories (OT) and in Israel itself motivated this in the hearts of many. Some answered this dilemma by deciding to openly refuse to serve, while others limited their refusal to tasks being performed in the OT or to specific orders. Still others chose other ways of avoiding military service, or particular forms of it. Several Israeli organizations, including the Druze Initiative Committee, Yesh G'vul, signatories of the two Seniors' Letters, the Refusers' Parents Forum and Courage to Refuse[1] have successfully legitimized a growing public debate about draft resistance and refusal to serve in the military or in the OT.

One of these movements is New Profile, established in 1998 with the aim "To change the profile of Israeli society from a militarized society of war and might to an actively peacemaking community in which the rights of all its citizens are protected and promoted equally, and the human rights of all people residing inside and outside Israeli borders are respected."[2] Like other movements, New Profile takes as basic the assumption that conflicts between human beings can and should be resolved peacefully, and that the Israeli-Palestinian conflict is no exception to this rule. But as a feminist movement, it is also committed to a more self-aware and at times self-critical stance within the refusal movement in Israel.

As two New Profile activists, we would like to address the issue of conscience in Israeli society from the perspective of our movement's work and social analysis.

Israeli society puts enormous pressure on young people to enlist. On the more formal level, there is a very far-reaching official high-school curriculum of "preparation to military service," jointly run by the Israeli Ministry of Education and the military's Education and Youth Corps (see Givol, Rotem and Sandler, 2004; Shalev, 14 Jan. 2005).

But this is only the tip of an iceberg. The military is present in the Israeli formal educational system and in the culture in general, in many ways. The militarization of kindergarten education can serve as a good case to demonstrate our point here. The fact that in some Israeli kindergartens children mark the end of the year by performing a mock military parade was considered odd enough to have once made it into a minor critical press item (Lavie, June 28, 2002). On the other hand, the presence of soldiers during the school year inside kindergartens and schools is considered altogether normal and even desirable.

There are also special activities and ceremonies involving the military. In one typical such ceremony,[3] all the kindergarten pupils in town were transported to a public ground and brought presents for the soldiers of a particular military unit. The commander of the unit gave a short speech, thanking the children and the teaching staff, while noting what a great human potential these children are for the future of the army. In other such ceremonies tanks and other weaponry may be brought to the place for the children to climb on.

The soldier image is ubiquitous in Israel. It appears in ads, children's literature, school curricula, street names, etc. New Profile has long made a practice of identifying the use of this image in the cultural sphere. In 2001 New Profile activists collected some such images and created a roving exhibition: "Study War No More." Some items in the exhibit show how the soldier/hero image is used to sell cheese, cell phones, beer, and even tranquilizers for an anxious mother of a soldier son.[4]

But overt military presence is only part of the story. A main component of the educational process in Israel centers on the Jewish holidays. There is a pattern within the narrative: we, the Jews, fought against evil others: Greeks in Hanukkah, Persians in Purim, Egyptians in Passover, Germans on Holocaust Remembrance Day, "The Arabs" on Memorial Day and Independence Day. We won.

History curricula, field trips, and school ceremonies all work together to instill the seeds of the belief that no alternative exists to the constant state of war. History

[5] These issues have been discussed thoroughly in the papers collected in Gor (2005). This book grew out of a conference called *Militarism and Education: a Critical Perspective*, which took place in Jerusalem and Tel-Aviv in 2001. This conference, initiated by *New Profile*, brought together academics and activists from Israel and other countries to critically examine the various forms of military presence in education and to seek and support alternatives to it.

[6] The same tribunal tried these objectors in two parallel procedures. Jonathan Ben-Artzi was tried separately, as his refusal is based on pacifist beliefs, while Noam Bahat, Matan Kaminer, Adam Maor, Haggai Matar and Shimri Tzameret cited the occupation of the OT as their main reason for refusing.

[7] Up to recently, these figures were not made public. The little information that began reaching the press in the late 1990s was deliberately misrepresented (thus, the army would publish figures for "the enlistment rate," which in fact referred only to Jewish males). It required thorough and diligent research on our part to document and calculate the actual enlistment rates and to integrate the disparate pieces of information that appeared in different sources into a complete picture. Information published in the last two years (e.g. Harel, July 30, 2004; Yehoshua, May 20, 2005; Greenberg, July 24, 2005) tends to be more detailed, and less misleading, though still not complete.

The enlistment rate among Jewish men is relatively high – 77% as of 2003. However, only 60% of Jewish men complete their 3-year term of military service. Among Jewish women, the enlistment rate in 2004 was 57.7%. No data has yet been published on the number of women soldiers who get premature discharges. In the entire population, Jewish and non-Jewish, the enlistment rate is 53%, with somewhere around 44% finishing their mandatory military service as prescribed by law. All these rates have been dropping steadily since the early 1990s. Only fragmentary data have been published for the reserves: some 18% of all Jewish men and a few hundred Jewish women performed reserve service in 2004. In most cases, though, this service was almost nominal. The full month reserve service, which was standard for Jewish men up to some fifteen years ago, is now performed by about 3–5% of them.

Bibliography

Algazy, J. *Ha-korban* [The Victim], Haifa: Pardes, 2006.

Blatt, M., Davis, U. and Kleinbaum, P., eds. *Dissent and Ideology in Israel: Resistance to the Draft 1948–1973*, London: Ithaca Press, 1975.

Dor, D., *Intifada Hits the Headlines: How the Israeli press misreported the outbreak of the second Palestinian uprising*, Bloomington, IN: Indiana University Press, 2004.

Givol, A., Rotem, N. and Sandler, S. *The New Profile Report on Child Recruitment in Israel.*, Tel-Aviv: New Profile, 2004. Available online at: http://www.newprofile.org/data/uploads/child_soldiers/English.pdf.

Gor, H., ed. *Militarism be-khinuch* [Militarism in Education]. Tel-Aviv: Babel, 2005.

Greenberg, H., "Deaga be-tsahal: ha-banot memaatot lehitgayes" ["Concern in the IDF: Few Girls Enlist"], Y-Net, 24 July 2005, http://www.ynet.co.il/articles/0,7340, L-3117323,00.html.

Harel, A., "Be-maarechet ha-bitakhon nifradim me-raayon tsva ha-am" ["The Defense Establishment Departs from the Idea of a People's Army"], *Haaretz*, 30 July 2004.

Khenin, D., Sphard, M. and Rotbard, S. eds. *Mishpatei ha-sarvanim* [Trials of the Objectors], Tel-Aviv: Babel, 2004.

Kidron, P., ed. *Refusenik!: Israel's Soldiers of Conscience*, London: Zed Books, 2004.

Rappaport, A. "Khalalim Almonim" ["The unknown fallen"], Maariv, 18 June 2005. Available online at: http://www.nrg.co.il/online/1/ART/947/550.html.

Shalev, M. "Manhig Khinuch Rashi" ["Chief Education Leader"], *Yedioth Aharonoth*, Musaf le-Shabat [Weekend Supplement], 14 Jan. 2005. English translation available online at: http://www.newprofile.org/showdata.asp?pid=737.

Yehoshua, Y., "Rak 1 mi-5 ose miluim" ["Only 1 in 5 Does Reserves Service"], Yedioth Aharonoth, 25 May 2005.

Pacifoid Jew

Rabbi Albert S. Axelrad

Years ago, I found myself attracted as a peace activist to such fine groups as the Fellowship of Reconciliation and the War Resisters League. I was certain that it was within the ranks of pacifists that I would find my kindred spirits and that it was there that I belonged. So I enlisted.

A measure of uneasiness and reserve, however, attached itself to my joining on several counts. With an eye toward qualifying my membership in line with my honest convictions, I entered into a lengthy and candid correspondence with an FOR leader and national staffer. In that exchange, I clarified my doubts and reservations.

To begin with, I told her that as a parent I might conceivably find physical discipline a necessity sometimes. Is that not at loggerheads with pacifism, I wondered? As a parent, she assured me that many a pacifist found spankings a necessary tool in child rearing, and that many of them also wrestled uneasily with the dilemma.

On another level that threatened to pose a far more irreconcilable difference between us. I told her that as a Jew I stand committed to the continuity and survival with the Jewish people and to the Jewish State of Israel as an instrumentality of the Jewish people, even by means of force and violence if necessary as a last resort. I explained that as a humanist I felt committed to the self-determination, liberation, and continuity of every people/nation, provided each recognizes these same rights for others.

Moreover, as a theistic, religious Jew I believe that Jewish (and Israeli) continuity is a necessary and central vehicle for the unfolding of God's messianic plan in history. Jewish survival on two equal fronts, i.e., as a leavening- force community in the Diaspora and as a model nation-state, is, to me, a theological indispensability. That survival must be assured and defended, even by force if need be. Jews are especially duty-bound, I believe, to join in that survival struggle and are to "leave the rest to God" only after exerting in that direction their own creative spiritual and physical energies. In the face of a Holocaust or an attack on Israel's very existence, I would resort to violence given the opportunity, and I would support my Jewish brothers and sisters in doing so. Such is my understanding of Jewish ethical values and imperatives, on the one hand, and of historical reality on the other. Meanwhile, however, my inclination—based likewise on Jewish ethical values and imperatives and on historical reality—was to devote myself wholeheartedly to the struggle for peace.

She understood and sympathized with my dilemma. Our views differed, she admitted, adding that under the duress of a life-and-death assault, not even a committed pacifist knows with certainty what he/she would really do. In the meanwhile, she said, with inspirational impact, we need to join hands and work for peace and reconciliation, actively, creatively, with zeal and commitment, setting aside our theoretical differences, particularly where they relate to hypothetical situations. Agreeing with her, I moved my theory and theology to a rear burner for the moment and linked arms.

At a 1974 Danforth Foundation conference of Underwood Fellows, I had occasion to depict myself as a "near pacifist." I explained that my major commitment is to peace activism in all spheres, including the Israeli-Palestinian conflict, and that my posture is more than "dovish" and peace loving. After all, war strategists and defense secretaries also claim to be peace lovers! "No one wants war!" they say. While the generals prepare for war, I share with pacifists in a real and active commitment to pursue peace. On the other hand, however, given an attack against Israel's existence, I accept and support violence. Such an orientation makes me a "near" rather than a sheer pacifist. A friend later suggested that for such peace-activist Jews who stop just short of out-and-out pacifism we coin the term "pacifoid," with an "oid" suffix signifying "like, resembling" (though one of my students suggested it would sound like a combination of pacifist and paranoid"!).*

A Quaker colleague at Danforth Foundation conference attacked my self-definition. Being a "near pacifist," he charged, is akin to be "just a little pregnant." Internally inconsistent. Impossible.

Logically, my Quaker colleague may be quite right. There is more to life, through, than logic and consistency. Jewish ethical values are at one and the same time both visionary and rooted in reality, idealistic and realistic together—anomalous though that may be. This singular dimension to Jewish ethics, and, equally to the point, the problematics of Jewish survival in the perennially hostile world make the pacifoid posture the only justifiable and viable one for the Jews. With the advent of the messianic day, this will change. At that time, the Jew will finally be able to take hold of what is unfortunately a luxury thus far, sheer pacifism.

Theory alone, however, is inadequate. It tends to leave things in an ambiguous, nebulous state. And terming pacifism a luxury, as we Jews do, but stopping at that, albeit with a sigh of lament and resignation, is a cop out. It will be more instructive and constructive, then, to go further and to translate the pacifoid posture into some concrete principles. How better to accomplish the task than by applying the posture to the Israeli-Palestinian conflict?

Unlike pacifism, the pacifoid posture recognizes the need for Israel to be militarily prepared to repel an Arab attempt to destroy it, as in 1948 and 1967. In the context of American politics and foreign policy, the pacifoid Jew urges US political support for Israel in the frequently hostile UN and other deliberative and negotiating bodies, and advocates for American aid in enabling Israel to be militarily prepared to meet all exigencies. The pacifoid Jew is totally committed to Israel's security, however we may differ from Israeli and Diaspora leaders on its achievement. If all this means a parting of ways between us pacifoid Jews and pacifists, as many seem to think, so be it.

But like my Fellowship of Reconcilliation (FOR) advisor, I would set theory and ideology aside at such an urgent time, forging an activist alliance in pursuit of peace. The pacifoid Jew will try to prevail upon pacifists to join in to demand that Israel's right to survival as a Jewish state be accepted by all—Palestinians, Arab nations, and others—and that it be assured by the world's nations. Such a minimalist moral posture is vital. It is, in fact, both immoral and destructive to the cause of peace that some pacifist elements, including the American Friends Service Committee, have maintained muted and equivocating voices in this regard.

At the same time and likewise in pursuit of peace, the pacifoid Jew would propose peace correctives to Israeli policy. In so doing, we would no doubt come to be at odds with many Israeli and Diaspora Jewish leaders.

True, we would not preach pacifism to Israel. On the other hand, we would refuse to make of Israel a "sacred cow," which our Diaspora leaders do, mindlessly, and worse, idolatrously. Within the framework of commitment to Jewish statehood and, more important, to Judaism and the Jewish people, we would be impelled to go further and to press forward with peace activism.

We demand that our leaders in Israel and in the Diaspora get untracked. We demand that they seriously assume the responsibility of moving the Jewish state toward ethical "model-hood" and the Diaspora community to the state of a leavening force, in the prophetic mold. We find bloodthirstiness, expansionism, and reliance upon might alone to be abominations to the Jewish spirit. We reject the clenched fist in favor of the outstretched arm. Not unilaterally, but within the context of a genuine peace settlement and normal relations, we demand that Israel proclaim a commitment to relinquish and return all conquered territory, with the possible exception of the Golan Heights' bluffs, which should become a demilitarized zone. We insist that Israel recognize the right of the Palestinian people to self-determination and to non-belligerent, autonomous statehood in the West Bank and the Gaza Strip. We advocate Israeli openness to sharing Jerusalem, termed "holy city" both in Hebrew and Arabic, as a dual capital with a Palestinian state. We urge that Israel take the initiative of offering to recognize and negotiate with any representative element of the Palestinian people on the basis of precondition of mutual recognition, acceptance and to the renunciation of terrorism, violence, and force.

All this flows from our basic presupposition that the Arab-Israeli conflict is a clash of two nationalisms, Israeli and Palestinian, each of which is in the right and each of which must be accommodated. In all this, the pacifoid Jew and the pacifist must coalesce, forging an alliance that will have the credibility it needs in the Jewish world only if the pacifist partner comes out squarely for Israel's continuity as a Jewish state. Together we would have Israel, as the powerful party and as the Jewish state (i.e. a state to be governed not just by *Realpolitik*, like all other states, but by Jewish ethical values and ideals), take bold and creative initiatives toward peace, heretofore lacking, rather than rest secure in military strength and preparedness alone.

In these priorities and emphases, we would join with Israeli Zionist "doves" and peace activists who seek our solidarity and support. Our fervent hope would be for the emergence of growing, like-minded elements in Arab and Palestinian circles. Strengthening one another and gaining ascendancy, such forces will become increasingly pervasive, leading the way to peace.

A. J. Muste was right: "There is no way to peace—peace is the way." In this pursuit, the pacifoid Jew and the pacifist must join, however different may be our underlying orientations and concepts.

Note

* For the term *pacifoid* I am indebted to Richard Israel, my colleague in the Hillel Rabbinate.

Was the Vietnam-Era Peace Movement Effective?

Jerry Elmer

Was the multifaceted Vietnam-era peace movement in the United States a success? Did we end the war? Did we even help to end the war? Were we successful in achieving our goals? If so, what goals did we achieve?

Professional historians and peace-studies scholars have chronicled the Vietnam era from a variety of perspectives, but their conclusions about the efficacy of the peace movement as an undifferentiated whole, or of specific, narrower tactics within the wider movement, are elusive. Professor Lawrence S. Wittner's conclusion in *Rebels Against War: The American Peace Movement, 1933–1983* is typical: "Beginning in the 1960s, the peace movement emerged as a powerful force in American life . . . the peace movement was no longer a marginal force in American politics, but an important participant, a serious contender for power."

A reader who looks for specific peace movement tactics being tied to specific (positive) responses by the government will not find much in the extant literature (with two notable exceptions that I discuss below, one of which was attested to by a remarkable and unexpected source).

It is easy to see why the historians and scholars are reluctant to posit cause and effect between actions of the peace movement and governmental responses. Causation in world affairs—what specific event led to what specific result—is almost always impossible to prove with any degree of certainty. To be sure, on some narrow issues it is sometimes possible to draw such a link. We know that the picture of

Chris Kearns burning his draft card, printed in the August 20, 1965 issue of *Life* magazine, led to the swift passage of the draft-card burning bill in the Senate the following week, because the senators who took to the Senate floor told us so. But such obvious correlations are rare. Moreover, part of the reason that the question of the Vietnam peace movement's overall effectiveness is such a difficult one is that the natural concomitant of the question "Were we effective?" is "Were we effective *at doing what*?" Depending on what one thinks we were trying to accomplish, we were more or less effective. At least for those of us in the pacifist wing of the wider peace movement, our interest in peace activity during the Vietnam War was always in part wider than only affecting this or that specific American policy.

I do not pretend to be a historian; to the extent that I can bring a useful perspective to such questions, it is as an activist, not as a scholar.

Certainly, the Vietnam-era peace movement accomplished a number of very specific goals. The government used Selective Service to conscript hundreds of thousands of men to fight, kill, and die in an undeclared war. At the same time, the government provided draft-age men with little or no help in negotiating the arcane maze of sixteen separate classifications, exemptions, and deferments that existed under Selective Service law. The peace movement—most notably AFSC and Women Strike for Peace at the national level, but also hundreds of unaffiliated local peace organizations and centers—stepped in and provided thousands of draft counselors at hundreds of locations nationwide who gave vital, often life-saving information to millions of men. I was never involved in draft counseling because I did not see my role as providing objective information about deferments to draft-age men; I was more interested in organizing total resistance to the draft. Still, to the millions of men that were helped, the creation of this nationwide network of draft counselors was not a small accomplishment.

Later in the war, peace activists set up coffeehouses outside military bases to provide information on conscientious objection and desertion to soldiers. An underground railroad was established to help spirit deserters (as well as draft evaders) to Canada. A stream of such deserters passed through my apartment when I lived in Manhattan, and I was only one tiny cog in a large and sprawling operation. (Professor Wittner puts the number of military deserters at 40,000 in 1968 and 53,000 in 1969.) Again, for the many men we helped, this was not a small accomplishment.

But what about changing American policy in Vietnam? Did the peace movement ever have an effect on changing US policy? One of the clearest examples of the direct effect of the peace movement on US Vietnam policy was the eleventh-hour aborting of Operation Duck Hook by President Nixon in response to the Moratorium activities of autumn 1969.

Shortly after taking office in January 1969, Nixon, who had won the election in large part based on his promise that he had a "secret plan" to end the war, directed his aides to prepare a major escalation of the war, Operation Duck Hook. Nixon gave the Vietnamese until November 1 to capitulate at the Paris negotiations. If Nixon's ultimatum were not met, the United States would mine Haiphong Harbor, bomb Hanoi, and destroy North Vietnam's agricultural dikes. These actions were to be followed by a US ground invasion of North Vietnam and the use of nuclear weapons. The specific plans called for the use of two atomic bombs. As activist-scholar Joseph Gerson recounts in his book, *With Hiroshima Eyes* (1995), Nixon's threats were conveyed to the Vietnamese in July through a French diplomat in Hanoi, and in August by Henry Kissinger on one of his secret trips to the Paris negotiations. The threat of American use of nuclear weapons in Vietnam at that time was confirmed by Daniel Ellsberg, writing in the March 1975 issue of *Fellowship* magazine. On October 1, 1969, Nixon signaled the seriousness of his intentions by raising the alert status of US military forces worldwide.

A range of scholars agree that it was the autumn Moratorium demonstrations that year that stayed Nixon's hand. On October 15, literally millions of Americans participated in hundreds of separate events in cities and towns across the country. On November 15, 500,000 people rallied in Washington, DC. (This was the demonstration at which the Boston Eight surfaced, over my objections, with stolen draft files.) The huge demonstration was preceded by a three-day March Against Death, conceived and organized by Ron Young. For three days and nights, 45,000 demonstrators walked in single file from Arlington National Cemetery, past the White House, to the steps of the Capitol. Each demonstrator carried a candle and a placard bearing the name of an American or Vietnamese who had been killed in the war. At the Capitol, the placards were placed into coffins. To many participants and observers, the power and quiet dignity of the March Against Death made this the most moving demonstration of the entire war.

Those of us who participated in these events were frustrated at the time. Nixon, in a show of bravado, let it be known that his administration would not be swayed by protests and that he had spent November 15 watching a football game on television rather than meeting with a delegation from the anti-war movement. Only later did we learn of the effect that those demonstrations had. Professor Melvin Small, in *Johnson, Nixon, and the Doves,* concludes that "The Moratorium helped to convince Nixon that Americans would not accept the savage blows envisioned in Operation Duck Hook." Nixon himself substantially corroborated this account in his own writing after leaving office. Both Ellsberg and Joseph Gerson go further, concluding that the autumn 1969 demonstrations led *directly* to the abandonment of the plan by the Nixon administration. Ellsberg concludes:

Those who demonstrated against the war saved hundreds of thousands of lives, certainly. But we are in their debt for having avoided a probable nuclear war. The benefits to humanity of having avoided nuclear war are simply incalculable.

Yet, in other important ways, the peace movement surely failed. Between 1967 and 1968, the slogan of the umbrella National Mobilization Committee to End the War was "From Dissent to Resistance." During this period, huge demonstrations were held, individual draft resistance soared, acts of draft-file destruction multiplied, there was a nationally coordinated academic strike, and the Columbia University uprising occurred. There was lots of both dissent *and* resistance. Meanwhile, US troop levels in Vietnam increased from 485,000 to 536,000.

Some of the worst and most fundamental attitudes of Americans—attitudes that allowed the war to happen in the first place—were not changed by the long efforts of the peace movement either. For example, the change of American attitude that came about at the time of the Tet Offensive in 1968 was a shallow one.

The Tet Offensive in Vietnam, launched by the liberation forces on January 29, 1968, was a turning point in the war—perhaps not in the actual military situation on the ground in Vietnam, but certainly in the attitude of the American public toward US intervention.

In a nationwide Gallup poll released on December 7, 1967, just before the Tet Offensive, 52% of the people polled described themselves as "hawks" and only 35% described themselves as "doves." Less than a year later, in a Gallup poll released on August 7, 1968, when asked "Do you think the US made a mistake sending troops to fight in Vietnam?" 53% answered yes and only 35% answered no. This was the first time that a respected national poll reflected an anti-war majority.

Americans' change of heart, however, was in fact shallow. The problem for most Americans was mainly that it now appeared we could not win. As the *New York Times* put it in a lead editorial on March 24, 1968, "The futility of escalation has long been evident . . . the search for a military solution is futile . . ." A very similar tone emerges from the much-ballyhooed editorial against the war by CBS News anchorman Walter Cronkite, widely viewed at the time as "the most trusted man in America." On February 27, 1968, shortly after returning from a news-gathering trip to Vietnam, Cronkite startled hawks and doves alike by broadcasting an editorial critical of the war. But Cronkite's criticism, too, was rooted in the fact that the war did not seem to be working: "It seems now more certain than ever that the bloody experience of Vietnam is a stalemate."

To the *Times*, to Cronkite, and to many Americans, the problem with the war was not that the US was perpetrating crimes against humanity, but rather that the crimes did not seem to be achieving their intended goal. In their view, it was the futility of the war, not its immorality that was the central problem. Even the wording of the August 1968 Gallup poll was troubling because it failed to distinguish between the views of those who thought it a "mistake" to have sent troops to Vietnam because to do so was wrong and immoral, and those who thought it a "mistake" because it appeared we were not winning.

To be sure, there were a great many problems with the war, but the factor perceived by too many Americans at that time, that we were not winning, was emphatically not one of them. One actual problem was that we had gone in on the wrong side, fighting against the side struggling for freedom and independence for their country. We were supporting an unpopular and totalitarian puppet government whose own people were immolating themselves in the streets in protest against that government. We were committing atrocities beyond number and pursuing policies, including targeting civilians, which were internationally recognized as war crimes.

Very much the same shallow attitude can be seen in the public's response to the US invasion of Iraq in 2003. Most of those who did dissent raised superficial issues: the cost of postwar reconstruction is too steep, Bush may have lied about the presence of weapons of mass destruction, and it is impractical to think that we can pacify Iraq. Immediately after the US invasion of Iraq, President Bush's war policy was wildly popular with the American people. As had been the case with Vietnam, it was only later, when it seemed that the war policy was not really working, that the American public soured on the war in Iraq. In 2003, the few who dared to say the truth about the US invasion of Iraq were viewed by the mainstream as a kooky fringe but the simple truth was that for the US to invade Iraq was a crime against humanity. Indeed, waging a "war of aggression"—that is, attacking another country that had not attacked you first—was the heart of the Nuremberg indictment.

For better or for worse, activists like me seem to have a different perspective on events than the scholars do. For example, in *Johnson, Nixon, and the Doves*, Professor Small describes at some length the demise of the anti-war movement after protests in the spring of 1970:

The nationwide response to the Cambodian invasion and the Kent
State killings was the last success for the anti-war movement during
the Nixon administration, at least in terms of the quantity, quality,
and impact of mass demonstrations . . .

When the North Vietnamese launched a major offensive in the
spring of [1972] and Nixon responded with stepped-up bombing
and the mining of the Haiphong harbor, he met little serious opposition. The boys were almost all home, the movement was in disarray,
radicals and hippies were discredited. . . .

The life had gone out of the movement.

In fact, from the perspective of one who was involved in the movement in
1972 and thereafter, very much the opposite appears to have been true. More
than forty national organizations joined together to form the Coalition to Stop
Funding the War. These included the traditional pacifist organizations like AFSC,
WRL, and FOR that had been in the Fifth Avenue Vietnam Peace Parade Committee in 1965, then the Mobilization Committee to End the War, and then the
New Mobilization Committee—the successive coalitions that had sponsored the
mass demonstrations—but also the Coalition to Stop Funding the War included mainline religious denominations such as the United Methodist Church, the
Union of American Hebrew Congregations, and the United Presbyterian Church
in the USA, and liberal groups such as Americans for Democratic Action. Professor Small is correct that peace movement strategy shifted away from mass demonstrations after 1972, but visibility in the press by means of mass demonstrations is
not the only way to measure the strength of a movement. The forty national organizations that made up the Coalition mounted a nationwide lobbying effort aimed
at cutting funding for the ongoing American war effort. The effort was both sophisticated and, more to the point, successful. For fiscal year 1975 (beginning October 1, 1974), the effort succeeded in getting Congress to cut the administration's
request for aid to Saigon by more than 50%, from $1.6 billion to $700 million.

The Tiger Cage Vigil and Fast in Washington during the summer of 1974 was
coordinated closely with the Coalition to Stop Funding the War. The Tiger Cage
Project was a centralized project in which participants came to Washington, DC,
and lobbied members of Congress. Immediately after the conclusion of the Tiger
Cage Project, many of its sponsors participated in a decentralized effort called the
"Week of Concern," September 29 through October 6, 1974. In Rhode Island,
where I was an organizer during the Week of Concern, we took the tiger cage

display to a different city in the state each day. On Thursday evening, October 3, we sponsored a Religious Convocation for Peace at a local church, and on Friday evening, October 4, we sponsored a Vietnamese dinner with guest speaker Marj Nelson, a physician recently returned from service at the AFSC medical facility at Quang Ngai, Vietnam.

Similar events were held in about fifty cities nationwide. In Pasadena, California, a tiger cage was erected on the City Hall steps during the city art fair. In Holly Spring, Mississippi, signatures were collected on anti-war petitions addressed to members of Congress. In Connecticut, tiger cage displays appeared in New Britain, Bristol, Waterbury, New London, Storrs, Winsted, New Haven, Fairfield, Hartford, and Middletown. In Denver, Colorado, Joan Baez sat chained inside a tiger cage replica before singing at an anti-war event. An anti-war vigil in Chapel Hill, North Carolina, received front-page coverage in the local newspaper. In Davenport, Iowa, John Young, a former Vietnam prisoner of war, and Peg Mullen, a Gold Star mother, spoke at an anti-war program. Press conferences, public meetings, and church services were held in Indiana and Kentucky. A centerpiece for all of these events was lobbying members of Congress to cut off funds for the war. Where the Tiger Cage Project had brought participants to Washington to lobby members of Congress on the war, the Week of Concern brought lobbyists to senators' and representatives' home offices.

Thousands of activists attended the Assembly to Save the Peace Agreement. We chartered a bus to bring fifty Rhode Islanders to Washington for the event, and there was similar participation from all parts of the country. Over the weekend, a series of speakers including Don Luce trained participants in how to lobby Congress effectively. The climax of the Assembly was on Monday, January 27, when thousands of activists fanned out and visited nearly every senator and representative's office, urging a cutoff in funds for the war. The Tiger Cage Project, the Week of Concern, and the Assembly to Save the Peace Agreement were all complementary efforts. All focused on members of Congress, all involved extensive lobbying by constituents to cut American funds for Saigon.

When the liberation forces launched their final offensive in the spring of 1975, the administration's hands were tied. That spring, the administration repeatedly, and with increasing desperation and then panic, sought supplemental spending authority to try to avert the coming defeat in Vietnam. Under tremendous, effective, coordinated lobbying pressure from the peace movement, Congress held fast. No more funds were forthcoming, and the war ended on April 30, 1975, with the victory of the liberation forces. While the public visibility of the movement may have faded with the end of the mass demonstrations, the life had surely not gone out of the movement. Far from being in disarray, the peace movement was surely at its most organized and perhaps at its most effective. Far from being discredited and marginalized as radicals and hippies, the peace movement worked more closely and more successfully during this period than ever before with mainline churches.

The singular effectiveness of the peace movement during this period was powerfully attested to shortly after the war ended by a most unexpected source. On January 27, 1976, the last US Ambassador to Saigon, Graham Martin, testified before the House Committee on International Relations. In describing the reason for the American defeat in April 1975, Ambassador Martin said: "Military assistance for fiscal year 1975 had been reduced [by Congress] from the $1.6 billion original request to $1 billion in the fiscal year 1975 authorization . . . to $700 million in the final appropriation." Speaking of the effects of the peace movement during the period of the Tiger Cage Project and Week of Concern, Martin said, "In the United States the erosion of public support [for the war] was a progressive, palpable, almost measurable phenomena [sic] in the late summer and fall of 1974." Martin spoke of "the mounting crescendo of organized campaign" that came "to a focus with the December 'pastoral letter' convoking on January 29, 1975, [sic] in Washington the celebration of the second anniversary of the 1973 [Paris] accords."

Ambassador Martin went on to say that the decision of Congress to cut funds for the war "was made inevitable by one of the best propaganda and pressure organizations the world has ever seen . . . The main organization I think is the Indochina Resources Center [sic], and I really think that another principal element would be the multifaceted activities of Mr. Don Luce . . . It's the constancy of the drumming in day after day after day of particular themes." Then the following exchange took place between Congressman Hamilton and Ambassador Martin:

> Mr. Hamilton. You impressed me with the great compliment you pay these people [peace activists], they have the resources to sway the whole country, 220 million Americans and the US Congress.
>
> Ambassador Martin. I would fully concur with your statement that I am paying these people an enormous compliment. I mean it to be that. They deserve it . . . This is an enormously effective organization and I do think that they deserve the compliment I have paid them.

In the Heady Seventies of the Women's Movement

Naomi Goodman

When the world was changing,
I took off my wedding ring.
My logic simple: If
He won't wear a wedding band
Why should I
Advertise my personal life?
My bonding made public by banding
As birds are banded.

After he died, I felt the need
To put back on my wedding band
To reaffirm our life.
This second time,
I placed it on my hand myself.
There was no struggle left
Only memory.

War Remembrance

Ira Katz

Human history, it might be said, is simply a series of wars. Virtually all cultures have put war and warriors on a pedestal; literally on monuments, but also figuratively in art, literature, and museums. Through these means we remember war. I have been thinking about how we should remember war. What kind of war museum could depict the ultimate horror of war?

A couple of years ago I taught American engineering students in Brussels. I lived near the Cinquantenaire Park where there is a rather quaint military museum. It is quaint, because the displays are amateurish by typical US standards; however, the collection is good, especially with pieces from the Napoleonic wars (Waterloo is nearby) and the two world wars. It is pleasant to visit on a quiet afternoon to watch the Belgian school children as well as to view the exhibits. In a manner, the museum makes war seem fun, a great game

Our group visited the American Military Cemetery at Hamm, Luxembourg. The immaculate rows of graves, the chapel, the monuments depicting the campaigns of the fallen, and the grave of General Patton make this a special place. The majority of these valiant soldiers had perished during the Battle of the Bulge as the cemetery is located in the Arden Forest. One could not help but to desire to die for the US and be buried at a place like this.

Only about one mile away is a Cemetery for German Soldiers at Sandweiler. Here the grounds are not so immaculate, there are four corpses buried under each stone, and of course they were the enemy fighting for Hitler's Germany. Yet it is still moving, especially noting the young age of many of the victims, younger than the college students with whom I was traveling.

War is certainly not all fun, nor even all honor and glory. There are victims, not only enemy soldiers, but totally innocent and defenseless civilians. I saw this depicted in two very famous paintings on a trip to Madrid to visit another group of students. In the Prado Museum is the painting the *Execution on May 3rd, 1808* by Francisco de Goya. In this scene French soldiers are executing Spanish citizens after a rebellion. Nearby at the Reina Sofía, Spain's national museum of modern art is the mural *Guernica* by Pablo Picasso. This abstract vision of the population of the town of Guernica being bombed by the German Luftwaffe during the Spanish civil war is perhaps the most well known image depicting the horror of modern war.

A very different wartime museum is located a few miles north of Brussels in the small but prosperous Flemish town of Mechelen. The dean of the college at which I was teaching was a proud citizen; so he wanted me to see his town. The Mechelen Museum of Deportation and Resistance is located in the very building that was the starting point for the road to Auschwitz. What are most poignant for me are the pictures and stories of the individual victims. The victims depicted by Picasso are abstract, by Goya foreign; but the family photos with victims tinted in red, are horrifying because you can easily imagine your own photos so marked. To personalize the events gives them the most impact.

All of these experiences have crystallized in my mind the design for a different type of museum for war remembrance. What people should remember is that in war one's soul can be in greater danger than one's life. Even when fighting for a righteous cause, the nature of war is to kill or be killed, true enemies or innocent victims. Fighting in a foreign land within a foreign culture, differentiation is difficult if not impossible. What is the greater horror, to be the victim or the perpetrator of a war crime?

Murder in war is not by faceless, evil people, but by you and me if put into a similar situation. Goya does not show us the faces of the firing squad. Picasso shows no cause for the horror and anguish. But those French soldiers might have been artists themselves. The German bomber crews certainly loved their own mothers, wives, and children who resembled their victims. The soldiers rationalize the murders because they are taught to do so by politicians. It is literally part of their training to dehumanize the enemy, soldiers and civilians alike. We should know now that those rationalizations have been shown historically to be largely fabrications. For example, the British propagandized that the Germans were killing Belgian babies to convince the US to enter WWI. Similarly, we were told that Iraqi soldiers were pulling the plugs on child incubators in Kuwait during the Gulf War.

We should understand that our troops are in serious moral danger after Hurricane Katrina when Louisiana Governor Kathleen Blanco could state with no irony and none taken, that National Guard troops recently returned from Iraq "have M-16s, and they're locked and loaded . . . these troops know how to shoot and kill [alleged looters], and they are more than willing to do so if necessary, and I expect they will." How can we train fellow citizens to be *more than willing* to kill!

A proper war museum would be like the one in Mechelen, but now it would follow the lives, even the personalities, of soldiers who in war became murderers. Perhaps we could read the poignant letter of a soldier to his mother the day before he murders someone else's mother. The point is to make society, individual citizens, be afraid of war. To make people always remember that war should not be natural but is evil, that it is the antithesis of civilization, that we should not look for glory and honor in killing an enemy thousands of miles from home. This museum should remind us to pray to "forgive us our trespasses, as we forgive those who trespass against us; and lead us not into temptation, but deliver us from evil."

Facing a Test of Faith: Jewish Pacifists During World War II

Michael Young

Sometimes between July and September of 1943, Moshe Kallner, a strictly Orthodox Jew who had fled Hitler's Germany during the 1930s, asked for a transfer from the Civilian Public Service Camp, where he had already worked for seventeen months. In a letter to Evan Thomas of the War Resisters League, Kallner expressed his distress:

> The dilemma in which I find myself is that although I detest war, conscription, the hypocrisy with which this war is being fought by the Allies, etc., still it seems to me that conditions would be even worse under Hitler and, despite the dark future, which is being prepared by the Allies, I have to cooperate with them, because under Hitler there is no future at all. . . . I find myself torn between the desire to refuse to cooperate with conscription and between my remorse, which tells me that refusing to participate in war means not to make a stand on the basic problem.[1]

As a conscientious objector he could not countenance war as a solution but as a Jew, he could not passively accept the slaughter of his European brethren. Kallner felt that he had no alternative but to join the army, yet even then, he would continue to support the efforts of the pacifist movement.

tions became more hesitant in proclaiming it as the war dragged on. This reflects a latent distrust of Jews who would refuse to fight against Hitler and a lingering fear of the anti-Semitic accusations that the Jews were shrinking their responsibility to take part in "their war."

Indeed, more than 500,000 men and women of the Jewish faith responded to the call of war, and more than 7,000 of these people died in combat.[20] As in World War I, the Jews participated disproportionately to their numbers; they now intensely believed that the defeat of the Nazis was a moral cause. With their brethren being persecuted in Europe, most of the Jewish laymen could not understand and would not tolerate those who refused to fight. Some Jewish conscientious objectors were disowned by their families and shunned by their neighbors. Even in prison "the Jewish CO finds the going a bit rough at times, because the normal Jewish inmate population consists of many 'jail house patriots' who look upon their pacifist fellow Jews as 'queers,' cowards or psychopaths."[21] An article in the March 6, 1942, issue of the American Jewish Congress' *Congress Weekly* explicitly condemned Rabbi Isidor B. Hoffman, the pacifist advisor to the Jewish students at Columbia University:

> But do the Jewish students obtain the best spiritual guidance when their spiritual leader is candidly opposed to what the nation is fighting for? . . . As leaders of nations all over the world have always said: If you are not with us, you are against us.[22]

As news of the true extent of Hitler's atrocities began to leak out in 1943, the isolation of the Jewish pacifist became even more pronounced and some, like Moshe Kallner, began to waver in their pacifist faith. Judah Magnes [Chancellor and later President of Hebrew University], who had withstood the official ostracism placed upon him because of his unswerving and outspoken opposition to World War I, lamented his realization "that what one thought was part of one's religion is subject to change because of what a single man can do." By 1939, after years of public agony, he had chosen armed resistance to Hitler as the lesser of two evils.[23]

Like many other radical pacifists, the Jewish objectors who maintained their witness tended at first to disbelieve stories of the concentration camps, suspecting that the government was trying to stir up hatred of the Germans with atrocity stories as it had during World War I. Yet, when forced to come to grips with the truth, most Jewish pacifists resolved their dilemma in terms of their pacifism and not their Jewishness. The slaughter of the European Jews was seen as the inevitable result of hatred and war. Their true battle was against fascism, not Hitler, as an idea cannot be destroyed merely by destroying those who believe in it. To participate in the war would only help perpetuate the conditions that originally could spawn a Hitler. Finally, many Jewish pacifists could not kill even to save themselves and they refused to kill to save others.

The pacifist community and the Jewish objectors in particular, however, did not ignore the need to find an immediate solution to the problems faced by European Jewry. As early as 1933, some pacifists were calling for a boycott of German goods and for more relaxed immigration policy in the United States for European refugees. They sought to raise money for "guarantees" for individual refugee families, which the US government required to insure that the immigrant did not become a burden on the economy. In 1939, the Subcommittee on Refugee Problems of the War Resisters League, a pacifist group with many Jewish members, urged the pacifist movement to lobby for a liberalized refugee policy.[24] Most Americans opposed this measure, primarily from a fear that an infusion of cheap labor would put additional pressure on a tight job market. Many Jews were also afraid that increased immigration would generate more anti-Semitism. The WRL-affiliated newspaper, the *Conscientious Objector*, decried the hypocrisy of the Allies who fought for freedom and then refused the refugees entrance either into their own countries or to Palestine.[25] The Jewish pacifist believed that he or she had a twofold duty to their brethren in Europe:

> [We] must strive for the earliest possible settlement of this war as an early peace would not only make an end to the world-wide slaughter, but might also, by the stipulation of the rescue of the Jews as one of the armistice terms, prevent their extermination; which might otherwise result from the fury of the Nazis as they near a bitter defeat; [We] must strive to stir the United Nations to open Palestine for free entry of Jews with full opportunity for colonization, so that a free an democratic Palestine may stimulate the cultural and spiritual regeneration of Judaism throughout the world. [26]

Most Zionists supported the war effort, in part because they believed that an Allied victory would further their cause. While there were some pacifists who were ardent Zionists, most objectors saw the need for a Jewish homeland but advocated that it be a bi-national state. Jewish nationalism, like any other nationalism, was wrong since it was both a cause of war and antithetical to the pacifist vision of a broader human fellowship.

The Jewish objector was also sensitive to the fear that pervaded the Jewish establishment that their stand would compromise the position of the Jews as loyal American citizens and exacerbate an anti-Semitism, which had arisen during the Depression. Rabbi Solomon Fineberg, a non-pacifist member of the Central Conference of American Rabbis, expressed this fear during the organization's debate on the conscientious objector support statement. He argued that approval of the statement would lend credence to the belief then being widely expounded by William Dudley Pelley, leader of the fascist Silvershirts, that the Jews brought the country into war then deserted the effort:

> Had the request come from the United States government that we register conscientious objectors, it would have been a different problem. By taking the initiative now, we would appear to suggest to Jews that they avoid service at such a time as other young men will be called to the colors. [27]

The Jewish pacifists were conscious of this anti-Semitism and of the feeling of the Jewish establishment that the status and security of the Jew could only be assured if he is seen as a conspicuous "hundred percenter." Yet, while they dreaded providing the anti-Semite with any pretext of his claims that the Jews were disloyal, the pacifist searched for a solution other than enlistment. Some insisted that the Jewish pacifist maintain a very quiet witness against the war; others, like Bernard Gross, believed that if evidence of their dissent from the general Jewish patriotic chorus were made known, it would deflate the accusations that the Jews dragged the country into war.[28] Finally, the pacifists argued that this war, like all wars, was a futile exercise and once it ended the disenchantment of the population would lead to a search for a scapegoat and to an even greater anti-Semitism:

> Disillusioned and desperate Americans are in no way different form disillusioned and desperate Germans. "The Jews did it! They took us into war because they hated Hitler. They own the newspapers. They run the movies, they control the banks. The Jews did it. Down with the Jews!" [29]

Only by refusing to fight could Jews try to put an end to this vicious cycle of war and hatred. The Jewish pacifist attempted to counteract his sense of isolation from the community by joining with other pacifists in groups such as the War Resisters League, and, to a more limited extent, the Fellowship of Reconciliation. Their recognition of the unique burden they carried, however, led some to work towards the establishment of a separate Jewish organization. In November 1941, Rabbi Abraham Cronbach, a leading Jewish pacifist and a professor at the Hebrew Union College in Cincinnati, attempted to form a "fellowship of Jewish pacifists," but his efforts were aborted, possibly by Pearl Harbor and the US entrance into the war.[30] The original impetus for what would be the Jewish Peace Fellowship came from Bernard Gross, a Philadelphia resister, who felt the need to maintain the Jewish identity that he was in danger of losing because of the pro-war stand and icy intolerance of his fellow Jews. Gross corresponded with Rabbi Isidor B. Hoffman of the WRL, who initially saw little value in the idea:

> I am sorry to say that Rabbi [Sidney E.] Goldstein—and I too now—are not very sympathetic to the idea of organizing either a "Jews Against War" or a "Hebrew Service Committee." Of course, I very much regret that the number of Jewish pacifists is so small and the facilities and personnel are so limited that it looks as though the results of such an attempt of organization would be small and discouraging. At present, a substantial proportion of Jewish COs feel they have some anchorage in the WRL and a few in the FOR. [31]

Four factors led to a change of heart in Rabbi Hoffman and in other Jewish pacifists as well; a growing isolation aggravated, in part, by the lack of a well-known Jewish peace leaders; the feeling that a Jewish rationale for pacifism had to be developed in answer to the assertion that a Jew could not be a pacifist; the need to find a source of financial support for the Jewish conscientious objectors in Civilian Public Service Camps or in prison and for their dependents on the outside, and, finally, a growing dissatisfaction with the WRL's increasing emphasis on resistance to conscription to the exclusion of more service-oriented projects.

In 1941, the government had established Civilian Public Service (CPS) Camps where those men who had been classified as conscientious objectors would perform alternative service. The Historic Peace Churches, who were to administer the camps, welcomed them as an opportunity for service and as an experiment in the pacifist way of life. Within a year, however, many of the non-Mennonite and non-

Brethren pacifists in the camps began to object to the insignificant jobs delegated to them and the lack of compensation. The WRL had tentatively sanctioned the CPS by affiliating with the Consultative Council of the National Service Board for Religious Objectors, which coordinated the system, but by 1943, with the addition of some younger members to its Executive Committee, the League slowly began to shift towards a position of radical war resistance and of opposition to all conscription and to the availability of only one type of alternative service. In March 1943, the organization withdrew from the consultative Council. Rabbi Hoffman, a vice-chairman, along with former Executive Committee Chairman Rabbi Sidney E. Goldstein and Reverend John Haynes Holmes, a former national chairman, resigned. Rabbi Hoffman's reason went deeper than simple disagreement over the CPS policy and reflected his definition of the proper role for the Jewish Peace Fellowship: "You and other members of the Board know very well of my distress at what seems to be the League's preoccupation with the fight against conscription at the expense of both the implementation of a pacifist philosophy of life among its members and the effort to remove the causes of war."[32]

By 1943, the more activist Jewish members of the WRL were defining their pacifism in secular political terms and for these the resistant role was consistent with the nature of their objection. Some, like Abraham Kaufman, although they disagreed with the League's changing orientation, could not leave the organization within which they themselves had matured. Those pacifists who gravitated towards the Jewish Peace Fellowship, while they may have maintained membership in the WRL if they had ever belonged, and may have even agreed with its policy decision to withdraw from the National Service Board's Consultative Council, were more committed to their Jewishness; for them, the service role was an expression of their search to integrate their pacifism and their Judaism. Rabbi Hoffman had been unhappy with the WRL's direction for nearly a year, a disillusionment shared by Bernard Gross who was unable to support the WRL in its "so-called 'political actions.'"[33] During this year of growing disaffection, and largely as a result of this disaffection, Rabbi Hoffman, along with a group of Columbia University graduate students, joined together with the pacifist members of the Central Conference of American Rabbis to organize the Jewish Peace Fellowship.

The group started out [in 1941] with forty members and a single chapter in New York City, but within a year had grown to over 100 members and with new chapters in Philadelphia and Los Angeles. They believed that a specifically Jewish organization of pacifists would enable Jews and non-Jews to know the contribution that Judaism and the Jewish experience had to offer to pacifist philosophy and would strengthen the devotion to peace of the non-pacifist Jews. [34] According to its "Statement of Purpose," the JPF would venture to apply the pacifist way of life to all human affairs, both public and private, to assist financially and spiritually the Jewish conscientious objector in camps or in prison and to engage in constructive social action on behalf of peace and justice. [35]

> No self-respecting member of the JPF can merely *refrain* from buying war bonds. If his neighbors are giving 10% to this cause, he must give more than 10% to the feeding of the victims of war, to the relief of civilian populations, to the support of CPS and to all the manifold causes which look to us for aid. We can answer the charge that we are 'aloof pacifists' only by being vigorous 'activists' in service and sacrifice. This is why our organization is exploring opportunities for social action. [36]

Finally, while quietly spreading the pacifist message, the JPF would try to be a tempering influence on the inevitable hatred and cries for revenge, which would arise as the war went on. Since the "peace" would almost certainly be "bad," the pacifist must do his best to ameliorate its consequences. [37]

The Jewish Peace Fellowship, like the WRL, and other pacifist groups, was most successful when it turned inwards and focused its efforts on the support of the conscientious objector. Most Jewish pacifists went to CPS camps run by the American Friends Service Committee and unless their families could provide for their maintenance, the Quakers had to incur expenses on their behalf. The JPF believed that they had a responsibility to "take care of their own." By playing on this sentiment and by maintaining a low profile, the group was successful in raising money from such establishment organizations as the Jewish Welfare Board. Since June 1943, however, the JPF had not contributed any money to the National Service Board for the support of the Jewish conscientious objectors in CPS. The Executive Board had promulgated this policy partly because of budgetary priorities and partly because the Joint Rabbinical Committee, which had been established by the members of the Central Conference of American Rabbis and the Rabbinical Assembly, was in a better position to raise substantial sums. Rabbi Arthur Lelyveld, who was the first chairman of the JPF, and Rabbi Hoffman, administered the bulk of the Committee's work. Finally, some members of the JPF, while disagreeing with the general direction in which the WRL was moving, agreed with the League's specific protest against the CPS concept of unpaid labor. In April 1944, the JPF decided to resume its support for the National Service Board since many members felt that the maintenance cost was an obligation, which the JPF was morally bound to meet despite the objections of some of its members to CPS policies.[38] Throughout this period of non-support they had continued to send books, speakers and periodicals of Jewish interest to the camps and had been corresponding as individuals with the men.

In its response to the events of the war and in the role it played, the identity of the Jewish Peace Fellowship was pacifist first and Jewish second. The very existence of a JPF, however, testifies to the uniqueness of the pressures felt by the Jewish pacifist. When Moshe Kallner confessed to his agonizing dilemma and his eventual renunciation of his pacifism, he was writing for all pacifists, but as a Jew he confronted the problem more acutely. He felt the conscious and unconscious tug of his cultural identity; nor would his family and friends, gripped by an emotional and moral imperative, let him forget it. As Abraham Cronbach wrote in 1937: "Of all the outrages committed against the Jews by Hitler, none is more calamitous than this—he has banished from the hearts of many Jews the will to peace." [39]

While some Jews like Kallner gave up their pacifist witness, others attempted to escape their isolation by joining secular war resisters' groups. Those who were more committed to their Jewish identity organized a separate group. They believed that as Jews they experienced distinct pressures and would benefit by confronting those problems together. The members of the Jewish Peace Fellowship were searching for a way to integrate their Jewish background with their pacifist beliefs and instincts. Like John Haynes Holmes, in his call for Jews to join the pacifist ranks, many would ask whether the Jews, because of their diasporean tradition of internationalism and their historic reliance on the strength of God rather than the strength of force, were not the supreme pacifists?[40] But, history had provided its greatest test of faith and only a few had maintained it.

Notes

(Rabbi Isidor B. Hoffman Papers include personal papers and papers of the Jewish Peace Fellowship)

1. Moshe Kallner to Evan Thomas, July 24, 1943. War Resisters League (WRL, MSS, Box 17. Swarthmore College Peace Collection (SCPC).

2. Abraham Kaufman's Form 47 – Special Form for Conscientious Objectors –1941. Loaned to author by Abraham Kaufman.

3. Bernard Gross's Form 47 -- Special Form for Conscientious Objectors –1941. Hoffman Papers.

4. I have tried to draw a composite portrait of Jewish pacifists by generalizing from the files of Jewish objectors in the papers of attorney Julien Cornell and the Metropolitan Board for Conscientious Objectors – and from the papers of the Jewish Peace Fellowship in Rabbi Hoffman's possession.

5. *Tidings* II (Feb., 1944), p. 1

6. Bernard Gross to Rabbi Isidor Hoffman, July 21,1942. Hoffman Papers.

7. Abraham Cronbach, *The Quest for Peace* (Cincinnati, 1937), pp. 151, 158.

8. Vernon Hollaway, "American Pacifism Between the Two Wars, 1914-41," (Unpublished Dissertation, 1949), p. 8.

9. Emergency Peace Campaign, MSS, SCPC.

10. Cronbach, p. 162

11. Carl Herman Voss, *Rabbi and Minister: The Friendship of Stephen Wise and John Haynes Holmes* (Cleveland, 1964), pp. 309 – 13

12. Ray H. Abrams, "The Churches and the Clergy in World War II," *Annals of the American Academy of Political and Social Science*, CCLVI (March 1948), p. 117.

13. Central Conference of American Rabbi (CCAR) *Yearbook*, LII (1940), pp.106 – 10.

14. R.R. Russell, "Development of Conscientious Objector Recognition in the United Sates, " *George Washington University Law Review*, XX (March, 1952) p. 424.

15. For a discussion of the pacifist interpretation of the Jewish tradition, see Abraham Cronbach, *The Jewish Peace Book* (Cincinnati, 1932); Abraham Cronbach, *The Quest for Peace* (Cincinnati, 1937); Abraham Cronbach, "War and Peace in the Jewish Tradition," in *Yearbook of the CCAR*, XLVI (1936); Allan Solomonow, editor, *Roots of Jewish Nonviolence* (Jewish Peace Fellowship, Nyack, N.Y., 1971); Marcus Wald, *Jewish Teachings on Peace* (New York, 1944) and *Shalom: The Jewish Peace Letter, since 1968* the publication of the Jewish Peace Fellowship.

16. Interview with Herman Adlerstein, attorney for many Jewish conscientious objectors.

17. CCAR, *Yearbook,* L (1940), p. 131.

18. Open Letter from the Rabbinical Assembly, October 1940, Hoffman Papers.

19. *Tidings*, I (Feb., 1943) p.1.

20. George Freedman and Louis Falk, *Jews in American Wars* (New York, 1954), p. 105.

21. *Tidings,* II (April, 1944), p.3.

22. Harold Ribalow, "Jews at Columbia University," p. 7. Hoffman Papers.

23. "Judah Magnes: A Tragic Dilemma," Christian Century, LVII (March 27, 1940), p. 406.

24. WRL MSS Box 2 at SCPC.

25. *Conscientious Objector,* V (May, 1943), p.4.

26. *Tidings,* II (Feb., 1944), p.1.

27. CCAR *Yearbook*, L (1940), p.128.

28. Bernard Gross, Open Letter, March 1941. Hoffman Papers.

29. John Haynes Holmes, "Should Jews be Pacifists?" Reprint in JPF Papers at SCPC.

30. Abraham Kaufman to Abraham Cronbach, Nov. 19, 1941. WRL MSS at SCPC.

31. Rabbi Isidor Hoffman to Bernard Gross, Feb. 14, 1941. Hoffman Papers.

32. WRL MSS Box 16 at SCPC.

33. Bernard Gross to Rabbi Hoffman, June 10, 1943. Hoffman Papers.

34. JPF News, I (August, 1942), p.1.

35. JPG "Statement of Purpose," JPF papers at SCPC

36. *Tidings, I* (October, 1942), p.1.

37. *Tidings, I* (February, 1944), p.3.

38. *Tidings, I* (February, 1944), p.1

39. Cronbach, *The Quest for Peace*. P. 47

40. Holmes, "Should Jews be Pacifists?" See Wald, *Jewish Teachings on Peace.*

Jewish Conscientious Objectors in the US and Israel

Murray Polner

Between 1967 and 1970, while researching a book on Vietnam veterans, I naturally spent a lot of time with many ex-GIs. I was quickly struck by how different they were from my former army buddies of a previous era. A surprising number expressed a profound sense of grievance that they had been lied to, manipulated and then abandoned by the men and institutions which had sent them off to southeast Asia to fight people who had never threatened them or their country. For many, the delicate bond between rulers and the ruled had been ruptured. And I concluded:

> "Never before in American history have as many brave and loyal
> young men been as shabbily treated by the government that sent
> them to war; never before have so many of them questioned as
> much, as these veterans have, the essential rightness of what they
> were forced to do."[1]

But it was hard for me to think in rigid categories. What of those other "brave and loyal young men" who refused to serve? It was hardly an easy decision to risk imprisonment, or go into exile. Those who courageously refused to serve in a pointless and brutal war were always in danger of becoming victims of their own government.

During World War I thousands of Americans were sent to prison for refusing to serve in a war whose primary purpose was to defend and expand European empires. The famous labor leader and Socialist Party presidential candidate Eugene Victor Debs was among the most notable of those who received draconian sentences for daring to oppose or even question Woodrow Wilson's (and the US government's) draconian Espionage Law. This was the same Wilson who invaded Mexico and was undeniably racist. Many others were jailed for draft dodging, were refused CO status, or suffered because of their motley backgrounds of radicalism, liberalism, socialism, pacifism, or religious principles. Others were caught up in the mindless pro-war flag waving and jingoism that shamefully swept the United States and led directly to the infamous Red Scare and Palmer Raids of the postwar era.

World War II, however, posed a perplexing dilemma for many Jewish young men who opted for CO status or simply refused to report for induction when the first peacetime draft was established in October 1940. By 1943, when it became widely known that the Germans and their allies were killing Jews en masse, fewer Americans Jews who received draft notices chose to request an exemption based on their pacifist or political views.

Since the end of WWII, however, it is fair to ask whether one should always willingly serve a government fighting or threatening to fight unjust wars. And to what extent do conscience and personal morality matter? It's obviously a question with no simple answer. But to ask whether every citizen owes it to his nation to put on a uniform if called to military service has always been an intimidating question too often posed to young people by men living in safety decades away from having had to make their own life and death decisions. With very few exceptions no child or grandchild of Washington's pro-war elite during the Vietnam and Iraq wars ever served on active military duty. Meanwhile, wars continue to be instigated and backed by those benefiting materially, as well as by excessive nationalist, ethnic, ideological or religious hatreds that are easily aroused by sophisticated manipulation of the populace.

In the end, as the proud voices in this book explain, it was and remains a matter of conscience, ethical behavior, and tradition that permits and upholds a Jew's (and anyone else, for that matter) right to say no to war. It also requires courage.

In the United States, many young men (and who knows, a future draft or mandatory universal national service may also include young women) discovered they could be "peacemakers" (Martin Buber's term, or possibly selective pacifists or "pacifoids," in Rabbi Richard Israel's felicitous description which Rabbi Albert S. Axelrad cites in his essay, "Pacifoid Jew").

Take Rabbi Roland B. Gittelsohn for example. He was a chaplain who served on Iwo Jima during WWII. "Combat itself was the most unspeakably horrendous hell I have ever known or could possibly imagine . . . How a single one of us left Iwo Jima alive is a miracle," he wrote in a sadly forgotten but searing account of his combat experiences and his struggle to help the troops somehow survive in the midst of so much destruction and madness. Yet having experienced the barbarism man and governments are capable of, and while he will always rightly honor the memory of the gallant marines who stood alongside him on that blood-soaked island, well after the war he considered the CO claims filed by many young men during the Vietnam War. Distinguishing between two kinds of war found in Judaism's teachings, the compulsory war and the optional war, he draws the reader's attention to Deuteronomy, which excuses those who have legitimate reasons for avoiding battle. Both the CO and those who joined the military can find that Judaism supports their position, he wrote. While conceding, "Judaism doesn't offer simple, easy answers to any of life's crucial dilemmas," he concluded that our faith "gives even higher priority to responsibly motivated conscience than to government and law."[2]

Can a Jew in good conscience, then, professing Judaism's ethical, moral, historical and religious principles be a pacifist after the Holocaust? The answer is—yes, absolutely! Even in Israel.

"In a non-dogmatic tradition such as Judaism," the Jewish Peace Fellowship has stated, "there is much room for individual intuition and understanding. . . . For while Judaism is not in any absolute sense a 'pacifist' tradition, some of its basic teachings, when applied to modern warfare, raise grave doubts about the permissibility of participation in war today."

In Israel today, there are a growing number of young men and women, reservists, pilots and active duty members who refuse to bear arms against occupied Palestinians. A surprisingly large number have requested exemptions as conscientious objectors—some have been imprisoned. Others refused to serve with their military units on the occupied West Bank or in Gaza or else simply walked away to live or study in other countries. Still others serve but refuse to support the Occupation and the privations visited upon ordinary Palestinians.

250 Israeli high school students—the *shministim*—sent a letter in March 2005 to the then Israeli Prime Minister asserting their refusal to take part in the Occupation of Palestinian land and its people.

Reserve combat officers and IDF soldiers have also signed on to Courage to Resist, founded in 2002, as a form of selective conscientious refusal. They have stated publicly: "We, reserve combat officers and soldiers of the Israel Defense Forces . . . Have seen the bloody toll this Occupation exacts from both sides . . . We [while continuing to serve in the IDF 'in any mission that's serves Israel's defense'] "shall not continue to fight beyond the 1967 borders in order to dominate, expel, starve, and humiliate an entire people."

Other reservists who may report when called to duty but refuse to serve on the West Bank and in Gaza have joined together in Yesh G'vul ("There is a limit [to what an army can ask of its conscripts]"). "We the undersigned," went their Declaration of Refusal, "IDF soldiers, declare that we will not take part in the continued oppression of the Palestinian people in the occupied territories, and will not take a hand in the policing and defense of the settlements serving that end." [3]

In the US, during the Korean and Vietnam wars, everyone who asked for CO status had to complete a lengthy biographical questionnaire, which challenge the petitioner to explain in detail why he believed as he did. It required them to write about their families, beliefs, sources of inspiration, and ideals. In short, it asked them—and will do the same if a draft is in our future—to explain why and how they had become believers in nonviolence and why they wish to avoid military service. In the end, to be a conscientious objector demands the same moral courage and inner strength demanded of those who choose military service.

Following are several excerpts from CO forms submitted to and collected by the Jewish Peace Fellowship during the Vietnam War era when a draft was still in effect. Because it is no longer possible to locate all the writers we have chosen to identify them by their first initial.

> "Pacifist" and "Conscientious Objector" are just words. However, these words also represent a way of life and a system of values. The fact that I have only recently begun to apply these words to myself does not mean that I have only yesterday begun to follow pacifist beliefs and a nonviolent life style. On the contrary, I have always generally held these pacifist beliefs and lived in the same nonviolent manner...beliefs [that] are the products of twenty years of life experience, religious training, and study of great men and ideas.
>
> —R.

> I am frightened as I stand here, I do not know what will happen to me. . . . For at this moment before all you [the Selective Service System's draft board] who are witnessing my act of resistance, I am

affirming those ideals—love and justice—that men in general and Judaism in particular hold sacred. And I am ashamed as I stand here, ashamed that I am the first Rabbinical student ever to turn in his draft card. . . . Yet I wonder, does the Judaism of the prophets, the Judaism that suffered so much whenever the State ruled men's consciences mean so little to us that even I can be the first to speak up with my life and future against the genocide of another people?

—J.

"By far one of the most influential experiences in the process of realizing my religious objections to war was exposure to Army ROTC at college. I joined voluntarily at the beginning of my freshman year with the idea of making my almost inevitable two years of service in the armed forces more productive and bearable as an officer. After a year in which I spent one hour a week in the classroom and one hour a week in drill, I quit the Corps in October 1966. . . . I felt confusion and uneasiness as those values I had been brought up to respect came in conflict with military attitudes and actions. I began to know that war could never bring about a world in which human beings could live in brotherhood and peace. I felt something I never expected to, shame in wearing the Army uniform.

—D.

From my father, who is a doctor, and from my mother, who is an artist, I learned to cherish the spiritual values of life in the Jewish tradition. The practice of resolving conflicts between individuals by discussion and debate, which I learned from my family, is a fundamental tenet of my life. I cannot serve in the armed forces as a non-combatant because to do so would contribute to the waging of war and the destruction of human life. It is not sufficient merely to refrain from pulling the trigger; one must not aim the gun, or repair the gun if it is broken.

—S.

Following are two excerpts in which two contemporary brothers not facing a draft have nevertheless discovered pacifism and nonviolence.

"Religion is the basis for my belief in nonviolence and my opposition to war. Judaism has led my life in the direction of peace and to respect the sanctity of life...Instead of killing for my country, I will provide my country with a more peaceful and productive service... I will do this by pursuing my dreams and goals in life. I will enrich a young life with the gift of education, in a way that they can and will want to learn. I plan to attend and graduate...with a degree in elementary education, bring success to children's futures as an elementary school teacher [and] also continue my community service by providing for the sick and hungry, as well as visiting and helping out in hospitals. I will do my service to my country and its people through peaceful pursuits as a proud citizen of the USA."

—Greg Gingold

I am conscientiously opposed to war and participation in war in all forms. I have always believed that the most important aspect of life is our interaction with other human beings. How people connect, communicate, and live with each other on an everyday basis is why I believe God put us here on Earth. I believe we are here for each other, to make the lives around us richer while helping others...I am a peaceful person.

"I believe God wants me to help others in a peaceful way, to follow the teachings of Judaism 'to seek peace & pursue it" (Psalms 34:15) and that 'whoever saves a life, it is considered as if he saved an entire world.' (Jerusalem Talmud, Sanhedrin 4:1). These teachings are ways for one to live his life...It is written in Isaiah 2:4, 'They shall beat their swords into plowshares and their spears into pruning hooks. Nation shall not lift up sword against nation, neither shall they learn war anymore.'"

—Scott Gingold

Though there is no draft in the United States now; the sentiments arising from refusing to go to war remain powerful. Since World War II, the children of the powerful rarely serve on active military duty. No congressional son was drafted during the Vietnam War and there are virtually no congressional or White House sons or daughters serving as enlisted combat personnel in Iraq. The truth is, no draft can ever be fair. Anyone with political pull and family connections will always be able to avoid active military duty, or in the very rare instance when he or she does not, will surely receive safe jobs.

All a draft can do is help transform yet another generation of Americans into potential cannon fodder. It also contributes mightily to the further militarization of the United States. Since World War I the world has experienced continuous bloodletting, always enhanced by conscription.

Americans should oppose any future draft because it is a form of slavery and tramples on our freedom, which should never be sacrificed for ideological pipe dreams and political manipulation.

Notes

[1] Murray Polner. No Victory Parades: *The Return of the Vietnam Veteran* (N.Y.: Holt, Rinehart & Winston, 1971), p.165.

[2] Roland B. Gittelson, *Here I Am: Harnessed to Hope* (N.Y.: Vantage Press, 1988), pp.93-100 and pp.101-124 for his unforgettable experiences as a Chaplain on Iwo Jima during WWII.

[3] Peretz Kidron, Compiler and Editor, Refusenik: *Israel's Soldiers of Conscience.* Foreword by Susan Sontag. (London & NY: Zed Books, 204), p. 82.

Torah, War, and the "Gentle Heart" Today: Israeli Soldiers' Refusal to Serve in the Occupation Army

Rabbi Arthur Waskow

The Torah teaches: "The officials shall go on addressing the troops and say, "Is there anyone afraid or gentle-hearted? [Some translate "rakh halevav" as "disheartened" or "softhearted"] let him go back to his home, lest he melt the heart of his brothers, like his heart!" (Deuteronomy 20:8; Parashat Shoftim)

More than 450 Israeli reserve soldiers and officers have publicly announced that they will serve in defense of Israel's boundaries but refuse to serve in the army of Occupation in the West Bank and Gaza. They have named themselves *Omets Lesarev*/Courage to Refuse.

Adding also the previous group "Yesh G'vul" ("There is a border/ There is a limit") and the *shiministim* (students on the verge of conscription) who have also said they will defend Israel but refuse to serve in the Occupation Army, there are more than 1,500 such Israelis.

This essay will examine the Torah-related and ethical questions involved in the present Refusal movement and in the biblical and Rabbinic view of this question. First, it is noteworthy that the biblical tradition has a place for individual exemption from national military service (Deut. 20: 5-8):

Then the officials shall address the troops: "Is there anyone who has built a new home but not yet dedicated it? Let him go back to his home, lest he die in battle and another dedicate it.

"Is there anyone who has planted a vineyard but has never harvested it? Let him go back to his home, lest he die in battle and another initiate it.

"Is there anyone who has paid the bride-price for a wife, but who has not yet married her? Let him return to his home, lest he die in battle and another marry her.

The officials shall go on addressing the troops and say, "Is there anyone afraid or gentle-hearted? Let him go back to his home, lest he melt the heart of his brothers, like his heart!"

I Maccabees 3:56 reports that even in the moment of resistance to the Syrio-Hellenistic empire ruled by Antiochus, Judah Maccabee applied this passage of Torah and ordered back to their homes the newly married, the new homebuilders, and others as well as the gentle-hearted.

Notice that this war was being fought against an imperial Occupation of the Land of Israel, against an enemy that had desecrated the Temple and commanded idolatry.

About three centuries after the Maccabeean wars, when the Rabbis took up the question of interpreting this Torah passage, some of them asked why the last verse specified both "afraid" and "gentle-hearted" as reasons to exempt a man from military service. According to one interpretation, those who must be exempted from army service are not only those who are afraid to be killed but also those who are gentle of heart lest they become killers.

The *Tosefta Sotah* 7:22 quotes Rabbi Akiva as saying, "Why does the verse then say 'and the disheartened'? To teach that even to the mightiest and strongest of men if he is compassionate (Rachaman) he should turn back."*

Notice that the gentle-hearted MUST be exempted if that is how they feel, there is no discretion, not the Army's and not theirs, to conscript them. And notice that the Torah's concern is both for conscience and for practicality: if they stay in the Army, their example may bring other soldiers to become unwilling to kill, or to die.

This provision operates also as a rough public check-and-balance to measure whether the people really believe a specific war is worth dying for and killing for. If many soldiers begin to take the position that a specific war is not worth their dying or killing, the war may become impossible for the nation to fight.

If on the other hand, most eligible fighters rally vigorously to the cause, the war can probably be fought. In the Talmud (see especially Sanhedrin 2a [the Mishna], 16a, and 20b, and Sotah 44a-b), the rabbis limited the exemptions by distinguishing different types of wars—an "obligatory war" from a "voluntary war" (milchemet chovah vs. milchemet reshut)—and said that the exemptions named by the Torah applied in the second case but not in the first.

But what is an obligatory war? Not so easy:

Raba said (Sotah 44b): The wars waged by Joshua to conquer Canaan were obligatory in the opinion of all; the wars waged by the House of David for territorial expansion were voluntary in the opinion of all; where they differ is with regard to wars against heathens so that these should not march against them.

Note that there was a real difference of opinion about whether a preventive/defensive war was voluntary or obligatory.

So one could argue that only a war to establish a Jewish place in the Land of Israel, like Joshua's wars and the war of 1948, was obligatory; once that place for sustainable self-government was carved out, all other wars were (thought by some to be) voluntary. So in our own day, the Occupation of the West Bank and Gaza could be argued to be an expansion of territory beyond what is necessary for a sustainable self-governing Jewish community, and therefore a voluntary war in which the exemptions would apply.

It is certainly not an open-and-shut case that the Occupation is a *milchemet reshut*; but it seems a reasonable extrapolation.

The fact that the electorate and Knesset may have authorized the present level of war to control the West Bank/Gaza does not settle the matter. To declare a voluntary war, according to the Talmud, required the approval of a Sanhedrin of 71. So even if the Sanhedrin (or an elected analogue today) voted for such an expansionist war, the exemptions would still apply.

In assessing the situation we face today, there is a second dimension to apply: There are many aspects of our lives, and this is one, that is profoundly different from the context in which the Talmud evolved.

Indeed, the Maccabees, far more nearly than most later Rabbinic communities, lived in the situation of a state or state-in-the-making in the Land of Israel that would have to decide whether and how to make war. One would think that if ever there was a war the rabbis might have defined as "obligatory," in which the Deuteronomic exemptions would have been suspended, it would have been the kind of war the Maccabees were fighting against Antiochus. Yet the Maccabees understood the Deuteronomy text to apply even in their extreme situation. They applied the Torah, and evidently because many of the people did support that war, they fought and won.

Of course "the Book of Maccabees" does not control the halakha, and was not even canonized by the Rabbis as sacred text. But it does make clear what Jews who lived in this situation thought and did. So today we might take their responses into account.

Another of the most important differences between our lives and those of the Rabbis is that today we are intertwined with an effort by the human race to develop an international law of war which includes the UN Charter, the Geneva Conventions, etc., and includes not only an Israeli state but a law of that state itself *requiring* a soldier to disobey an unlawful order, including one unlawful under international law.

This does not end our questioning, but does enrich and complicate it a great deal. We might even, borrowing from but not necessarily standing inside the Rabbinic mindset, think of this whole weave of international law as the effort of the Children of Noah to develop the *sheva* mitzvot—the seven commandments—by which, according to the Rabbinic mind, the whole human race is bound. So the Talmudic law of *milchemet chovah* and *reshut* may not for us exhaust the question.

Finally, what weight and value do we give the life-experience of our own generation(s)? Some of us would say that our lives continue to distill Torah, if we open our experience to God.

In that case for sure, and probably even if we would not go so far, it behooves us to listen to the direct reports of those involved. The reservist refuseniks that have signed the recent statement do not think that the State of Israel is under occupation or in any danger of being occupied. Just the reverse. They do not believe that the Occupation army is acting in a way that protects Israel. Just the reverse.

Two reports:

- Shuki Sadeh, a paratrooper reservist who was among the signers, told a newspaper how he had seen an Israeli soldier kill a young Palestinian boy at a distance of 150 meters. "What angered me at the time," Sadeh explained, "was that our soldiers said, 'Well, that's another Arab who has disappeared.'"
- Ariel Shatil, an artillery master sergeant recently on duty in the Gaza Strip, recalled that while it's claimed that the Palestinians shoot first and Israelis just respond, in reality, "We would start shooting and they would fire back."

Today, some Israeli soldiers are in a new situation, applying much the same basic sense of values that are marked out in Torah, attempting to distinguish defense from a war of conquest and occupation—and appealing to the individual "heart" as one of the crucial elements in making that decision.

At the level of reexamining, revitalizing, and renewing Torah, we might imagine bringing together some members of Courage to Refuse with rabbis of various streams of Jewish life and as well with ethicists who have addressed the questions of just war, nonviolence, and civil disobedience.

Note

* See Jacob Milgrom, ed., *The JPS Torah Commentart: Deuteronomy,* note 22 on p. 379, citing *Tosefta 7:22.* See also Midrash *B'reshit Rabbah 76:2 and Rashi on Genesis 32:8,* which uuse similar logic to understand Jacob's feeling both "fear" and "distress" at Esau's approach—fear lest he be killed and distress lest he kill. Thanks to Rabbis Everetter Genler and Marc Gopin and also to Deborah Shubowitz for helping guide me along this midrashic path.

The Political Rehabilitation of Joseph Rotblat

Lawrence S. Wittner

By the time of his death on August 31, 2005, Joseph Roblat was a revered figure. A top nuclear physicist, Rotblat received—among many other honors and awards—a British knighthood and, together with the Pugwash Conferences on Science and World Affairs (an organization that he had helped to initiate), the Nobel Peace Prize (1995). As the president of the Pugwash conferences recalled: "Joseph Rotblat was a towering figure in the search for peace in the world, who dedicated his life to trying to rid the world of nuclear weapons, and ultimately to rid the world of war itself."

But Rotblat's steadfast support for nuclear disarmament and peace did not always receive such plaudits. Born in Warsaw on November 4, 1908, Rotblat was the fifth of seven children of Jewish parents. Although his father was a prosperous paper merchant, the business collapsed during World War I. To escape starvation, the Rotblat family was reduced to selling vodka that they distilled illegally in their basement.

Young Joseph Rotblat proved an excellent student and, in 1939, after attending classes at the University of Warsaw, he won a research fellowship in physics to Liverpool University. Accordingly, he moved to Britain, where he studied with James Chadwick, one of the world's top physicists. Though Rotblat returned to Poland to fetch his wife, Tola Gryn, also Jewish, she was too ill to leave and, thus, remained there. This proved a terrible mistake. The day after he departed again for

Britain, German troops invaded Poland and World War II began. Although Rotblat sought thereafter to rescue his wife, he was unsuccessful. She disappeared and, despite repeated inquiries, he was never able to learn what had happened to her. Ultimately, he concluded that she must have died in a Nazi concentration camp.

Fearing that Nazi Germany might develop the atomic bomb, Rotblat, now a promising physicist, came to the US to work on the Manhattan Project, America's own atomic bomb program that he—like many other scientists—hoped would deter Germany's launching of a nuclear war. But, in late 1944, when Rotblat learned that the German bomb program had been a failure, he resigned from the Manhattan Project and returned to London to engage in non-military work. This decision, taken for humanitarian reasons, plunged him into hot water with the authorities. Shortly after telling his US supervisor of his plan to leave Los Alamos, he was accused by US intelligence of being a Soviet spy. The charge, totally without merit, was eventually dropped.

Back in Britain, Rotblat engaged in peaceful research and, in the postwar years, helped to organize the Atomic Scientists' Association (ASA), which drew together some of that country's top scientists. Much like America's Federation of American Scientists, the ASA promoted nuclear arms control and disarmament. However, British government officials, then more interested in building nuclear weapons than in eliminating them looked askance at its activities. In 1947-1948, when the ASA organized an Atomic Train to bring the dangers of nuclear weapons (and the supposed benefits of peaceful nuclear power) to the attention of the British public, Prime Minister Clement Attlee objected strongly to plans for government cooperation with it. In March 1948, when Rotblat invited Attlee to visit the Atomic Train during its stay in London, the foreign secretary and the defense minister advised the prime minister to reject the offer, which he did.

Rotblat's relations with the British government continued to follow a difficult course in the 1950s. Working closely with the philosopher Bertrand Russell, Rotblat signed the Russell-Einstein Manifesto of July 9, 1955, which warned nations that if they persisted in their plans for nuclear war, civilization would be utterly destroyed. This venture, in turn, led to the Pugwash conferences—so named because they began in 1957 at a private estate in Pugwash, Nova Scotia. Designed to bring together scientists on both sides of the "iron curtain" for serious, non-polemical discussions of the nuclear menace, these conferences were low-key operations, with little publicity outside of scientific circles. Nevertheless, British officials were deeply suspicious of the Pugwash conferences and of Rotblat, who did most of the organizational work for them and, in 1959, became Pugwash secretary-general.

Convinced that "the Communists" wanted to use the 1958 Pugwash conference "to secure support for the Soviet demand for the banning of nuclear weapons," the British Foreign Office initially sought to promote an attitude of skepticism toward it. But, when Rotblat asked J. D. Cockcroft, a member of Britain's Atomic Energy Authority, to suggest who might be invited to it, Cockcroft and the Foreign Office decided that a better strategy would be to go with the flow and arrange for the participation of a staunch proponent of the British government's position in the meeting, which they did.

Although one British diplomat noted that the conference "passed off quietly enough and not too unsuccessfully from our point of view," the British government remained on guard. Learning of plans for another Pugwash conference in Vienna, the Foreign Office warned of the possibility "that this will be more dangerous from our point of view than its predecessors." Communist participants might launch "a major propaganda drive against nuclear weapons," and "the organizing committee consists of Lord Russell and Professor Rotblat." From the British government's standpoint, the Pugwash conferences were little better than "Communist front gatherings."

British policy gradually began to shift, however, as the government grew more interested in nuclear arms controls. Asked by Rotblat if he would like to join the advisory body of the British Pugwash committee, Cockcroft referred the matter to the Foreign Office, which responded that he should do so, as it would help prevent Pugwash from "being exploited for propaganda purposes." Although the Foreign Office did not think he should attend the next Pugwash conference, in Moscow, during 1960, it reversed course that summer and urged him to recruit additional politically reliable scientists to attend. Indeed, it now sought to take over the Pugwash movement for its own purposes. In response to a suggestion by Cockcroft, a Foreign Office official opined that "it would be most helpful if the Royal Society could be persuaded to sponsor British participation . . . and if this were to lead to the winding up of the present Pugwash Committee."

But the plans for a takeover failed. When the British government suggested topics for Pugwash meetings and more government officials who should be invited to them, Rotblat resisted, much to government dismay. In October 1963, a Foreign Office official complained, "the difficulty is to get Prof. Rotblat to pay any attention to what we think. . . . He is no doubt jealous of his independence and scientific integrity." Securing "a new organizer for the British delegation seems to be the first need, but I do not know if there is any hope of this."

Nonetheless, despite lingering resentment at Rotblat's independence and integrity, the British government had arrived at a positive appraisal of the Pugwash conferences. As a British defense ministry official declared in January 1962: Pugwash was "now a very respectable organization." When the Home Office, clinging to past policy, advised that Pugwash was "a dirty word," the Foreign Office retorted that the movement now enjoyed "official blessing." Explaining the turnabout, a Foreign Office official stated, "The process of educating" Soviet experts is "bound to be of some use to us." Furthermore, "we ourselves may pick up some useful ideas from our own scientists . . . and are not likely to be embarrassed by anything which they suggest." Finally, "if there is ever to be a breakthrough, it is not inconceivable that the way might be prepared by a conference of this kind."

In fact, there soon was a breakthrough: the Partial Test Ban Treaty of 1963—a nuclear arms control measure that the Pugwash conferences played a key part in generating. The British government had no doubt about the connection, and in 1964 it honored Rotblat with a CBE—Commander of the British Empire—for his organization of the Pugwash conferences.

In the following years, Rotblat continued his role as a prominent critic of nuclear weapons, particularly as a leader of the ongoing Pugwash movement. Not noticeably religious or involved with Jewish organizations, he did not shy away from the heated debate over the Israeli nuclear weapons program. In 1965, when Rotblat met with Prime Minister David Ben-Gurion, he expressed his misgivings over the prospect of Israel's acquisition of nuclear weapons. Three decades later, in his Nobel Peace Prize address, Rotblat praised Israeli engineer Mordechai Vanunu's revelation of Israel's nuclear weapons program as an act of courage and condemned the eighteen-year prison term given to him as excessively severe.

The 1995 Nobel Peace Prize, of course, provided the final act in Rotblat's political rehabilitation. Few could any longer doubt his steadfast, consistent support for nuclear disarmament and world peace.

And so it goes. Today's dangerously peace-minded heretic is tomorrow's hero. Abraham Lincoln—that staunch critic of the Mexican War—became America's best-loved President. Robert LaFollette—reviled and burned in effigy for his opposition to World War I—emerged as one of this nation's most respected Senators. Martin Luther King, Jr.—condemned for his protests against the Vietnam War—is now honored as this country's great peacemaker.

Perhaps today, when governments promise us endless military buildups and wars, people should take note of this phenomenon.

THE MIDDLE EAST

When Arik was fifteen, his fellow classmates started
chanting "death to the Arabs, death to the Arabs."
Upon hearing this, Arik reacted by climbing onto his
desk and yelling "Heil Hitler!" The class fell silent and
his friends, stunned, asked him if everything was alright. He then pointed out that such chanting was
exactly how the Holocaust had begun, except that
in Nazi Germany the chant called for the death of
the Jews.

—Yitzhak Frankenthal,
"To Be a Free Nation in Our Land"

Not Yet A Season For Peace

Dan Leon

A popular Hebrew song starts with the words, "We have come to the Land to build it and to be rebuilt by it." This expressed something of the spirit in which I came to Israel from England in the spring of 1951 to live on a newly founded kibbutz in Galilee. This may sound pretentious but in my kibbutz, two flags flew high over the water tower: the blue-white flag of Israel and the red flag of the workers. I was twenty-five years old and in spite of the many problems, there seemed much to celebrate in Israel's third Independence Day.

In that period, Israel's population was made up of 684,000 Jews and 120,000 Arabs, about one-seventh the number compared with the population in 2006. Jewish society was constantly changing under the impact of mass immigration.

In the early 1950s, my first years in the country, years which now seem infinitely distant in every sense, Israel was still striving to retain its pioneering image and to foster in its diverse population an overall sense of solidarity and common purpose. Agricultural work in the countryside, manual labor in the towns and efforts to open up the Negev, were held in high respect. (I myself worked for many years as a shepherd though I was a university graduate and this was a common thing). Because nowadays our society is characterized by a massive socio-economic gap, it is notable that in those days there was a relatively egalitarian Jewish population, in which while there were no doubt richer and poorer, at least the better off didn't flaunt their wealth, as they do today.

As we shall see, Israel's record in its early days contains failures as well achievements. Nevertheless, all in all these were exciting times. In reborn Israel everything was happening "for the first time in two thousand years." In this sense, though the country faced formidable difficulties, Israelis found good reason to take pride in their new state.

Wars "of choice"

After the 1948 War of Independence there were still real problems of security since our neighbors had not recognized Israel's borders, which at the end of the fighting were one-third broader that those stipulated in the 1947 UN partition proposal. (On the map, my kibbutz, on the road from Acre to Safed, near what was later to become the town of Carmiel, was just outside the 1947 borders). Yet we who strove for peace didn't anticipate that only eight years after 1948, Israel would be again at war. In the summer of 1956, in what was called the Sinai campaign, the Israeli army went into action in collusion with the doomed Anglo-French colonial attempt to control the Suez Canal after the Egyptian President Nasser had nationalized it.

We on the left opposed the war, which though it was fought by what was called the Israel Defense Forces (IDF) was, like the Lebanon war some twenty-five years later, a "war of choice" and not a war of self-defense. The Sinai campaign was mercifully short because its initiators were so isolated in the world, but as its opponents we found ourselves in a minority in an Israeli public opinion, which already saw what was regarded as security as its first priority. Yet this foolhardy and ultimately ineffective misuse of Israel's armed forces in an action condemned both by the US and the USSR was of considerable historical significance. It convinced the Egyptians and the whole Arab world, as well as a large section of international public opinion that the State of Israel was not an integral part of the Middle Eastern scene, but a foreign element planted in the region by outside powers. This shadow cast over Israel's image is still visible today.

With all this, one cannot but once again recall Israelis' sense of national pride half a century ago, in the late 1940s and the early 1950s. (Some think it lasted even until 1967). Israelis had won their independence and saw that it was used in attempts both to develop the length and breadth of the country and to absorb mass immigration. Between May 1948 and the end of 1951 nearly 650,000 immigrants arrived, more than the entire Jewish population of 1948. Subsequently, there were over a half million immigrants between 1951 and 1967. The Declaration of Independence had stated, "Israel will be open for Jewish immigration and the Ingathering of the Exiles." And it was.

of unemployment compared to 9.9% among the Jews. There is no industry in the villages where most Arabs live and no new Arab town has been built. Only 6.6% of the Arabs work in the civil service, while 40.4% work in construction. As for their earnings, over half are in the two lowest wage decimals while only 2.6% are in the two top decimals. The disparity between Jews and Arabs in education has been decreasing over the years yet it is still evident at all age levels, including the numbers accepted for university studies. (All the above data refer to the year 2002).

Third, Israel's contribution to "peace and good neighborliness:" Apologists for Israeli policies see the Jewish state as living in a constant state of siege, surrounded by neighbors who strive for its destruction. (Hence the tendency to rely on military men like Rabin, Barak, and Sharon as prime ministers, though the strong influence of the military on Israel's political culture doesn't depend on having a general as prime minister) In this perception, what counts is only maintaining military superiority since there exists no viable option for peace-oriented political initiatives. When the "security" argument always has priority, the belief that "there is no partner for peace" becomes a self-fulfilling prophecy. In fact, however difficult the implementation, there was always a peace option, symbolized by the famous handshake on the White House lawn between Rabin and Arafat in 1993.

Not a "liberal Occupation"

According to the peace option, the victory in the Six-Day war of 1967 could have been used not to occupy and colonize the Palestinian lands but to offer the Palestinians the right to realize their own self-determination. A genuine concern for Israel's security would have understood that a lengthy occupation contradicts Israel's real security interests. This turned out to be the truth. After some forty years of Israel's occupation of the West Bank and the Gaza Strip, one no longer hears talk of "a liberal occupation." More than a million Palestinians found themselves under Israel occupation in 1967. The Palestinian population, highly educated and politically conscious, was determined to resist the occupation by every means, including years of negotiations and two Intifadas. Inevitably, therefore, the Israeli occupation regime was characterized by harsh military measures, mass arrests (there are 9,000 Palestinian political prisoners in Israeli prisons) and an iron fist against all signs of resistance. It also had grave repercussions on the moral fiber of Israel society itself, a subject of its own that needs separate treatment.

When Israeli journalist Amira Hass, who writes on the occupied territories in *Ha'aretz*, received an international award for courageous journalism in 2004, she said that in winning the prize "I find myself benefiting from the reality of an ongoing ruthless Israeli Occupation and an apartheid sort of domination that my state, Israel, exercises over the Palestinians—a domination which robs them of their chances of free human development, and endangers the normal future of my people, the Israelis."

On the actual workings of the Occupation, on the endless expansion of settlements on Palestinian land, and on the way all this is too often misrepresented in the Israeli media, she states that "it would take days to cite the reports from the field—be me and by others—that refute the Israeli official military presentation of events." To their credit, Amira Hass, together with her *Ha'aretz* colleagues Gideon Levy and Akiva Eldar, maintain their independence as journalists whose only commitment is to write the truth as they see it. Their importance lies not only in what they say but also no less in their right to say it.

"Nobody to Talk to"

It is still in fashion to quote Abba Eban's famous remark that "the Palestinians never miss an opportunity to miss an opportunity." There can be little doubt that in the course of the conflict, the Palestinian record includes many incorrect evaluations and wrong decisions at various stages of negotiations. The same applies to the Israeli side and it bears particular responsibility because it is by far the strongest party (and has generally enjoyed American support). As I write, the Israelis claim that "there is nobody to talk to" on the other side. While Arafat was alive he was demonized and seen as an obstacle to peace. His successor, Mahmoud Abbas (Abu Mazen) was derided by Ariel Sharon as a "plucked chicken."

Though lacking Arafat's charisma and authority, Abu Mazen was elected to lead the Palestinian Authority, is a believer in peace and compromise and should have been afforded maximum Israeli support. He has not received this. At this writing Prime Minister Olmert has been reluctant even to meet him. Observers have noted that those who didn't want Abbas got Hamas. Pessimists add that perhaps those who don't want Hamas will get Islamic Jihad. As the conflict becomes more extreme and more violent, both sides seem to move further from the peace option—a viable and independent Palestinian state living alongside a secure Israel.

Where is the Peace Movement?

As a peace activist in Jerusalem since 1967, and the former editor of two peace-oriented publications, *New Outlook* and the *Palestine-Israel Journal*, one of the questions posed for me in today's situation is: where is the Israeli peace movement? As an extra-parliamentary movement in the past it exercised important influence on Israel's political scene. Peace Now had emerged in an open letter to Prime Minister Menachem Begin signed by 350 reserve officers in 1978 supporting the concept of territories for peace. Succeeding in the 1980s in mobilizing mass public support for peace, its activities reached a peak in the famous 400,000 demonstration in Tel-Aviv in 1982 against the Lebanon war. The movement still monitors the growth of settlements in the occupied territories and was associated with the 2003 Geneva Accord, a detailed blueprint for peace agreed upon by leaders of the Israeli and Palestinian peace movements. However, if in the recent period there have been mass demonstrations, they belonged not to the left but to the right and the settlers. The radical peace group Gush Shalom is active but remains a small movement. Vital work is being done by a number of human rights organizations like B'Tselem but this depends on a limited core of activists rather than the broadly based political activism which characterized the peace movement in its heyday.

Why? Could it be that the mainstream peace movement, too, has been influenced by the sense that there is nobody to talk to on the other side?

Peace and Social Justice

Yet the need in Israeli society for an alternative, in terms both of peace and of social justice, remains as pressing as ever. Its message has been enunciated so often and so well that we choose only two of examples. The first is by Professor Martin Buber (1876–1975), the great Jewish philosopher of dialogue, who, though not a pacifist, as far back as 1918 rejected what he called "a Jewish state with cannons, flags and military decorations." In 1949 he warned against the dangers of "extreme nationalism" and the "spirit of militarism" in the young State of Israel.

In 1939, Buber had written in a letter to the Indian leader Mohandas Gandhi that in Palestine, Jews, and Arabs:

> Must develop the land together, without one imposing his will on the other. We consider it a fundamental point that in this case two

vital claims are opposed to each other, two claims of a different nature and a different origin, which cannot be pitted one against the
other and between which no objective decision can be made as to
which is just and which is unjust. We consider it our duty to understand and to honor the claim which is opposed to ours and to
endeavor to reconcile both claims. We are convinced that it must
be possible to find some form of agreement between this claim and
the other; for we love this country and believe in its future; and
seeing that such love and faith are surely present on the other side,
a union in the common service of the land must be within the
range of the possible.

The second was written by Amos Oz, one of Israel's outstanding authors, after
the 1967 war:

"I believe in a Zionism that faces facts, that exercises strength with
restraint . . . that sees the Palestinian Arabs as Palestinian Arabs
(not) as a shapeless mass of humanity waiting for us to form it as we
see fit; a Zionism also capable of seeing itself as others may see it;
and finally, a Zionism that accepts both the spiritual implications
and the political consequences of the fact that this small but precious land is the homeland of two peoples fated to live facing each
other willy-nilly, because no God or angel will descend to judge
between right and right."

Israel as an independent political entity is recognized today by its enemies as
well as by its friends. It is militarily strong and economically dynamic. Moreover,
it is widely believed that it is here that the Zionist idea was realized and that Israel
as a Jewish state is today the central factor in the life of the whole Jewish people.
Perhaps, however, the late British philosopher Bertrand Russell had a point when
he wrote in 1929, "it seems to be the fate of idealists to obtain what they have
struggled for in a form which destroys their ideals."

Seeing the state today, we in the Israeli peace camp cannot say that its image
corresponds with the ideas for which we struggled for so many years. Like me,
many believed, and still believe, with Buber that peace "must be within the range
of the possible." But from the Psalmist we learned that "to every thing there is a
season, and a time for every purpose under the heaven. . . . a time to love, and

a time to hate; a time of war, and a time of peace." Though our commitment to peace remains firm, we have to admit that at the present time, the season of peace has yet to come.

A Prophetic Judaism of Human Rights: Rene Cassin and Resistance to the Israeli Occupation

Jeff Halper

The European Enlightenment had a profound if uneven impact on world Jewry as it moved steadily throughout the nineteenth century from Western through Central and finally to Eastern Europe, where the vast majority of Jews lived. By the time Russian Jews, including my grandparents, established themselves in the US, Talmudic-based ultra-Orthodoxy had given way to more secular forms based, if on anything beyond a vague sense of Jewish "culture," "tradition" and "community," and then on universalistic values generally associated with the prophets. When I taught Sunday School in our rabbi-less Conservative synagogue in Hibbing, Minnesota, I learned that Judaism can best be defined as "ethical monotheism." Although the monotheism never took root in me, a Judaism defined by ethics certainly did. And I found confirmation in the movements for social justice, civil rights, and anti-war during the Sixties, in which I proudly noted the disproportionate number of Jews who participated along with me.

One of the books issued by the Conservative movement was entitled *Jewish Heroes*. If I remember correctly it dealt with truly formidable figures such as Rabbi Akiva, Maimonides, Hannah Senesh, and David Ben-Gurion. Written in the 1950s, it could not yet have included such Jewish civil rights martyrs as Michael Schwerner and Andrew Goodman, or Abby Hoffman, or Betty Friedan or *the* Jewish hero of my day, Sandy Koufax. Nor did it mention the five whites arrested with Nelson Mandela, all of whom were Jews or—well, the list goes on. Yet one of the great Jewish heroes, perhaps the greatest, Rene Cassin, could have been included by that time. Instead, he has been forgotten by all except perhaps his own French Jewish community.

Rene Cassin was the embodiment of all that modern Jewry could aspire to. A French Jew who for many years served as the President of the League of European Jurists, he was the chief author of the Universal Declaration of Human Rights, called the "Magna Carta of All Humankind." And the "Jewish element" of this story does not end here. The fundamental human rights conventions, which form the basis of international law, managed to gain acceptance in the rare window of opportunity from 1945–1952, before the Cold War descended. During those years the Holocaust and its aftermath weighed heavily upon the international community. Rene Cassin, together with Eleanor Roosevelt, spearheaded the UN's adoption of the Declaration in 1948 over the opposition of governments jealous of surrendering any of their sovereign powers. It is worth noting that without vigorous lobbying of American Jewish groups—those very organizations today defending Israel's massive violations of human rights—the Declaration and the subsequent Geneva Conventions might never have been adopted. Cassin was the founder and first president of the Consultative Council of Jewish Organizations (CCJO), an organization linking French, British and American Jewry in the conviction that "support for the human rights of all people is an obligation incumbent upon all Jews, as we believe that universal human rights are intrinsic to Jewish values."

In 1968 Rene Cassin, then serving as president of the European Court of Human Rights, was awarded the Nobel Peace Prize for his part in drafting the Universal Declaration of Human Rights. He is buried in the Pantheon in Paris together with other illustrious heroes of the French Republic, among them Voltaire, Rousseau, Victor Hugo, Émile Zola, and Jean Jaures.

Cassin had grasped what most Jews, at least in the post-Holocaust Diaspora, realized intuitively: that only in a world based on universal human rights would Jews find the security and equality that had so long eluded them. Hence the disproportionate Jewish involvement in the labor, civil rights, and anti-war movements. Prophetic Judaism had finally linked up not only with its natural extension, the notion of universal human rights, but with an emerging set of practical instruments of implementation—human rights conventions covering a wide range of issues, an ever expanding corpus of international humanitarian law and institutions of enforcement such as the International Court of Justice and the recently created International Criminal Court (which Cassin dreamed of and which Israel, accompanied by China and Bush's America, has refused to recognize). And a Jewish hero, together with a once-heroic organized Jewish community, had played a key role—indeed, the only role a responsible Jewish community could be expected to play.

Israel, part of whose rationale was to protect and provide refuge for Jews, ironically threatens all of this. Its demand that world Jewry uncritically support policies that perpetuate its Occupation is bad enough. As long as a genuine two-state solution was possible with the Palestinians and not a "two-state solution" in which an expanded Israel dominates forever a Palestinian Bantustan, a balance could have been found between the right to (and need for) a Jewish state and the equally just rights, claims and needs of the Palestinians. But given the fact that Israel's settlement project has progressed to the point that it forecloses a viable Palestinian state, Diaspora Jews are further called upon to uphold one of the last expressions of the very 19th century's "organic" nationalism of Eastern and Central Europe of which they were the chief victims. There's an unspoken element of Zionism that Diaspora Jewry would reject outright if it was ever proclaimed in their own countries that underlies Israeli aggressiveness towards the Palestinians, and which took me years to fully grasp. This is the role that exclusivity and privilege played in the Zionist framing of things. This element, seldom if ever stated explicitly (and then only by settlers and the extreme right), can be put as follows:

The Land of Israel [from the Mediterranean to the Jordan River] belongs exclusively to the Jewish people. There is no other people with valid national rights over or claims to the country. Although Arabs live in the Land of Israel, they do not constitute a collectivity that in any way challenges Jewish exclusivity. Since the Land belongs to the Jews, only they have the prerogative to decide its fate. Any political solution to the conflict, even one in which a Palestinian state may emerge, will be decided solely by Israeli Jews. Arabs might be consulted, but genuine negotiations based upon the notion that the Palestinians have a right of self-determination in the Land of Israel are out of the question.

If this is the case, then "supporting Israel" does *not* mean supporting the Jewish right to self-determination, but rather Israel's pro-active and exclusive claim to the entire country between the Mediterranean and the Jordan River, pockmarked by islands of Arab autonomy. Although Israel wins international (and Diaspora Jewish) support by invoking "security" as the basis of its policies, in fact almost no element of the Occupation can be explained by security: not the establishment of some 300 settlements, not the annexation of East Jerusalem, not the expropriation of most West Bank land, not the demolition of 12,000 Palestinian homes, not the uprooting of more than a million olive and fruit trees, not the tortuous route of the Separation Barrier deep into Palestinian areas—none of it. Something else is going on here. The matrix of control that Israel has laid over the Palestinian areas, I would submit, has only one purpose: to ensure permanent Israeli hegemony and control over the entire country. This is the only way to read the so-called "convergence" (or "realignment") plan, a plan based by necessity on oppression, an ever-expanding violation of Palestinian human rights and, ultimately, the institutionalization of as permanent regime of domination—apartheid. It is *the* nightmare for any Jew, in which the Jews of Israel become the new Afrikaners.

Now little of what I have written above was evident to me when I moved to Israel in 1973. The Zionist paradigm made sense to me, especially the notion of Jewish national self-determination (another Zionist ideal supported by Diaspora Jews only in the breach.

Fewer than 1% of American Jews ever emigrated to Israel.) In the years immediately following the 1967 war, the Occupation had not yet become entrenched, Israel still exuded a progressive socialism, Begin and Sharon were not considered serious candidates for power and the two-state solution was still alive (though, at that time, it was anathema to Israel and the organized Jewish community abroad). I knew, of course, about the conflict with the Arabs and immediately upon landing in Israel I joined *Siakh*, the Israeli New Left, where I met my wife Shoshana. For all its flaws, Zionism might still have worked out had Israel relinquished the West Bank, East Jerusalem and Gaza and allowed a Palestinian state to emerge there. As it turned out, the Labor government soon asserted its claim to half of the Occupied Territories, and whatever legitimate security concerns did exist were overrun by the settlement project, the most explicit indication of Israel's pro-active claims to the entire country west of the Jordan, especially evident following Menachem Begin's victory in 1977 but pursued vigorously by subsequent Labor governments as well.

But "Arabs" (we generally don't use the word "Palestinian" in Israel) are largely invisible, and are certainly irrelevant to us. The vehicle that propelled me beyond the purely Jewish space inhabited by Israeli Jews and into the seething, angry yet unseen poltergeist of our Arab victims was ICAHD, the Israeli Committee Against House Demolitions, which I helped found in mid-1997. The election of Binyamin Netanyahu in May of 1996 clearly spelled the decline, if not the end, of the Oslo peace process. The mainstream Israeli peace movement had become dormant, hoping against hope that peace might yet emerge from the roller coaster of negotiations, but under Netanyahu the Occupation brutally reasserted itself. Seeking to re-engage in resistance, a number of us sought the views of Palestinian activists over how we might best cooperate. Israel's policy of house demolitions, now on the rise again, arose repeatedly in those conversations, and in a meeting attended by people representing the Israeli women's peace group Bat Shalom; Yesh G'vul, the movement of reservists who refuse to serve in the Occupied Territories; Rabbis for Human Rights, representing some 100 Israeli rabbis; the Public Committee Against Torture; and Palestinians and Israelis for Nonviolence; as well as several members of the Meretz party and Peace Now, it was decided to establish ICAHD.

The decision to pursue the issue of house demolitions marked not only a return of the Israeli peace movement to active opposition to the Occupation but fundamentally changed the very way we worked. Palestinians needed neither our "solidarity" nor our symbolic protests. Facing the demolition of their homes, they wanted to know what we would actually do for them. Could we prevent the demolitions? If the bulldozers arrived at 5 A.M., could they call us and expect us to come running? Would we actually resist demolitions together with them, putting ourselves at risk to save their homes? And if demolitions did take place, would we, could we, help them secure legal building permits? Would we help refinance and rebuild the homes? And what were we prepared to do to change Israeli government policy? How would we let the world know what was happening?

Suddenly protest was no longer sufficient; we had to deliver. In 95% of the cases of houses destroyed by the Israelis, there has been no security reason: the people neither committed any security offense nor were ever charged with any. After more than twenty years of political involvement, I discovered how little I knew about the Occupation. The Civil Administration, Israel's military government in the West Bank, seemed to be the source of much of the suffering, but I didn't even know where it was located. I couldn't have told you who actually issues demolition orders, on what authority, and why this particular house was targeted from among the thousands targeted for demolition. In the West Bank it is the Civil Administration that demolished; in Jerusalem there are two government bodies—the Ministry of Interior and the municipality. Nor could I have explained the connection between the "facts on the ground" and Israel's overall political aims. In fact, it took us more than a year before we even witnessed a demolition. That finally happened on July 9, 1998, the day my Palestinian friend Salim calls "the black day in my life and in the life of my family," the day the bulldozers of Israel's Civil Administration demolished his home for the first time. The reality of Israel's Occupation was finally brought home to me. That was the day my protest against the Occupation turned into resistance.

The knock on the door informing the Shawamreh family that their home was about to be demolished had caught them by surprise as they were sitting down for lunch. Salim, who had tried to reason, and then argue with the soldiers, had been beaten and thrown out the door. In the commotion, his wife Arabiya had locked the door shut, closing herself and her six small children inside. In the few desperate minutes she had before the army lobbed tear gas canisters into the house (canisters, I later found, were made by a company in Philadelphia and clearly marked with the warning: "For outdoor use only") and smashed open the door, she managed to make a few calls for help, one of them to me as a member of ICAHD. By chance I happened to be close by, attending a demonstration against Israel's demolition policy we had organized opposite the Civil Administration offices in the nearby settlement of Beit El. As I rushed down the hill towards the house, the bulldozer suddenly appeared before me. Almost instinctively I did what I have done many times since: I threw myself in front of it to stop the demolition. This was the first time anyone had ever done anything like that. No one knew what to do. It was clear, however, that I was an Israeli Jew, so no one was ready to shoot me. After trying to coax me to get out of the way, the soldiers brusquely (but not too roughly) pushed me down the hill, where I found myself lying in the gravel and dirt next to Salim. Wiping the perspiration from his pained face, trying to find words of awkward consolation, I promised him that the world would hear his story.

More to the point, the Jewish community in Israel and abroad should hear his story and draw lessons from it. Rene Cassins did not reject the idea of Zionism; in fact, he was distressed when, in 1975, soon before he died, the General Assembly of the UN passed the resolution declaring that Zionism is racism. But he would have insisted that Israel's existence be reconciled with the notion of human rights. I am not aware of any statement he made regarding the Occupation. He died a year before Begin came to power, before Sharon was charged by the Israeli government to do all that is possible "on the ground" to incorporate Judea and Samaria (and Gaza) into Israeli proper and to foreclose forever the establishment of a viable Palestinian state. But seeing the absolute impossibility of removing a half million Israelis from the Occupied Territories, he might well have reached the conclusion I have: that a viable two-state solution is no longer possible. If that be the case, he would have been at a loss to explain how permanent Israeli control over millions of Palestinians could ever be transformed into what he would undoubtedly have pronounced the only just and sustainable solution to the conflict, one that insists on Palestinian rights to self-determination in a viable state of their own. Being a French patriot (Cassin was one of de Gaulle's closest advisors in WWII), a cosmopolitan Jew who rejected communitarianism in favor of Jews' involvement in progressive human affairs and an advocate of human rights, Cassin might have come around to a one-state solution. He may even have come to support the vision of Monnet, the father of modern Europe with whom he shares a vault in the Pantheon, of a Middle East Union in which self-determination is integrated with wider concerns of economic and political life more in tune with our contemporary global reality.

A turn to human rights and international law offers the best—I would say the only—hope of rescuing an Israel gone fundamentally wrong. But insisting on the primacy of human rights is of prime importance to Diaspora Jews as well. Israel may enjoy short-term benefits from avoiding accountability under international law, but that runs counter to the long-term interests of the Jewish people whose security depends upon a world order based upon universal human rights. The jurist Cassin realized that persecution against the Jews over the centuries derived, in large part, from their exclusion from all forms of law, be it tribal, ecclesiastical, or civil. They were history's ultimate "Others," strangers, aliens. Universal human rights finally bring the Jews "under the umbrella" as an integral part of the human family. The fundamental question for world Jewry vis-à-vis Israel, then, is whether we want to step outside the umbrella once more. Is it in the broader Jewish interest to claim, as Israel does, that human rights covenants and international law do not apply to us? Do we really want to be a "special case" again?

As an Israeli peace activist I am fighting for an Israel that conforms to human rights and international law, whatever fundamental changes in Israel's existence that may engender. I am honored to have been nominated for the 2006 Nobel Peace Prize by the American Friends Service Committee, together with the Palestinian intellectual and activist Ghassan Andoni, for my work with ICAHD. The nomination is especially meaningful in that it draws me closer to Cassin. It would have been nice, however, to have that nomination seconded by a Jewish organization, if only to show that Jews, too, understood the crucial connection among resistance to the Occupation, helping Israel make the transition from an ethnocracy to a democracy, and saving the very soul of the Jewish people. For this is what I believe is at stake, nothing less. If Diaspora Jews take the path their religious and organizations leaders are urging on them, namely support for Israel's violations of Palestinian human rights and international law with no genuine security justification, they will alienate themselves from the very ground of our collective moral being, namely the ethical monotheism that defines our people. After Rene Cassin, no one can represent Judaism—be they Israelis or Jews of the Diaspora—without reference to human rights.

To Be a Free Nation in Our Land

Yitzhak Frankenthal

In July, 1994 my eldest son Arik was abducted and murdered by the Hamas organization. A young man of nineteen and a half, he was drafted into the army soon after graduating high school. His short life was terminated prematurely in a brutal murder within a hundred days of his recruitment.

Aside from his living in Israel, Arik dreamt of becoming an historian and educator. This wasn't his only dream, as he had so many, but I can only speak of those he discussed with me. Another of his dreams was to see peace between Israelis and Palestinians. The peace of which he spoke of included an independent Palestinian state.

When Arik was fifteen, his fellow classmates started chanting "death to the Arabs, death to the Arabs." Upon hearing this, Arik reacted by climbing onto his desk and yelled "Heil Hitler!" The class fell silent and his friends, stunned, asked him if everything was alright. He then pointed out that such chanting was exactly how the Holocaust had begun, except that in Nazi Germany the chant called for the death of the Jews. His friends at his funeral told this story to me.

Arik's death was a major changing point in my life. The old Yitzhak died, and a new Yitzhak was born. The *new* Yitzhak was no longer willing to continue living as just another father whose son was murdered but decided, from that point on, to live as a father who fights for the lives of his children and grandchildren—to live as a father who fights for reconciliation and peace between the two nations.

I felt I had failed as a father by bringing a child into the world—a child that was no longer alive; his death, I believed, was not a result of illness or accident, but simply a result of the absence of peace. It was at that point that I decided to get up and act and work towards realizing peace and reconciliation.

I, Yitzhak, am a religious and Zionist Jew. I worship G-d regardless of the situation, good or bad. Each day, I put on my *tefillin* and pray to G-d three times. For me, being a Jew is a commitment to uphold the commandments dealing with interpersonal relations. Judaism is the internalization of the Hazal saying: "Man (i.e. all men and women) is beloved because he was created in the image." My Judaism is based on the wisdom of King David who says, "Depart from evil, and do good; seek peace, and pursue it." (Psalms 34:14) When I encounter injustice or cruelty, I immediately speak out against it.

I lost my son Arik because of our cruel and unjust behavior vis-à-vis the Palestinians. Not knowing him from Adam, Arik's murderers killed him because there was no peace and because of the horrible Occupation which has been going on for nearly forty years. We must realize what occupation is before we can comprehend its cruelty. We need to see, clearly and honestly, the atrocities the Occupation causes.

For decades most Palestinians have been unemployed and without income. Their schools are dysfunctional and their kindergartens are poor and severely lacking in playground facilities. There is no recreational culture to speak of, as there are no public libraries, no recreational areas, no pools or community centers, no malls, no theaters or concert halls—and the list goes on and on.

The hospitals are ill-equipped, understaffed and unsophisticated. The universities lack finances and facilities. The entire life of the Palestinian, in fact, is a life of need and suffering.

For the past decades, hundreds of Israeli roadblocks hinder the Palestinians for hours every day. Their roads are in ruins and sidewalks are a luxury. The Occupation is the worst form of terror, cultural terror, but one that is sadly perceived by the world and Israel as an occupation—not terrorism. But to the Palestinians the worst terroriusts are their Israeli occupiers. In the Palestinian perception, Israelis have murdered thousands of their fellow citizens—including children, women and the elderly. Palestinians feel an obligation to fight the Occupation, and the *Occupier*.

According to their view, Israel has perhaps the strongest army in the world, while they, the Palestinians, have but one main weapon with which to fight—the most intelligent "smart bomb" in any arsenal, the weapon of the despaired—the suicide bomber.

Indeed, how terrible must be the feeling of the Palestinians to know that the only weapon with which to fight their oppressor and obtain their national goal, i.e.

the end of the Occupation and an independent state, is to commit suicide attacks with explosives, killing as many Israelis as possible in the process. In writing this, I do *not* support (or even rationalize or comprehend) the Palestinians' behavior in this regard. I am opposed to violence of all forms, be it Israeli or Palestinian. I am unwilling to justify the Palestinian logic of despair, as I am an Israeli—and it is my family and I that these attacks are aimed at.

Hatred of Israel in the Muslim world is fueled and aggravated in direct relation to Palestinian suffering. The entire world, including the US, is suffering from Muslim fundamentalism that is in no small part due to American support of Israel. Peace between Israel, Syria, and Lebanon—a lasting peace based on reconciliation—would minimize and marginalize this fundamentalism.

The situation for the past forty years has always been on the verge of either great opportunity or catastrophic detonation. Ever since Ariel Sharon proceeded to evacuate the entire Gaza Strip of all its settlers (including Netzarim, a small Gaza Strip settlement), we were presented with a real opportunity in the Middle East to attain a peace based on reconciliation.

For nearly forty years, Israelis and the world have been led to believe that the settlements served as a safety mechanism, a buffer of sorts, while Israeli peace activists were up in arms, contending that these settlements brought nothing but bereavement, grief, and terror to both Israelis and Palestinians. Yet we even saw Sharon show that it *is* possible to "let go" of these settlements.

Out of the hundreds of settlements in the West bank, only 130 are legal, sanctioned by the Israeli government. The rest were established in contradiction to the will of the Israeli government, and are by-and-large examples of the brute-force mentality of the settlement movement. For years, the settlers were treated as Israeli heroes. Considered as the "true" Israelis, their occasional shenanigans were overlooked with tolerant and lenient overtones. For years, the "sheriff" of Hebron was Rabbi Moshe Levinger, who killed a Palestinian shopkeeper but served only thirteen weeks imprisonment. This man established a (legal) settlement in Hebron with a few dozen Jewish families, which caused a local Palestinian population of nearly 150,000 to live under constant Israeli terror. There are entire streets in Hebron that are closed to Palestinian travel. Hundreds (!) of stores in Hebron have been closed for years, all in the supposed interest of this Jewish settlement. Not for the first time, I will note that their Zionism has become a destructive force alien to Judaism. The daily human suffering in the occupied territories in general, and in Hebron in particular, is indescribable. Soldiers have testified to opening fire at Palestinians out of sheer boredom. There are scores of testimonials of Israeli "defense" forces vandalizing solar heater tanks on the roofs of Palestinian houses—ruined for "the fun of it." Others tell stories of sadistic abuse and structural vandalism, committed for sheer amusement.

Settlers have been above the law for decades. Ever since the evacuation of Amona, which showcased the underlying attitude of rebellion in the settler mindset, the Israeli government has awakened to a new understanding that these Jewish law-breakers—2006 versions of pogromists and hooligans—pose a very real problem. Settlers and their children have for decades been handled with silk gloves. I would hope that, with the recent harassment of Israeli security forces by the settlers, the Israeli government will realize that this treatment might have been misguided.

Hamas has recently been chosen to lead the Palestinian Government, and has established a majority parliament. It is critical to realize that this is not a "Hamas" government, but the *Palestinian* government. This government is not recognized by the free world or by Israel. Hamas has been articulating its defiant refusal to recognize Israel whenever it has the opportunity to do so, but we must be honest with ourselves and ask—have we ever *truly* recognized Palestine as an independent country? Was the state of Palestine established or has Israeli occupation continued to this day?

The Palestinian government recognized Israel some fifteen years ago—so what is the true nature of the daily statements and claims regarding the Palestinian non-recognition of Israel? Yasser Arafat died in late 2004. It had been argued for years that this man, Yasser Arafat, was the source of all evil in the Middle East and that he alone was responsible for the terrorism and, consequently, the lack of peace. Remembering the many meetings I held with Arafat, I recall a leader who could have realistically led his nation to achieving historic peace and reconciliation.

If only he had had an Israeli partner.

During the Camp David meetings, Arafat was led astray, tricked by the Israeli Prime Minister Ehud Barak and by Bill Clinton, on the other. This is a true shame, as a real agreement could have been achieved at that time with Arafat. Today we are witnessing the same process repeat itself, with the Israeli side stating, "There is no one to talk to." What nonsense! There was someone to talk to, and there *is* someone to talk to today—the *real* problem is that there is nothing to talk *about*.

To achieve historical peace, we (Israel) must be first willing to accept the 1967 borders, with negotiable amendments. On a scale of difficulty that runs from one to ten, where ten is impossible and one is unavoidable the difficulty to discuss such an agreement has decreased from ten to nine—from impossible to extremely difficult. The increased ease (or should I say decreased difficulty) is due to the evacuation of settlements in the Gaza Strip: Every Israeli leader knows that the difficulty inherent in evacuating settlements is astounding and that it is not "fun," or easy to discuss. We must remember, however, that this is the only path to peace. There are no other options if we strive to eventually reach the ultimate goal, peace.

As I write this article, a wall is being built between Israelis and Palestinians. This wall will not fulfill its acclaimed purpose, i.e. providing Israel with increased security. It will instead serve to deepen and entrench the schisms, hatred, and cruelties of the Occupation of the Palestinians. No wall can stop Kassam rockets, and even the highest wall will not be immune from tunnels dug beneath it. An eleven-kilometer long wall was built along the Egyptian border. Hundreds of tunnels were discovered beneath it. How many tunnels should we expect to find underneath an 800-kilometer long wall? Doesn't the Israeli leadership understand this? They do. But the desire to prove that there is no partner for peace takes precedence over common sense.

Ever since Arik was murdered, I have dedicated all of my time—night and day—to reconciliation and peace. The task is difficult, harsh, and it tears the soul apart. To see my brethren behave in such a cruel manner against the Palestinians; to see the suicidal Palestinians killing off my brethren; to be in a position whereby, hearing the news, I know that the killing of Israelis will inevitably continue—so long as the Occupation continues—is emotional torture of the worst kind. I believe it is important to mention, again and again, that *both* nations have amazing individuals and despicable ones, as every society does. In spite of this, only the Israeli side has occupiers.

To see religious Jews and rabbis avidly supporting continual occupation is also torturous. As a religious Jew who worships G-d, I know how many people today suit the Talmudic definition "*Naval bereshut haTorah*" (loosely translated as a glutton "sanctioned" by the Torah).

The last phrase in *HaTikva* (the Israeli national anthem) which was sung on Independence Day, reads "Our hope is not yet lost, it is two thousand years old, to be a free people in our land—the land of Zion and Jerusalem." Indeed, may we truly be free in Israel. Free of occupation, free of evil and callousness. It is up to us—and only us—to end the continued suffering.

Long live the State of Israel.

Long live the People of Israel.

May we finally understand that Palestinians are people, no different from you and me.

Two Poems

Ada Aharoni

Not Returning Home

I'm so sorry, my love,
I'm not returning home
for I can't return
home

I love you so
want to be with you so,
but somewhere there in a tank
in Gaza, under speared palm trees,
so far from you my love—
a murderous bullet hit me
in the very fallow of the center of
of my heart
where I first fell for you—
and now I am falling forever

I so want to be with you my love,
so want to hug you
my love, my life—
but cannot return home.

They have uselessly spilled
my young life, my young blood
under Gaza's blue skies—
and now I will not
just cannot
return home to you my love
Shalom my love, my life

My Sister, Daughter of Ishmael

"They shall sit every man under his vine and under his fig tree, and none shall make them afraid." (The Bible, Michah 4:4)

"He who walks in the peace, walk with him." (The Koran, Sura 48)

My Arab sister, daughter of Ishmael,
Let us build a sturdy bridge
Form your olive world to mine,
From my orange world to yours,
Above the boiling pain
Of acid rain prejudice—
And hold human hands high
Full of free stars
Of twinkling peace

I do not want to be your oppressor
You do not want to be my oppressor,
Or your jailer
Or my jailer,
We do not want to make each other afraid
Under our vines
And under our fig trees
Blossoming on a silvered horizon
Above the bruising and the bleeding
Of Poison gases and scuds.

So, my Arab sister,
Let us build a bridge of
Jasmine understanding
Where each shall sit with her baby
Under her vine and under her fig tree—
And none shall make them afraid
AND NONE SHALL MAKE THEM AFRAID

Machsomwatch (CheckpointWatch): Women, Protest, and the Fight for Human Rights in the Occupied Territories

Nura Resh

We are now entering the 40th year of an occupation regime, the result of the "Six-Day War" (June, 1967) when Israel occupied the West Bank and the Gaza Strip.

The second Intifada that broke out at the end of 2000 was characterized by mass demonstrations and later, by an intensification of violent suicide bombings. In response, the Israeli army tried to control Palestinian movement by erecting roadblocks /barriers/ checkpoints, first around Jerusalem, and soon mostly inside the West Bank.[1] The checkpoints, about sixty of them manned by soldiers who control the movement of people and vehicles between Palestinian communities, have become an institutionalized phenomenon of the Occupation scenery, disrupting every aspect of the daily life of the Palestinian community: economic activity, education, health, and social contacts. They are overshadowed by the harsh, and sometime arbitrary, limitations of the checkpoints[2] (e.g. World Bank, 2002; Rosenfeld, 2002; Keshet, 2005). Repeated stories and reports about humiliations, violence, arbitrariness, and human rights abuses at the checkpoints provided the stimulus for the protest action of Machsomwatch.

Machsomwatch (here after, CheckpointWatch) is an Israeli women's protest organization, established at the wake of the second Intifada (January, 2001), by a small group of Jerusalemite activists, who began to take shifts at the checkpoints around Jerusalem, witnessing and reporting what they saw. During the five years of its existence, it grew to about 400 participants, organized regionally in four groups: Jerusalem, Tel Aviv/center, Be'er Sheva/south, and Haifa/north. It is the largest civilian protest group consistently present at these Palestinian-Israeli Army encounters in the West Bank. It is also the largest organization in the Coalition of Women for Peace, an umbrella group of nine feminist organizations, founded at about the same time (2001). Its main activity is organized around watching checkpoints along the Green Line and (mostly) inside the West Bank in groups of 2 to 4 women, usually in two shifts every day. A report summarizing the organization's activity in 2004 tallied about 3000 shifts at various checkpoints during that year. (Machsomwatch, 2005)

The "founding mothers" have framed the organization's goals, which are basically accepted by all and declare that in the context of protesting the Occupation and the very existence of the checkpoints, women will:

- Monitor the behavior of soldiers and police at checkpoints
- Ensure that the human and civil rights of Palestinians attempting to enter Israel are protected [3]
- Record and report the results of our observations to the widest possible audience, within and without Israel.

Embedded in these goals, is an immanent tension between the protest function (eyewitnessing and reporting) and the humanitarian action ensuing from the second aim. I will return to this point later.

The Organizations' Social Composition

The decision to be an exclusively women's organization was taken at the outset by the "founding mothers," emulating other women's protest organizations, like Women in Black, Bat Shalom, and others. This decision was based on a combined ideological-practical argumentation: "Our quiet but assertive presence at checkpoints is a direct challenge to the dominant militaristic discourse that prevails in Israeli society. . . ." (www.machsomwatch.org. Kimmerling, 1993; Sasson-Levi, 2006). This decision rested also on experience in other bi-gender protest movements, which became "naturally" male-dominated, pushing women to marginal roles (Sasson-Levi and Rappoport, 2003; Keshet, 2005). Though many of the women interviewed declared that in principle they do not prefer a one-gender activity, this decision was never challenged and most of the members agree with its practicality, i.e., that the presence of women and their style of discourse vis-à-vis the soldiers, is more effective, and that it emphasizes a civilian presence.

By its social make-up, the group seems relatively homogeneous, coming from the center of Israeli hegemony: Ashkenazi, educated, middle-class, mostly Israeli-born or Israeli-educated. They are mostly non-religious, and there are a high proportion of middle-age women.[4] Many described their upbringing as being carried out in the typical, very consensual, Zionist, Israeli spirit. Obviously, they all are "left" (in the Israeli jargon), and anti-Occupation. However, this relative homogeneity covers a considerable variety of ideological views and motivational forces, which permeates the group discourses (in certain cases, heated discussions), soothes inherent tensions, and affects the decision-making process within the organization. At the risk of over-simplifying, and over-generalizing, and though the ideological spectrum could be described as a continuum, I classify members as "hard-liners," "radicals," a "critical" group, and the more "consensual" and humanitarian-oriented women, who care about human suffering and welfare. Though, not mutually exclusive, and usually mentioned by women interchangeably, the "hard-liners," those with an activist background, stress the protesting function and the importance of reporting and testifying about the "injustice and evils of the Occupation." The "humanitarians" emphasize modifying the soldiers' behavior and helping the Palestinians in specific circumstances as their major mission.

Motivation to Act

In describing their decision to join CheckpointWatch, many of the women speak of a painful process of their "awakening of awareness" and "disillusionment" after the euphoria of the Six-Day War, and more generally from their uncritical patriotic Zionism, once they realized the evils of the Occupation, and the resulting "destructive processes" in the Israeli society. Investigating further what motivated their decision to act, three types of emphases appear:

- A wish to protest and testify about the oppression and human rights violations:

"Most important is to be there [at the checkpoints] and to report" . . . to emphasize the illegality of the checkpoints and the Occupation that created them . . ." (R.H). "I am there because I want to protest the existence of the checkpoints.... the sharpest, most intense metaphor for the Occupation." (A. K., quoted by Kadmon, 2003)

- Concern about the destructive marks the Occupation leaves on soldiers, and its negative effects on the Israeli civil society as a whole

    "Democracy and human rights are indivisible and can't be stopped at a line, it [the violations] spreads to the Green Line; the soldiers are "infected" and will carry it back home . . ." (N.P.) "I am not the 'committee for the Palestinians', I worry about the horrible corrupting process that is going on in the Israeli society..." (H.B.)

- Concern about mal-treatment and compassion for human suffering at the checkpoints and a wish to help the Palestinians

    "I came for humanistic reasons. How can one behave like this? . . . . How is it possible that my country, my soldiers, my army, allow themselves this kind of behavior? . . . . " (S.K.)

Ideological and Organizational Dilemmas

Embedded in the definition of the organization's charter and reflected also in the motives of the members is an inherent tension between the political protest function, and the humanitarian care intervention, which constantly consumes the Watchers.

Introducing a civilian eye into a situation, otherwise controlled solely by soldiers, we try to have our reports disseminated as widely as possible, in effect declaring: "You can't say that you didn't know."

At the same time, humanitarian concerns drive us to intervene in an attempt to alleviate the suffering of Palestinians. It is simply impossible to just stand in a shift at a checkpoint and write a detailed report about what is happening. Intervention may be specific: trying to modify soldiers' behavior or to solve a personal problem. It may be more general: trying to improve the appalling physical conditions at the checkpoints, or reverse illogical (and illegal) decisions, either at a local level, or by talking and meeting senior army officers.[5] At the request of Palestinians who approach us with their grievances we intervene in cases not directly related to the checkpoints. However, we realize that every "success" we experience is also some sort of co-optation: It helps institutionalize the checkpoints (and the Occupation), and the army uses us:

> " . . . In every action against the Occupation we get at a point to the dilemma: Where can we draw the line between protest and coopera- tion? When does trying to help the oppressed . . . turn into the fig leaf of the Occupation? Becomes part of its maintenance? . . . (A.K.) a fig leave, such as saying, "look how humanitarian we are. . ."

> "It is true, we collaborate with the Occupation, and I feel terrible about it. But, go tell the Palestinian woman who is being forbidden to cross the checkpoint with her sick baby on her way to the doctor that you do not collaborate with the Occupation, so she must some- how manage, or that she may apply to the high international court in The Hague. . . ." (D.B.) (E-mail exchange on the Checkpoint- Watch website)

There is also a gender facet to this inner contradiction: In carrying out the humanitarian function, women return to their stereotypical and more consensual role of "the caretaker," or the "nurturing mother," while in protesting the Occupa- tion and publicly reporting the events at the checkpoint, women are really acting as political activists.

There is yet another form of tension related to women and the soldiers we meet on our shifts. The question of "who are they" and how we relate to them is ex- pressed endlessly in oral and e-mail discussions. The more "critical" women would argue that soldiers are young adults, independent in their decisions, and thus fully responsible for the atrocities at the checkpoints, while the more "mothering" view will see them as "our (virtual) sons:" young, brain-washed, caught-up in an impos- sible situation that makes them indifferent to Palestinians as human beings and the resulting humiliations they receive and—in extreme cases—brutal reactions. Army service is (almost) universal for Israeli Jewish citizens. Indeed, most of us have paid our dues, having had husbands, sons, and brothers in the military. Para- doxically, women watchers often use these facts of life as a legitimizing factor in their confrontation with the soldiers. The strong identification with the army, the service in which is still considered a sign of affiliation with the national collective, and a legitimizing resource for membership in the civil society (Helman, 1997; Sasson-Levi, 2006), is a major source of ambivalence among some of our women.

"Successes and Failures"

What has CheckpointWatch achieved in its five years of activity?

First, it has made a major contribution in conveying the reality of the checkpoints to the Israeli public, in attracting attention and awareness to the "checkpoint regime," and its implications on every aspect of daily life of the civilian population. Even the mere fact that most checkpoints are located inside the West Bank separating *Palestinian communities* was a surprise to many Israelis, not to mention awareness of its use as collective punishment, and of violations of many human rights. In a world of fast-moving communications our reports also reach a wider international audience. And, in the long run, they will also serve as authentic testimonies to future investigators.

Second, though very limited and very problematic, the little humanitarian help that women manage to give by their intervention may alleviate somewhat the hardships and humiliations at the checkpoints and in some cases may be critical, making the difference between moving from one place to another, getting to the hospital or to the university, or being sent back, or worse, being detained for hours. We strongly believe though we can't prove—that our mere presence at the checkpoints has a modifying effect on soldiers' behavior.

Lastly, at the checkpoints, where only the army and military police represent Israel, we present to the Palestinians a different voice, a different face of Israel. The many thanks and welcoming greetings that we get from Palestinians, beyond the little we can do, strengthen the belief that this is another important facet of our contribution.

Still, however meaningful, the effect that CheckpointWatch has on Israeli society should not be exaggerated. We remain a small group, mocked by many Israelis, or considered "unpatriotic," "Arab lovers," and even "traitors." Most Israelis believe that the checkpoints are essential as a major contribution to security and we have not been able to change Israeli policy in regard to the Checkpoint regime, let alone to the Occupation.

Summary

Following Ferree and Meuller's (2005) classification of the women's movement as distinct from feminist movement, CheckpointWatch can best be defined as a women's civil movement: it mobilizes women to contest, protest or support a so-cial-political issue, rather than define issues related to gender relations as its major goal. However, our form of action—women standing opposite the soldiers at the checkpoints—challenges the existing definitions of gender roles and gender relations in the Israeli society. Hence, indirectly, it is a feminist movement *and* a political movement, calling for an end to the Israeli Occupation and the system of checkpoints that helps maintain it.

Continuous activity in CheckpointWatch is a very difficult, tiring, and at times frustrating routine. Vigils at the checkpoints are carried out in small groups far from Israeli eyes. We witness a sea of troubles and are unable to change the situation or help in individual cases. Many of the women are faced with indifference or even rejection in an Israeli environment that does not want to know, does not care, or worse, think "they (the Palestinians) deserve what they get" (Levi, 2006). Thus, words such as "shame," "rage," "desperation," and "frustration" are repeated in women's description of their feelings about the checkpoints and about the soldiers' and Israeli citizens' response to them.

Despite this and while some ideological and procedural conflicts are unresolved, the work of watching and reporting continues. Moreover, having a closer look on the multiple hardships and limitations faced by Palestinians and accentuated with the construction of the separation wall, women have begun varying their activities. They now follow (and fight for) the regular opening of gates in the separation wall to allow children and farmers crossing to schools and to their land; follow and report the detention procedures confronting Palestinians at military courts; try to help process Palestinian requests for work permits (in Israel), and the like. Worth noting is the evolvement of a separate NGO, Yesh Din (There is a Law), which collects evidence about settlers' violence against their Palestinian neighbors, helps victims to file their complaints to the police, and follow its inquiry (or rather, avoidance from a proper inquiry) of their cases.

Regardless of differences in political persuasion, all CheckpointWatchers are women who decided that, as Israeli citizens, they "should break the silence" and are willing to protest injustice in the hope that in a long run justice (and peace) will be restored.

Notes

1 The term "checkpoint" does not convey accurately the meaning of the Hebrew word "Machsom." "Barrier" or "road-block" would be more accurate, both literally and in describing their real function. I will, however, use "checkpoint" that became accepted in the daily discourse. Checkpoints were used by the army since the first Intifada (1989), but became an institutionalized measure of control since 2000.

2 The number of manned checkpoints changes from time to time. In addition, there are hundreds of unmanned barriers and roadblocks around and between villages and small communities within the West Bank and every now and then "flying checkpoints" are situated at various roads intersections for limited periods. Moreover, about 700 km. of roads within the area, turned into "apartheid roads," are banned to Palestinian vehicles.

3 The text was formulated when checkpoints were located around Jerusalem. Spreading very soon to *within* the West Bank, they mostly control movement *between Palestinians communities.*

4 Very interestingly, the founding group does not fit this description: they are mostly immigrants, who were educated outside Israel, they have a history of protest activism, and two of them are religious.

5 Using personal networks and the public reputation we managed to achieve, representatives of Checkpointwatch met with the IDF advocate general, with the West Bank commander, and with the Chief of Staff, as well as with regional generals and the "civil" governor of the West Bank.

Bibliography

Ferree, Myra M. & Carol McClurg Mueller. "Feminism and Women's Movement: A Global Perspective." In D. A. Snow, S. A. Soule & H. Kriesi (eds.) *The Blackwell Companion of Social Movements.* London: Blackwell, 2004. pp. 576–607.

Helman, Sara. "Militarism and the Construction of Community." *Journal of Political and Military Sociology* 25:305 332, 1997.

Kadmon, Sima. "Many Mothers" *Yediot Achronot, Nov.21.* (Hebrew), 2002.

Machsomwatch. *A Counterview: Checkpoints, 2005.*

Keshet, Yehudit, K. *CheckpointWatch: Testimonies from Occupied Palestine.* London: Zed Books, 2005.

Kimmerling, Baruch. "Patterns of Militarism in Israel." *European Journal of Sociology* 34, 1994. pp. 196-223.

Levi, Gideon. "When the Israeli society will Really Know." In H. Herzog & K. Lahad (eds.) *Knowledge and Silence: On Mechanism of Denial and Repression in Israeli Society* Jerusalem: Van Leer, 1996. pp. 75-82.

Nirgad, Lea. *Winter in Kalandia.* Tel Aviv: Chargol Press, 2004. (Hebrew).

Rosenfeld, Maya. "Sunday Morning at the Checkpoints: The "Compulsory Pleasure" of the Ruler, the "Compulsory Resilience" of the Ruled." *Politica, Israel Journal of Political Science* 11/12, 2004. pp. 41–55. (Hebrew).

Sasson-Levi Orna. *Identities in Uniform.* Jerusalem: Magnes, 2006. (Hebrew).

Sasson-Levi, Orna & Tamar Rapoport. "Body, Gender and Knowledge in Protest Movements." *Gender and Society* 17(3), 2003. pp. 379–403.

World Bank. *Fifteen month— Intifada, Closures and Palestinian Economic Crisis: An Assessment.* March 2003.

Descent into Violence

Milton Viorst

During my Jewish boyhood, I rarely encountered the super-devout, those we call Ultra-Orthodox today, whose appearance was so different from ours. Occasionally, two or three bearded men in black coats and hats, wearing side curls, knocked on our door to ask for a donation for some distant yeshiva, where others who looked like them studied the Torah and the Talmud.

We called them Hasidim, a term that in retrospect may not have been accurate. I have since learned that, though most Ultra-Orthodox may belong to Hasidic sects, many do not.

Israelis call all Ultra-Orthodox Jews by the term Haredim. It is derived from a verse in Isaiah, "Hear the word of the Lord, you who tremble (Haredim) at His word." Ultra-Orthodox Jews accept the designation for themselves. They understand it to mean those not only who tremble but to whom God pays heed.

I frequently encountered Haredim during extended visits to Israel, where I worked as a journalist. My initial disposition surely bred of my upbringing, was affectionate. At Mea Shearim, Jerusalem's Haredi quarter, for example, I was invariably exalted by a feeling of being on a wonderful voyage to the world from which my ancestors came. I recall the pleasure of buying a *tallith* in a tiny Mea Shearim shop and presenting it to my first son for his Bar Mitzvah.

Only later, as a regular observer of the intensifying conflicts between Jews, did I acquire less favorable opinions of the Ultra-Orthodox. My quarrel was not with their values or practices. My quarrel was in their contention that theirs was the only legitimate Judaism and their insistence that all Jews acknowledge this legitimacy.

My work in those days, took me not just to Israel but also to the Arab world, where I often encountered super-devout Muslims. They evoked in me no historical memories. But they were, I found, much like Ultra-Orthodox Jews. The term *fundamentalist* can apply to both. They both divided human society not by nationality, a secular standard, but according to faith. They rejected the temptations of modernity, believed all truth lay in ancient texts and yearned for a putative golden age of the distant past. They were both male-dominated, imposed restrictive dress codes and enforced strong sexual taboos. They also tended to be religiously and politically authoritarian.

When I began routinely journeying to Israel in the 1960s, Israelis were likely to cite animosities between Ashkenazim, European Jews, and Sephardim, Jews who came from the Arab world, as the country's most divisive social issue. But soon afterward came the Six-Day War, and, as a by-product of the huge victory that Israel won, the society's foundation shifted. Many Ultra-Orthodox believers declared that God had sent a message to have all Jews submit to God's rules, which they interpreted as being synonymous with their own. This assertion of power widened the rift with secularized Jews, creating a breach of unprecedented breadth.

* * *

Religious disputes, however, were by no means limited to ritual matters. After the Six-Day War, the most contentious issue became territory. Orthodoxy had held historically that only the Messiah could restore Jewish sovereignty in the Holy Land. After the victory, many rabbis decided that the West Bank and the Gaza Strip, respectively ruled by Jordan and Egypt, belonged to the Jews alone.

In fact, Orthodoxy itself was divided on this question, at least at first. The Haredim, who condemned Zionism for its secular nature, were largely indifferent to territory. But religious Zionism, a movement that for nearly a century had preached the priority of the Jews' return to their homeland, saw the victory as an opportunity. Religious Zionism's position, long at the margins of Jews mysticism, held that Zionism, however secular, was God's way of preparing the land for the Messiah's arrival. To its rabbis, the victory of 1967 was a message from God to seize the land for all time.

"Under heavenly command, we have just returned home in the elevations of holiness and our holy city. We shall never move out of here," declared Rabbi Zvi Yehuda Kook, who spearheaded the religious Zionist movement. "We are living in the middle of the redemption. The entire Israeli army is holy. The Kingdom of Israel is being rebuilt. It symbolizes the rule of the [Jewish] people on its land."

Kook and his followers reshaped Halacha, religious law, to serve their political ideology. Not only did they insist the law required permanent Jewish rule in the territories but also they proclaimed its supremacy over secular law. Many Jews rejected these dubious claims, but, in the postwar euphoria, Rabbi Kook's beliefs became hugely popular creating a movement that became Israel's most dynamic political force.

Religious Zionism was not alone; it must be added, in urging Jewish hegemony over all Palestine. Since the 1920s, Zionism had contained a minority wing known as Revisionism, which then and now promoted the kind of territorial nationalism that pervaded Europe in the nineteenth and early twentieth centuries. Religious Zionism's role was to sanctify this nationalism, imparting huge energy to it by characterizing it as God's command.

Religious Zionism after 1967 sparked the Jewish settlement movement in the occupied territories. It built communities across the land and brought in thousands of Jewish immigrants to live in them. In doing so, it often acted in violation of Israel's civil law, justifying its acts by claiming a divine calling. Every stake driven into the soil, it maintained, served God's will. Over the opposition of the international community and much of the Jewish world, its ardor has been key to perpetuating Israeli rule over the populations of the conquered land.

Modern Orthodox, unlike Haredim, wore contemporary dress. As a sign of identity, most crowned themselves with a knitted *kippa* secured by a hairpin. Their women were not subject to Ultra-Orthodox constraints in dealing with the outside world. Their settlements were well designed and solidly built, their homes spacious and comfortable. Their worldview, far from nostalgic, was very present-day.

Religious Zionists did not share the Haredi disdain for the secular state; even in overriding its laws, they esteemed it as an agent of Jewish power. Only at some unspecified future time did they imagine attaining messianic redemption, in which rabbis would secure God's realm under the Torah's authority. Meanwhile, they focused on retaining the holy soil, reshaping Halacha with the single objective of barring territorial withdrawal.

In the years just after the Six-Day War, few Israelis understood religious Zionism's dynamism. Most accepted the UN resolution that called for Arab-Israeli negotiations based on the exchange of land for peace. They recognized that settlements were an unnecessary burden on any such talks and were even prohibited by international law. But as long as the Arabs refused to talk peace, they regarded the relentless creep of religious Zionism's settlements as essentially innocuous.

In 1977, Egyptian President Anwar al-Sadat shattered the stagnation in Arab-Israeli relations with a peacemaking mission to Jerusalem. In a speech to the Knesset, he promised Israel full peace in return for its withdrawal from Egypt's Sinai.

The religious Zionists opposed Sadat's offer as an effort to separate Israel from a sacred possession. But the Likud government, notwithstanding its nationalist ideology, was sensitive to the strategic advantages. In 1979 Israel signed a formal peace treaty with Egypt. Under the terms, it agreed to withdraw from the Sinai in steps, the last of which contained a small settlement town called Yamit.

On the eve of the scheduled evacuation, hundreds of zealots—Haredim and secular Revisionists as well as religious Zionists—took over Yamit. Chanting prayers and reading the Torah, they vowed to resist to the death efforts by the Israeli army to evict them. They finally capitulated in return for money and amnesty, but not before issuing solemn warnings to the government that they would die before surrendering even a stone of the West Bank. Events would corroborate that they were not bluffing.

In 1992, Yitzhak Rabin, a hero of Israel's War of Independence and commander of the army in the Six-Day War, was elected prime minister, promising a concerted effort to extend the peace treaty with Egypt to an agreement with the Palestinians. A year later, he signed the Oslo Accords with Yasser Arafat, chairman of the Palestine Liberation Organization. The Oslo Accords only aggravated the settlers' wrath, shifting their target from the Arabs to the traitors they perceived in their own society.

Rabin's proposal to evacuate a small settler enclave in Hebron, considered especially vulnerable to Arab attack, provoked a defining crisis. Hebron, where Abraham is said to be buried and which David made his first capital, is sacred to Judaism. Jews have almost always lived there; sixty-seven died there in an Arab attack in 1929. Rabin's plan to remove the settlers signaled to religious Zionism the defeat of it holy mission, and its forces mobilized to fight.

Led by a former chief rabbi of Israel, religious Zionism issued a Halachic ruling. Not only did God command the settlers to resist evacuation, it said, but He instructed Israeli soldiers to disobey any orders to withdraw. The ruling pitted Halachic judgments against democratic legitimacy. Rabin, fearing civil war, backed off, and the Hebron settlement remains on its site to this day.

Having humiliated the state, religious Zionism intensified its campaign. Some rabbis circulated charges through its network of *yeshivot* that Rabin, in proposing to surrender Jewish territory, was a religious outlaw. Orthodox circles debated whether, under religious law, he was guilty of capital crimes. In New York, hundreds of Orthodox rabbis signed a statement declaring that Rabin deserved to die.

On November 4, 1995, Yigal Amir, an Orthodox student, killed Rabin with two pistol shots in the back.

After his arrest, Amir told investigators, "According to the Jewish law, the minute a Jew gives his land and people to the enemy, he must be killed. . . . I do not have a problem with it." Amir, who was sentenced to life imprisonment, never expressed remorse. In killing Rabin, Amir was convinced he was doing God's work.

The fanaticism that produced this murder was far from the religion on which I—and, I think, the vast majority of Jews—had been raised. It certainly did not correspond with the ethics I had been taught were intrinsic to Judaism. Though I never claimed to be observant, I strongly believed I was being faithful to my religious heritage in respecting decent differences in outlook between people and for valuing a compassion for Jews and non-Jews alike.

Judaism faced an earlier defining crisis in the first century CE, when its state and its Temple were destroyed by Rome, scattering its believers across the globe. The cataclysm divided Jewish history into two periods: homeland and exile. To deal with exile, a Rabbinic elite rose from the ruins and created the law that remained unchallenged for some seventeen centuries.

But while Judaism was stable, the world around it was not. By the twelfth century, the Renaissance, having undermined the Dark Ages' God-centered universe with a culture that placed man at the center, had imposed a fresh crisis on Christianity. The secularism that emerged from the turmoil produced the dynamism of today's Western civilization. Islam, in contrast, remained mired in traditionalism. As for Judaism, which had kept secularism at bay until the eighteenth century, the Enlightenment shattered its historic unity, when a majority of Jews embraced Western beliefs while a minority held tenaciously to the ancient ways.

A century ago, Enlightenment Jews founded the Zionist movement as a remedy to Europe's anti-Semitism; Rabbinic Judaism declared Zionism a heresy. The secular state that Zionism created opened the third era of Jewish history. But, as Rabin's murder makes clear, the conflict between Judaism's two wings is far from over.

Is it valid to treat the Jews of Moses' time, after the passage of four thousand years, as the same people as the Jews of Rabin's? Conceding genetic changes after centuries of intermarriage, are the Jews of these two distant eras linked in any way?

Are there enduring cultural characteristics that shed light on the Jews of Israel and the Diaspora today? I believe the answer to these questions is, basically yes.

Jews—quite justly—are wary of efforts to describe them collectively. Anti-Semites have long abused this practice. They have burdened Jews with the crucifixion hex, the Fagin stigma, and countless other characterizations to impose suffering. But this aversion is not license to deny that there is a heritage that can genuinely be called Jewish. Some of it, I would contend, can even be traced back to the time of Moses.

This heritage is not synonymous with predestination. Though most Orthodox Jews believe God arranges all, I myself doubt it. Central as He has been in our culture, I suspect that God having created us turned us loose to make our own fate. That is not to say the responses of Jews are totally improvised. Jewish history reveals recurring patterns, a kind of cultural predisposition. The solutions Jews have devised to their problems over 4,000 years contain much consistency—and many warnings.

To cite one: Well before my own quest, eminent scholars pointed to parallels between Jewish zealotry in the first century, which led to the demise of Temple and state, and Jewish zealotry in our own. Many Jews see a scary portent in the parallel. There may be other warnings. In making the transition to our own time, Jews have revealed immoderations not unlike that demonstrated in the tumultuous Judean era.

Have we, for example, digested the right lesson of the Holocaust? A half-century ago the image of the Jews was of a passive people. In Europe, millions imbued with a sense of their weakness perished at the hands of evil with barely a struggle. We remember with tears the photos of yeshiva students digging their graves in the shadow of Hitler's guards, reciting the *Shema*. We promised ourselves "never again."

Jews are now perceived as tough, self-willed, and aggressive, and there is much to be said for the new image. But I question the value of what we have learned when yeshiva students now curse and spit at other Jews before Judaism's holiest shrine, when a zealot kills the elected leader of the Jewish state, claiming divine authority. Should Jews celebrate these changes, or is it that we have reverted to being as stiff-necked as God found when we defied Him in Sinai?

Jews would surely be wise to contemplate the warning that Rabin's murder contains. History may be telling us that the Jews' descent into violence casts doubt on the ability of the state, and perhaps the community itself, to survive.

Anti-Semitism and Zionism in the Debate on the Palestinian Issue: Personal Reflections

Herbert C. Kelman

The heated debate about the Palestinian issue and Israeli actions in the occupied territories often confronts me with a dilemma. To begin with, I have trouble with any attempt to structure the issue as one between supporters of Israel versus supporters of the Palestinian cause. I consider myself to be *both* pro-Israeli and pro-Palestinian. Moreover, I consider many of the protagonists in these debates—whichever side they claim to support—to be working against the interests of both sides in this tragic conflict. In particular, I am profoundly alienated by the rhetoric of some elements on both sides of the debate: both by those who use their totally legitimate criticism of Israeli policies and practices as a warrant for anti-Semitic pronouncements and by those who use the totally appropriate rejection of anti-Semitism and other forms of racism in any decent society as a weapon to delegitimize all criticism of Israeli policies and practices.

My perspective on the issue is informed by some of my personal experiences. I was born and raised in Vienna before World War II, in a Jewish family of East-European origin. Growing up in Austria, I was no stranger to anti-Semitism, even in the pre-Nazi days. I was eleven at the time of the Anschluss in 1938. I lived for a year under Nazi rule, a year that included Kristallnacht, among other horrors. In 1939, our family managed to escape to Belgium, where we lived as refugees for a year, while waiting for our visas to the US. The war had already started, and we got out of Europe just a few weeks before the invasion of Belgium.

I grew up in the Zionist youth movement in Vienna, Antwerp, and New York—specifically, the religious Kibbutz movement (Brit Hanoar Hadati in Vienna, Bnai Akiva in Antwerp, Hashomer Hadati in New York). By 1945, before the establishment of Israel, I had developed an active concern about the impact of the Zionist project on the Arab population, and I came to support the concept of a bi-national state—along the lines proposed by Ichud under the leadership of Martin Buber and Judah Magnes (though I do not support the concept of a bi-national or unitary state today). In the post-war years I became active in the civil rights and anti-war movements in the US. My interest in issues of peace, social justice, and social change steered me toward academic studies in social psychology. One of my special interests has been international conflict and conflict resolution, and for more than thirty years my primary focus in this work has been the Israeli-Palestinian conflict.

Perhaps I can convey the flavor of my approach to the Palestinian issue *as a Jew* by quoting from remarks I made at a Rosh Hashanah service in 1988, taking off from the central dialectic in Jewish religion between particularism and universalism:

> It is a great historic tragedy that the Jewish people, in affirming our peoplehood and expressing our national identity through a state of our own in our ancestral homeland, has displaced another people and contributed to its pain. The resulting breach can be healed only through a historic compromise, whereby the two peoples share the land to which both are so deeply attached.

> In promoting such a compromise, we must eschew political rhetoric that stresses the "demographic threat" or Israel's need to "rid itself" of the large Palestinian populations of the West Bank and Gaza Strip. Such language is dangerously dehumanizing. Moreover, it ignores the reality that Israel cannot be rid of Palestinians—at least not by means consistent with fundamental Jewish and human values. Even a smaller Israel will include a large Palestinian minority, whose individual and group rights will have to be respected and who will have to be incorporated into Israeli identity. And even a partitioned *Eretz Yisrael* will require close links between the two com-

munities inhabiting it. Both are tied to the whole of the land and to each other in so many ways that it would be impossible to maintain two hostile entities there, hermetically sealed off from one another. The two peoples must find a way of living *together* if either one is to prosper, develop, or survive at all.

What we need, therefore, is the courage to speak in a new political language that says: Yes, indeed, we favor a historic compromise because it is in Israel's interest—because it is the only way to preserve the Jewish and democratic character of the state and to maintain Israel's peace, security, and respect among the nations. But we favor a historic compromise also because it represents a just solution to this tragic conflict—because we recognize that there is another people with legitimate grievances that must be redressed and rights that must be fulfilled.

We respond to Palestinian suffering and we care about their human and national rights for the simple reason that the well-being of any part of the human family is of direct concern to all of us. To exclude any group from our community of concern is to diminish our own humanity. But beyond that, the well being of Palestinians is of particular concern to us *as Jews* for at least three reasons:

First, as Jews we have a special responsibility toward Palestinians because they have been, and are being, victimized by our own people.

Second, as Jews we can identify with the Palestinian experience of refugee status, discrimination, arbitrary treatment, homelessness, and statelessness—all of which have been so central to the Jewish experience.

And third, though it may seem paradoxical, our own *ahavat Yisrael*—love of Israel—creates a special bond to Palestinians. They are an integral part of the land we love and their fate is inextricably linked to the fate of our Jewish sisters and brothers. Though the history of our two peoples has been marked by deadly conflict, we cannot abandon the effort of building a future relationship based on

mutual respect, on peaceful co-existence, and on a shared commitment to the common homeland.

I hope that this quotation, along with the brief summary of my personal background, convey the perspective from which I approach the issue of anti-Semitism
and Zionism in the debate on the Palestinian issue. Let me address the issue itself
by offering three caveats for conducting the debate about Israeli policies and practices in relation to Palestinians—caveats concerning:

- the danger of relegitimizing anti-Semitism
- the danger of delegitimizing criticism of Israeli policies and practices
- the danger of slippage between anti-Zionism and anti-Semitism

Relegitimizing anti-Semitism

We must be very alert to the danger that legitimate criticisms of Israeli policies
and practices may provide the excuse and occasion for guilt-free expressions of
anti-Semitism—in other words, that they may relegitimize anti-Semitism (at a
time when it has become unacceptable among decent people) under the guise of
political criticism.[1]

The debate about Israeli policy often provides an ostensibly legitimate opportunity to express the latent anti-Semitism that continues to run deep in Christian
societies, where the identification of Jews as Christ-killers has not lost its hold on
the popular imagination. Beyond that, among Europeans, both on the right and
on the left of the political spectrum, a hypercritical, anti-Semitically–tinged attitude toward Israel may also be motivated by guilt over Europe's long history of
anti-Semitism, culminating in the Holocaust. If Israel, the Jewish state, can be accused of oppressing another people, and if its actions can be equated with the actions of Nazis (as some critics like to do), then the sense of guilt for what was done
to European Jewry can somehow be eased. Moreover, it can retrospectively justify
what was done to the Jews because they have shown that they deserved it. Alexander Pollak speaks of this phenomenon as "secondary anti-Semitism."[2]

As for the resort to anti-Semitic formulations by Arabs and Muslims, one can
assume that the motivation derives more directly from anger at the Jewish state
for its treatment of their Palestinian brothers and sisters. However, though the

motives for adopting anti-Semitic language and imagery may lie in the current political context, the language and imagery themselves often draw on the myths and stereotypes about Jews contained in traditional Islamic sources and appropriate the myths and stereotypes of European Christian sources in the service of the political struggle against Israeli policies and practices.

By what criteria can we determine whether criticisms—even strongly worded denunciations—of Israeli policies and practices vis-à-vis the Palestinians can be described as anti-Semitic? The line may be hard to draw at times but criticisms become anti-Semitic—and hence illegitimate—when they are directed at "the Jews" rather than at Israeli authorities and the policies and practices these authorities pursue and condone. Moreover, the charge of anti-Semitism is particularly appropriate when references to the Jews and criticisms of Israel (or indeed, of US policy in the Middle East) evoke—explicitly or implicitly—the traditional, centuries-old stereotypes of the Jew, whether drawn from Christian or Islamic sources, or from the "Protocols of Zion."

One example of a traditional stereotype with deep historical roots and a distinctly anti-Semitic odor—even when those who use it believe that they are only stating objective facts—is the attribution of vast power to Jews, as in the claim that Jews control the media, or international finance, or US foreign policy. Recourse to this stereotype is illustrated in the oft-repeated claim that US policy in the Middle East is an extension of Israeli policy: Israel is described as the tail that wags the American dog. The "kernel of truth" in this claim is the fact that some of the second- or third-ranking US officials who have provided ideological support for recent US policies in the Middle East are Jewish neoconservatives, who also support hawkish positions within Israel. But US policy is made, of course, by such top officials as Bush, Cheney, and Rumsfeld, who are far more beholden to and influenced by other interest groups, ranging from the oil industry to the Christian right, than the Jewish neoconservatives in their employ or, for that matter, the Israel lobby or the Jewish vote. Moreover, the implication that the US national leadership would place Israeli interests (as defined by the Israeli right) ahead of what they perceive to be American interests is an absurdity that echoes the classical anti-Semitic stereotype of pervasive Jewish control. As for the Jewish neoconservatives themselves, the charge that their policy recommendations are driven by the Likud's agenda is reminiscent of the old canard about the dual loyalties of Jewish citizens of the US and other countries. I see no reason to doubt that their recommendations flow from their view of the world and of the US role within it (views with which I thoroughly disagree). It is not surprising that they find the attitude of the Israeli right congenial with their worldview—as does President George W. Bush himself.

One does not have to be an anti-Semite to yield to the temptation of the stereotype of Jewish power when caught up in the polemics of the Israeli-Palestinian conflict. A Palestinian friend of mine, who is definitely not an anti-Semite, complained in a recent statement that Jews dominate US Middle East policy and demonstrated his point with a list of names ranging from Paul Wolfowitz to Dennis Ross. Next time I see him, I plan to present him with an equally long list of Jews, ranging from Noam Chomsky to Marc Ellis, whom I am sure he would be happy to see in influential positions helping to shape US Middle East policy. He has every right to be critical of US policy and of the ways in which it has been shaped or executed by the particular individuals he lists, but the fact that they are Jews is entirely irrelevant to his criticism. I would say that in his rhetorical zeal he has—inadvertently, I am sure—tripped into an anti-Semitic stereotype.

Another indicator often used to designate criticism of Israel as anti-Semitic is that Israel is being singled out for criticism, while more serious or pervasive violations of human rights in other parts of the world are being ignored. A case in point is the call for boycotting Israel, such as the divestment proposals by some Protestant denominations, or the academic boycott (since rescinded) of two Israeli universities by the British Association of University Teachers. I am inclined to agree with Yossi Alpher when he writes "this boycott brings us into the tenuous twilight zone between anti-Zionism and anti-Semitism."[3] I have no doubt that some of the proponents of boycotts are motivated by anti-Semitism, perhaps by the desire to assuage guilt by stressing that Jews are no better than the Europeans who actively or passively persecuted them—or, even worse, that Jews deserved their fate. But it *is* a twilight zone. The fact that Israel is being singled out for criticism or boycott does not *ipso facto* prove that anti-Semitism is at work—which brings me directly to my second caveat.

Delegitimizing criticism of Israeli policies and practices

We must be very careful not to delegitimize criticism of Israeli policies and practices by automatically equating such criticisms with anti-Semitism (or with Jewish self-hatred). Everyone—whether Christian, Muslim, or Jew—has a right to criticize Israeli policies and practices that they perceive as violations of human rights, or as obstacles to peace, or indeed as threats to the future of Israel itself, without being called anti-Semites or self-hating Jews. And legitimate criticisms include not only criticisms related to the Occupation, but also criticisms of institutionalized patterns, such as laws and practices that deny equal rights to Palestinian citizens of Israel. Nor, for that matter, is it appropriate to label criticism of Israeli policies as anti-Israel. Often, in fact, such criticisms are profoundly pro-Israel—in calling attention, for example, to such practices as the settlement project and the effort to incorporate large segments of the West Bank into Israel that seriously threaten the future of Israel as a democratic, Jewish state.

The tactic of labeling criticisms of Israeli policies and practices as anti-Semitic is an inappropriate attempt to delegitimize such criticism and cut off debate. It has been used, for example, in response to the academic boycott called by the British Association of University Teachers. I strongly opposed that boycott (and have opposed similar boycotts in the past) for a number of reasons. I considered it unjustified, unwise, even unfair, and counterproductive. But is such a boycott *anti-Semitic* and does the fact that the Jewish state is being singled out for boycott while similar or worse violations elsewhere are ignored prove that this is so? I think not. And while I suspect, as already mentioned, that some of the promoters of this and similar boycotts are anti-Semitically motivated, there is no basis for claiming that is necessarily the case.

People do not usually sit down to draw up a rank-ordered list of evildoers around the world and then start at the top of the list to declare a boycott or engage in some other form of protest. There are many reasons why people may take action in one particular case rather than another. They may do so because they have a special interest in that area of the world; because they have a strong identification with the population that is victimized; because the particular case is prominently featured in the news; because they are presented with an opportunity to act; because there is a greater likelihood that the action in that particular case will have an impact; or because they feel some complicity in causing the evil or allowing it to happen. We cannot assume, therefore, that the reason for singling out Israel for criticism or protest is anti-Semitism unless we have evidence—such as the use of anti-Semitic stereotypes—that this is the case. In general, I might add, the argument that it is unfair to take action against one wrong because you are not taking action against other, perhaps greater wrongs, is hardly persuasive.

I am against the tactic of delegitimizing criticisms of Israeli *policies and practices* by labeling them as anti-Semitic. The picture becomes more ambiguous when the criticism takes the form of generalized anti-Zionism and verges on denial of the very legitimacy of the State of Israel. Even criticisms at that level cannot be automatically equated with anti-Semitism, but they bring into play the danger of slippage between anti-Zionism and anti-Semitism, to which my third caveat is addressed.

Slippage between anti-Zionism and anti-Semitism

Criticisms of Zionism—as an ideology and as a historical project—are not necessarily anti-Semitic. It is certainly legitimate, in my view, to criticize the ways in which Zionist ideology has expressed itself in practice. I maintain, however, that certain criticisms of Zionism as such cross the line of legitimacy. I have in mind, in particular, the equation of Zionism with racism, as exemplified by the 1975 resolution of the UN General Assembly (rescinded only after the Oslo agreement) that declared Zionism to be "a form of racism or racial discrimination."

I can agree that some versions of Zionism may properly be called racist; that the way in which the Zionist project has fulfilled itself has had, arguably, some racist consequences; and that some of the policies and practices of the State of Israel (and the Jewish Agency) can legitimately be described as "racist." But Zionism *as such* is Jewish nationalism—the national liberation movement of the Jewish people. To be sure, all forms of nationalism have a racist potential and there are good historical reasons for viewing them with suspicion. But to single out the Jewish national movement as *inherently* racist strikes me as illegitimate and, in fact, racist in itself—in other words, anti-Semitic.

From its beginnings, Zionism has had many faces. Writers and thinkers like Ahad Ha'am and those following in his footsteps, like Martin Buber, Judah Magnes, Ernst Simon, and their colleagues in Brit Shalom and in the Ichud, cannot by any stretch of the imagination be accused of racism. Yet, they were unambiguously Zionists, even though their model of Zionism did not prevail. They and their spiritual and intellectual heirs today are the best argument against the position that Zionism is *inherently* racist. It is clear, both historically and currently, that Zionism does not imply racism and does not necessarily go hand in hand with it.

The equation of Zionism with racism—a doctrine that, by definition, is illegitimate—decrees that Jews do not have the same right as other peoples to identify with their national group and seek national self-determination. I believe that the exercise of the right of national self-determination—for Jews, as for any other people—is not unlimited. I have argued that any group's self-determination must be *negotiated,* because it affects the rights and welfare of other groups.[4] But to equate Zionism as such with racism says that the Jewish people's right to self-determination—no matter how it might be implemented—is inherently illegitimate. And that is a view I consider implicitly anti-Semitic and hence unacceptable.

In rejecting the equation of Zionism with racism, which has the effect of completely delegitimizing it, I am not taking an uncritical attitude toward Zionism. In fact, I believe that, with the establishment of Israel and its existence as a recognized state over many years, we are now in a post-Zionist era.[5] (I use the term post-Zionism to refer to the new historical reality, not in the sense in which it is used by Israeli revisionist historians and critical sociologists.)

The new situation requires the evolution of a different kind of nationalism, appropriate to an established state in contrast to a liberation movement. This process of evolution is taking place, though it is slowed down by the fact that the Israeli state remains incomplete—as long as the Israeli-Palestinian conflict is unresolved, the borders are not finalized, and the legitimacy of Israel is not universally accepted. But I see the need for a gradual change in the political ideology of the state, especially in two respects: "post-Zionism can be said to imply an upgrading in the status of non-Jewish citizens of Israel and a downgrading in the status of non-Israeli Jews."[6] In other words, it will be necessary to deconstruct the concept of Israel as the state of the Jewish people to allow for the fact that the state must belong to and serve all of its citizens and that it cannot claim to represent and speak for non-citizen populations.

Conclusion

The nature of the debate on the Palestinian issue is a direct reflection of the nature of the Israeli-Palestinian conflict itself. It is, in my view, a tragic conflict between two peoples, each of which has historic ties and profound emotional attachments to the same land and claims it as its national home. They have come to see the conflict in zero-sum terms, not only with respect to territory, but also with respect to national identity: Each perceives the national identity of the other as a threat to its own national identity. Thus, the conflict has been marked from its inception by systematic efforts to deny each other's national identity and hence each other's right to establish a national state in the disputed land.

In keeping with the agenda of mutual denial of the other's identity, proponents of the two sides may resort to various forms of delegitimization of the other—of the other's movement and ideology, the other's policies and practices. In this vein, the debate between the two camps often features charges designed to delegitimize the other. Palestinians and their advocates may accuse Israel of racism and—deliberately or carelessly—make use of classical anti-Semitic stereotypes in their criticisms of Israeli actions. Israelis and their advocates, in turn, may accuse Palestinians of anti-Semitism and invoke the stereotype of Palestinian terrorism.

In the short run, those of us dedicated to resolution of the Israeli-Palestinian conflict must call attention to these various attempts to delegitimize the other side and make it clear that such tactics are themselves illegitimate means of carrying on the debate. In the long run, we must encourage the two sides to move toward mutual acknowledgment of the other's national identity and authentic ties to the land. By accommodating each other's identity, they will become able to embrace a two-state solution as a historic compromise, whereby the two peoples agree to share the land that belongs to both of them and achieve their respective national aspirations within it.

Notes

1 The following analysis is influenced by John Bunzl's discussion of the motives underlying the exploitation of the political debate for anti-Semitic purposes and Brian Klug's specification of the criteria for designating criticisms of Israel as anti-Semitic. See, e.g., John Bunzl, "Spiegelbilder—Wahrnehmung und Interesse im Israel/Palästina Konflikt," in *Anti-Semitismus—Antizionismus—Israelkritik: Tel Aviver Jahrbuch für deutsche Geschichte* (Moshe Zuckermann, Ed.), Göttingen: Wallstein Verlag, 2005; and Brian Klug, "Implementing the Berlin Declaration: The importance of conceptual clarity," *Public Expert Forum on Implementation of the Final Declaration of the Berlin Anti-Semitism Conference,* Berlin, 22 November 2004.

2 Alexander Pollak, "Report on anti-Semitism in Europe (EUMC): Problems of definitions and methodology," paper presented at the International Workshop on *Perception of the Middle East: Between Anti-Semitism and Islamophobia,* Hebrew University of Jerusalem, May 2005. Pollak points out that philo-Semitism, in its own way, may be similarly motivated by the need to assuage the guilt over the Holocaust. See also Elisabeth Kübler, *Anti-Semitismusbekämpfung als gesamteuropäische Herausforderung,* Wien: Lit Verlag, 2004 (pp. 114–118).

3 In "Israeli-Palestinian crossfire on the academic boycott of Israel." *Bitter Lemons* <www.bitter-lemons.org>, May 16, 2005 (Edition 16).

4 "Negotiating national identity and self-determination in ethnic conflicts: The choice between pluralism and ethnic cleansing." *Negotiation Journal,* 13(4), 1997, 327–340.

5 See my article, "Israel in transition from Zionism to post-Zionism." In *Israel in Transition* (Gabriel Ben-Dor, Ed.). Vol. 555 of *The Annals of the American Academy of Political and Social Sciences* (pp. 46–61). Thousand Oaks, CA: Sage, 1998.

6 Ibid., p. 49.

Joseph Abileah: A Nonviolent Israeli

Scott Kennedy

Joseph Abileah (1915–1993) was an accomplished violinist and founder of the Haifa Symphony Orchestra. He has also been described as "the first Israeli refusenik." Abileah was born in Austria and moved with his family to Haifa in 1923. He studied alongside Arab students and later worked as a surveyor under the British Mandatory Authority defining Arab property holdings. When the Arab Revolt broke out in 1935, a group of Arabs threatened to kill him because he was Jewish. Joseph calmly responded that if it was their duty then they should proceed. They decided to consider him a Muslim and spared his life. Abileah later said that, "not a single one had the courage or the heart . . . [to] follow the order which they had received to kill any Jewish person that they met. . . . nobody wanted to kill me. . . . I saw I was saved by the power of nonviolence."

Abileah later refused to enlist in the Haganah or the Jewish Brigade, joining an estimated one hundred Jewish Israeli conscientious objectors and draft resisters from just before the establishment of Israel until 1970. When tried in 1949 for refusing to serve in the military, Abileah, a violinist, defended himself in court after asking his father, Ephraim, a Haifa piano merchant, "If I plan to tell the truth, why do I need my own lawyer?" At his trial he summed up his belief: "I have been educated with Arab children on the same school bench. Do you expect me to kill my schoolmates?"

Often described as a "Jewish Israeli," "Quaker," and "Gandhian pacifist," Abileah was briefly imprisoned and was repeatedly brought before Israeli authorities for his refusal to serve in the military. Still, as an absolutist objector, he refused non-combat service, rejected findings that would declare him "unfit" for military service and, following repeated delays and postponements, was finally too old to be conscripted.

In 1972, Abileah became the co-founder and the first Secretary of the Society for a Middle East Confederation. Abileah opposed the Israeli Occupation of the West Bank and Gaza Strip, appearing before a UN Commission to declare that military occupation inevitably led to violations of human rights. "As long as we continue to occupy and oppress the Palestinian people, soldiers will be compelled to face the necessity of obeying inhumane orders. Peace and compromise are the only solution. . . ." The Society for a Middle East Confederation composed of Israelis and Palestinians and their supporters around the world, advocated a tripartite confederation of Palestine, Israel and Jordan. Throughout his life, Joseph Abileah worked tirelessly to promote peace and reconciliation, equality of all, and for a Middle Eastern regional approach in economic development, water resources and security.

Anthony G. Bing has written an excellent biography, *Israeli Pacifist: The Life of Joseph Abileah.* (Syracuse University Press, 1990). See, too, Akiva Eldar, "The first Israeli refusenik," *Haaretz*, July 22, 2005. (www.haaretz.co.il)

A Prayer for Israel, for the Innocents, for Peace

Rabbi Victor Hillel Reinstein

Ribono Shel Olam, Master of the Universe, we pour our hearts out to you in anguish for the suffering of all your children. We cry to You Whose tears fall for us. We cry out in reflexive pain for attacks upon our own people Israel, feeling as one body the ache in any part of our being. Protect our people upon our Land, calm and soothe them, return our captives, and let terror be no more. Help us to remember that we are one people, for all of our different ways of response. Let not the wanton hatred that brought down the walls of Your House divide us yet again from each other and from You. Know that our hearts break for the suffering of the innocents who bear the wrath born of our own pain and fear. Yearning for surcease from terror, we lash out in destructive fury. Open our eyes to the illusions of military might, to see in the rising plumes of so much smoke the certain rise of hate that will divide for generations more your children from each other, and bring no peace. Of those who really are children, in all the lands of war, protect them please, their fragile bodies and tender souls like flowers bending in the storm. Ease their parents' fear and give them reason to hope, that in whatever of Your languages they speak, they may find words with which to comfort their children. Please protect and quickly bring home our soldiers, and those of every flag, and wake us from the strangest dream to see swords and guns and uniforms scattered on the ground. From the whirlwind of war's futility, guide us to the wisdom of another way. For the sake of the ways of peace, help us all to clothe in humility our words to each other and to You. And let us say, Amen.

Selected Bibliography

Axelrad, Albert S. *Call to Conscience: Jews, Judaism and Conscientious Objection.* Hoboken, NJ: Ktav, 1986.

Baeck, Leo. *The Essence of* Judaism. New York: Schocken, 1948.

Bentwich, Norman. *For Zion's Sake: A Biography of Judah L. Magnes.* Philadelphia: Jewish Publication Society, 1954.

Bing, Anthony G. *Israeli Pacifist: The Life of Joseph Abileah.* Syracuse, NY: Syracuse University Press, 1990.

Breines, Paul. *Tough Jews: Political Fantasies and the Moral Dilemma of American Jews.* New York: Basic Books, 1990.

Brinner, William M. and Moses Rischin, ed. *Like All the Nations? The Life and Legacy of Judah L. Magnes.* Albany, NY: State University of New York Press, 1987.

Browning, Christopher R. *Ordinary Men.* New York: HarperCollins, 1992.

Eller, Cynthia. *Conscientious Objectors and the World War II.* New York: Praeger, 1991.

Elon, Amos. *The Israelis: Founders and Sons.* New York: Holt, Rinehart & Winston, 1971.

Fein, Helen. *Accounting for Genocide: National Responses and Victimization During the Holocaust.* New York: Free Press, 1979.

Frankl, Victor. *Man's Search for Meaning.* New York: Washington Square Press, 1963.

Friedlander, Albert H. *Leo Baeck: Teacher of Theresienstadt.* Woodstock, NY: Overlook Press, 1991.

Friedman, Maurice. *Martin Buber's Life and Work: the Early Years 1878–1923; The Middle Years, 1923–1945; The Later Years, 1945–1965.* Detroit: Wayne State University Press, 1988.

Gittelsohn, Roland B. *Here I Am: Harnessed to Hope.* New York: Vantage Press, 1988.

Goldberg, J. J. *Jewish Power: Inside the American Jewish Establishment.* Reading, MA.: Addison-Wesley, 1996.

Gopin, Marc. *Between Eden and Armageddon: The Future of World Religion, Violence, and Peacemaking.* New York: Oxford University Press, 2000.

Goren, Arthur, ed. *Dissenter in Zion: From the Writings of Judah L. Magnes.* Cambridge, MA, Harvard University Press, 1982.

Hallie, Philip. *Lest Innocent Blood Be Shed.* New York: Harper & Row, 1979.

Hammer, Joshua. *A Season in Bethlehem-Unholy War in a Sacred Place.* New York: Free Press, 2004.

Hertzberg, Arthur. *Being Jewish in America.* New York: Schocken, 1979.

Heschel, Abraham Joshua. *The Prophets.* New York: Harper & Row 1962.

_____. *Moral Grandeur and the Spiritual Audacity.* Edited by Susannah Heschel. New York: Farrar, Straus & Giroux, 1996.

_____. *A Passion for Truth.* New York: Farrar, Straus & Giroux, 1973.

_____. *The Sabbath: Its Meaning for Modern Man.* New York: Farrar Straus Giroux, 1995.

Hodes, Aubrey. *Martin Buber: An Intimate Portrait.* New York: Viking, 1971.

Kalechofsky, Roberta. *Judaism and Animal Rights.* Marblehead, MA: Micah, 1992.

Kidron, Peretz. ed. and compiler. *Refusenik: Israel's Soldiers of Conscience.* London and New York: Zed Books, 2004.

Kimmerling, Baruch and Joel S, Migdal, *Palestinians: The Making of a People.* Cambridge, MA: Harvard University Press, 1994.

Kolsky, Thomas A. *Jews Against Zionism: The American Council for Judaism, 1942–1948.* Philadelphia: Temple University Press, 1990.

Laqueur, Walter. *History of Zionism.* New York: Holt, Rinehart & Winston, 1972.

Levi, Primo with Leonardo De Benedetti, *Auschwitz Report.* New York: Verso, 2006.

Merken, Stefan and Polner, Murray, eds. *Wrestling With Your Conscience: A Guide for Jewish Draft Registrants and Conscientious Objectors.* Nyack, NY: Jewish Peace Fellowship, 2000.

Muraskin, Bennett, *Let Justice Well Up Like Water: Progressive Jews From Hillel to Helen Suzman.* Richmond Heights, OH: Congress of Secular Jewish organizations and New York: The Center for Cultural Judaism, 2004.

Peri, Yoram, ed., *The Assassination of Yitzhak Rabin.* Stanford, CA: Stanford University Press, 2000.

Pick, Philip L., *Tree of Life: An Anthology of Articles Appearing in The Jewish Vegetarian.* South Brunswick and New York: A.S. Barnes, 1977.

Polner, Murray. *Rabbi: The American* Experience. New York: Holt, Rinehart & Winston, 1977.

_____, ed. *Jewish Profiles: Great Jewish Personalities and Institutions of the Twentieth Century.* Northvale, N.J.: Jason Aronson, 1991.

_____ and Goodman, Naomi, eds. *The Challenge of Shalom: The Jewish Tradition of Peace and Justice.* Philadelphia: New Society Publishers, 1994.

Rabinowitz, Dan and Khawla Abu-Baker, *Coffins on Our Shoulders: The Experience of the Palestinian Citizens of Israel.* Berkeley, CA: University of California Press, 2005.

Reimer, Jack and Nathaniel Stampfer, eds. *Ethical Wills.* New York: Schocken, 1983.

Schwartz, Richard H. *Judaism and Vegetarianism.* New York: Lantern Books, 2001.

Segev, Tom. *The Seventh Million: The Israelis and the Holocaust.* New York: Hill and Wang, 1993.

Shlaim, Avi. *The Iron Wall: Israel and the Arab World.* New York: W. W. Norton, 2000.

Simon, Leon. *Ahad Ha'am: A Biography.* London: East & West Library, 1960.

Solomonow, Allan, ed., *Roots of Jewish Nonviolence.* Revised edition. Nyack, NY: Jewish Peace Fellowship, 1981.

Tessler, Mark. *A History of the Israeli-Palestinian Conflict.* Bloomington, IN: Indiana University Press, 1994.

Walzer, Michael. *Just and Unjust Wars.* New York: Basic Books, 1977.

Waskow, Arthur. *Godwrestling.* New York: Schocken, 1978.

_____. *Tent of Abraham: Stories of Hope and Peace for Jews, Christians and Muslims.* Boston: Beacon Press, 2006.

Wilcock, Evelyn. *Pacifism and the Jews: Studies of Twentieth Century Jewish Pacifism.* Stroud, Glos., UK: Hawthorne Press, 1993.

Viorst, Milton. *What Shall I Do With This People: Jews and the Fractious Politics of Judaism.* New York: Free Press, 2002.

Index

CONTRIBUTORS

Ada Aharoni, an international writer, poet and peace researcher, was born in Cairo, Egypt, and now lives in Haifa, Israel. She earned a Ph.D. in Literature at the Hebrew University. She has dedicated her life's work to the promotion of building a world beyond war, through writing poetry and historical novels, and peace activity. Among her many books are *Women Creating a World Beyond War and Violence, the Second Exodus,* about the forced exile of Jews from Egypt, which she and her family were part of, and *Memoirs from Alexandria*.

Rabbi Albert Axelrad serves as Chair and adjunct Professor of Religion at the Center for Spiritual Life of Emerson College in Boston as well as Interfaith Chaplain at the Massachusetts Eye & Ear Infirmary in Boston. He was for many years Chaplain and Hillel Director at Brandeis University. His books include *Meditations of a Maverick Rabbi, Refusenik: Voices of Struggle and Hope* and *Call to Conscience: Jews, Judaism and Conscientious Objection.*

Rabbi Philip J. Bentley has served congregations in several states and abroad. In 2005 he became rabbi of Agudas Israel Congregation in Hendersonville, North Carolina. He has published articles on peace, human rights, the environment, and Rabbinic tradition in *Tikkun, Fellowship, Judaism* and the University of Chicago's Law Review. He chaired the Jewish Peace Fellowship from 1988–1998 and has served as its Honorary President since then. He is a member of the Rabbinic advisory boards of the Jewish Labor Committee and Meretz USA.

Ira Chernus is Professor of Religious Studies at the University of Colorado at Boulder. He received his Ph.D. in the history of Judaism from Temple University. He is the author of *Mysticism in Rabbinic Judaism* and numerous articles on the history of Rabbinic Judaism. He has also written six books and many articles on issues of war, peace, and national security in American culture. As a longtime commentator in the news media and public radio, he often speaks about the Israeli-Palestine conflict and American Jewish life.

Claudia Dreifus is an adjunct assistant professor at Columbia University's School of International and Public Policy where she teaches "Magazine Writing with an International Dateline." She is also a Senior Fellow at the World Policy Institute of the New School University. Her articles about science have appeared in the *New*

York Times, Scientific American and *Smithsonian.* Her most recent book is *Scientific Conversations: Interviews on Science from the New York Times.* She is currently co-authoring a book on the American way of higher education with political scientist Andrew Hacker, who is also her domestic partner.

Jerry Elmer was a Vietnam-era draft resister. During 1969 and 1970, he participated in the public, nonviolent destruction of draft files at fourteen draft boards in three cities. After working full-time in the nonviolent peace movement for almost twenty years, he attended Harvard Law School, where he was the only convicted felon in the graduating class of 1990. The book from which his essay was taken, *Felon for Peace,* has been translated into Vietnamese and was the first book by an American peace activist ever published in Vietnam.

Edward Feder, a businessman, was, until his death, deeply involved in writing about and working for justice, nonviolence and the peaceful settlement of conflicts. He was also an active supporter of Israeli peace groups. "A problem solved by war," he wrote, "is not a problem solved and the dustbin of history is full of causes and ideologies that turned sour, because the means used to achieve them were evil." A sampling of his writings was published in *Nonviolent Activist: The Heart & Mind of Edward Feder,* edited and introduced by Murray Polner and Naomi Goodman.

Dorothy Field is a visual artist, writer, and one of the founding members of Victoria, Canada's, Women in Black group. In 1998 she traveled to Israel and the West Bank with a Compassionate Listening Group, meeting Israelis and Palestinians and hearing their stories.

Helen Fein, Ph. D., is Executive Director of the Institute for the Study of Genocide (New York City) and an Associate of the Belfer Center for Science and International Affairs of the Kennedy School of Government of Harvard University. She is the author and editor of twelve books and monographs, including two prize-winning books on genocide, and more than fifty articles on genocide, human rights, collective violence, collective altruism, and anti-Semitism.

Yitzhak Frankenthal is director of the Arik Frankenthal Institutute for Reconciliation, Tolerance and Peace, situated in Jerusalem, It was established in memory of his late son, Arieh Zvi Frankenthal, who was abducted and murdered by the Hamas organization.

Kenny Freeman is currently a Baltimore-based writer who began publishing *Jewish Opinion* in 1978 on the Internet in response to the first Intifada. He later became "an e-messenger for peace" in 2000. Immigrating to Israel in 1978, he wrote editorials in the *Jerusalem Post*, and published *The Yearning of Nazareth*, a prayer book for tourists. He later worked for the Civil Administration in Gaza as a writer for the Health Ministry, and was also the English-language editor of *Israel Review*. Since returning to the US he has worked with the homeless and mentally ill and completed a book, *The Vow of Jesus*.

Greg Gingold is a student at Fitchburg State College in Massachusetts where he majors in video editing. He writes and directs short films and has competed in several film festivals. Greg believes that peace and understanding is the way to solve life's problems.

Scott Gingold is a professional animator and cartoonist. He graduated from the School of Visual Arts in New York City. He runs his own business drawing caricatures of children at birthday parties and Bar/Bat Mitzvahs. Scott embraces the peaceful nature of Judaism and applies it to all aspects of his life.

Naomi Goodman served as president of the Jewish Peace Fellowship for many years. She was a Fellow of the Institute for Research in History and has written on women in the Hebrew Scriptures. She was co-author of *The Good Book Cookbook*, a biblical cookbook and authored a collection of her poetry, *On Borrowed Times: Poems of Two Centuries,* which can be ordered from Fithian Press, POB 2790, McKinleyville, CA 95519; www.danielpublishing.com. Naomi Goodman died in 2005.

Leah Green, founder and director of The Compassionate Listening Project www.compassionatelistening.org holds master degrees in Public Policy and Middle Eastern Studies from the University of Washington. She has produced three documentaries, including *Children of Abraham*, and *Crossing the Lines: Palestinians and Israelis Speak with the Compassionate Listening Project*. Leah is a 2003 recipient of the Yoga Journal's "Karma Yoga Award" and teaches Compassionate Listening worldwide.

Jeff Halper is an Israeli professor of anthropology and coordinator of the Israeli Committee Against House Demolitions, a coalition of Israeli peace and human rights groups that resist the Israeli Occupation on the ground, and especially its policy of demolishing homes. The author of *Between Redemption and Revival: the Jewish Yishuv in Jerusalem in the Nineteenth Century* and *An Israeli in Palestine,* about his work against the Occupation, he was nominated by the American Friends Service Committee for the 2006 Nobel Peace Prize, together with the Palestinian intellectual and activist Ghassan Andoni.

Rabbi Abraham Joshua Heschel (1907–1972) was a preeminent theologian, writer and supporter of civil rights, peace, and social justice. From 1945 until his death, he served as Professor of Ethics and Mysticism at the Jewish Theological Seminary. Among his many books are *Man in Search of God, The Prophets, The Earth is the Lord's,* and *Israel: An Echo of* Eternity. He was a member of the Jewish Peace Fellowship.

Susannah Heschel is Eli Black Associate Professor of Jewish Studies at Dartmouth College. She is the author of *Abraham Geiger and the Jewish Jesus* (University of Chicago Press), edited *Moral Grandeur and Spiritual Audacity: Essays by Abraham Joshua Heschel* and On *Being a Jewish Feminist: A Reader,* among others.

Ruth Hiller, mother of six, is a longtime peace activist and one of the original founders of New Profile. Three of her sons have already refused to serve in the Israeli military. Her oldest son, Yinnon, was the first pacifist in Israel to receive an exemption from the military via an appeal to the High Court of Justice (though the army released him at the last minute—ostensibly on the grounds of "unfitness"—to avoid an actual court ruling, which would have established more of a legal precedent). On past occasions, she has represented New Profile before the European Parliament and peace and women's groups in the US and Europe.

David Howard is a teacher, translator, writer and author of *The Last Gospel*, a novel. He co-chairs Citizens for Peaceful Resolutions/CPR in Ojai, California that was formed in response to the Bush administration's 2001 Nuclear Posture Review. Since 2002, CPR has helped organize efforts to wage peace in Iraq, abolish nuclear weapons, and end capital punishment. He also supports the "I Will Not Kill Pledge" for conscientious objectors.

Roberta Kalechofsky is the author of seven works of fiction, a monograph on George Orwell, poetry, and two collections of essays. She is the recipient of literary fellowships from the National Endowment for the Arts and the Massachusetts Council on the Arts. She began Micah Publications in 1975, which has since published forty books of poetry, fiction, scholarship, vegetarianism, and animal rights. In addition, she established Jews for Animal Rights in 1985.

Ira Katz is professor of Mechanical Engineering at Lafayette College. He co-authored *Handling Mr. Hyde: Questions and Answers about Manic Depression* and *Introduction to Fluid Mechanics.*

Herbert C. Kelman is Richard Clarke Professor of Social Ethics, Emeritus, at Harvard University. Between 1993 and 2003, he directed the program on International Conflict Analysis and Resolution at Harvard's Weatherhead Center for International Affairs and now co-chairs the University's Middle East Seminar. His books include *A Time to Speak Out: on Human Values and Social Research* and *Crimes of Obedience: Toward a Social Psychology of Authority and Responsibility (*with V. Lee Hamilton). He is a longtime member of the Jewish Peace Fellowship.

Scott Kennedy staffs the Middle East Program of the Resource Center for Non-violence *www.rcnv.org* in Santa Cruz, California, where he served three terms on the city council and two terms as mayor of Santa Cruz. He has visited Israel and Palestine more than forty times and twice chaired the National Council of the Fellowship of Reconciliation and helped found and chair the FOR's Middle East Task Force.

E. James Lieberman, a JPF board member, is a retired psychiatrist in Washington, DC, Clinical Professor at George Washington School of Medicine and author of *Acts of Will: The Life and Work of Otto Rank.* He is past president of the Esperanto League of North America.

Dan Leon, who lives in Jerusalem, is a former senior editor of *New Outlook* and co-managing editor of the *Palestine-Israel Journal*. His books include *The Kibbutz: A New Way of Life* and *Who's Left in Israel?* (Sussex Academic Press, 2004).

Bennett Muraskin is the adult education chairperson of the Jewish Cultural School and Society in West Orange, NJ, and has served on the faculty of the International Institute for Secular Humanistic Judaism. He is also a union staff representative for state college faculty and other professionals in New Jersey. His books include *Humanistic Readings in Jewish Folklore, a Yiddish Short Story Sampler,* and *Let Justice Well Up Like Water: Progressive Jews From Hillel to Helen Suzman.*

Nina Natelson is the founding Director of Concern for Helping Animals in Israel (CHAI), www.chai-online.org. Prior to founding CHAI in March 1984, she worked as a Program Analyst in the Inspector General's Office of the General Services Administration (GSA) and the US Labor Department for eight years. She successfully sued the GSA for sex discrimination, compelling the agency to hire, train, and promote women nationwide in that office. She graduated from New York University with a degree in languages, attended language schools abroad, and did graduate work in business at NYU and George Washington University.

Rabbi Victor Hillel Reinstein is the founding rabbi of the *Nehar Shalom Community Synagogue* in Jamaica Plains, MA. Meaning "River of Peace," *Nehar Shalom* offers a progressive voice for social change that is rooted in a vibrant embrace of Jewish tradition. He was the rabbi of Congregation Emanu-El in Victoria, British Columbia, and later rabbi of the Solomon Schechter Day School of Greater Boston. A longtime social activist, he draws from Torah and Jewish life the inspiration and guidance, the "vision and the way," to help fulfill God's hope for a world of justice and wholeness in which peace shall flow like a river.

Nura Resh is a sociologist of education at the Hebrew University of Jerusalem, and an active member of MachsomWatch. The description and analysis of the group in her chapter are based on intensive interviews with women-members, on reports from the checkpoints, and on e-mail exchanges in the organization's network.

Rabbi Michael Robinson (1925-2006) was long associated with the Jewish Peace Fellowship and served as its president. Born in Ashville, NC, he joined the US Navy at age seventeen and served in the South Pacific during World War II. Upon his discharge, he chose to embrace pacifism. He also became a rabbi, graduating from Hebrew Union College and later earning a doctorate from Union Theological Seminary. An ardent supporter, speaker, and marcher for civil rights and against the Vietnam War, he worked for peace, justice, and reconciliation between Israeli Jews and Palestinians, once declaring, "I'm not pro-Palestinian and I'm not pro-Israeli. I'm pro-humanity."

Rabbi Michael Rothbaum began pursuing Jewish studies at the New College of Florida, that state's public honors college, where he went on to found the school's first Hillel chapter. It was his commitment to social justice that first drew him seriously to Judaism and the social implications of its sacred texts. In addition to his Rabbinical duties, he teaches at Congregation Kol Ami in White Plains, NY and frequently addresses students and faculties at colleges throughout New York State. His work also includes extensive experience with community and religious social justice organizations, such as the New York Forum of Concerned Religious Leaders, Jews for Economic and Racial Justice, Rabbinical Students for a Just Peace, the Committee for the Human Rights of Immigrants, Interfaith Worker Justice, and the Jewish Peace Fellowship.

Sergeiy Sandler was born in the USSR and immigrated to Israel as a child. He refused to serve in the Israeli military on conscientious grounds and as a result was imprisoned. He was one of the founders of the Association of Conscientious Objectors in Israel in 1996, and since 1999 is active in the Israeli anti-militarist New Profile. He is a Council member of the War Resisters International. He holds an M.A. degree in philosophy and is currently writing his Ph.D. dissertation in philosophy at Ben-Gurion University, Beersheba, Israel.

Richard H. Schwartz is Professor Emeritus of Mathematics at the College of Staten Island in New York City. He is the author of *Judaism and Vegetarianism, Judaism and Global Survival,* and *Mathematics and Global Survival* and more than 130 articles at JewishVeg.com/Schwartz. He is also President of the Jewish Vegetarians of North America and the Society of Ethical and Religious Vegetarians. In 2005 he was inducted into the Vegetarian Hall of Fame of the North American Vegetarian Society.

Mike Shapiro's cartoons have appeared in many publications including the *Wall Street Journal, Barron's,* the *Harvard Business Review,* and *Reader's Digest.* He is also a contributor to many legal, medical, and business journals, has done work for animation studios and advertising agencies, and frequently draws caricatures at live events.

Allan Solomonow is a pacifist who has devoted himself to working for Israeli-Palestinian peace since 1970. He served as National Program Director for the Jewish Peace Fellowship, where he edited *Roots of Jewish Nonviolence.* He has also worked on Middle East issues for the War Resisters League and the Fellowship of Reconciliation. Since 1983 he has directed the Middle East Peace Program of the American Friends Service Committee office in San Francisco. Allan and his wife Ofelia (Alayeto) are members of the Kehillah Community Synagogue. He regularly leads tours to the Middle East and brings Israeli and Palestinian voices of peace to the US.

David Sparenberg is a poet-playwright, Shakespearean actor, stage director, workshop facilitator, and mystic with roots and lifelong study in Kabbalah, alchemy and shamanism. His literary work has appeared in more than 100 periodicals and journals in eight countries. He offers a one-man Shakespearean performance in the US and Canada to creatively assist people coping with life threatening illnesses, in particular cancer, and/or the loss of a loved one.

Ken Stanton is a Registered Nurse with current clinical experience in emergency and psychiatric nursing. He worked as a planner for the Sick Fund of the General Federation of Labor in Israel, and as a consultant to the US Veterans Health Administration on health care reform and ambulatory care redesign. He holds a Ph.D. from the London School of Economics and Political Science.

Phyllis Taylor is a Correctional Chaplain in the Philadelphia Prison System, a hospice nurse and bereavement counselor. She is a member of the Executive Committee of the Jewish Peace Fellowship, the Liberty Center for Survivors of Torture and Face to Face, an agency in Philadelphia reaching out to marginalized men, women and children. She is married to Dick, whom she met forty-three years ago doing civil rights work. They continue working together on issues of justice and nonviolence and enjoy their children, grandchildren and friends.

Milton Viorst has spent his professional life combining the disciplines of journalism and scholarship. He covered the Middle East for three decades for *The New Yorker* and other publications. He has written on the Middle East for the *New York Times*, *Washington Post* and *Los Angeles Times* and his articles have appeared in *Foreign Affairs*, *The Nation*, *The Atlantic* and *Time*. His most recent book is *What Shall I Do With This People? Jews and the Fractious Politics of Judaism*.

Rabbi Arthur Waskow has been one of the creators and leaders of Jewish renewal since writing the original Freedom Seder in 1969. In 1983 he founded and has since been the director of The Shalom Center (www.shalomctr.org), a prophetic voice in Jewish, multireligious, and American life that draws on Jewish and other spiritual and religious teachings for work for justice, peace, and the healing of our wounded earth. His books include *Sermons of Joy, Godwrestling,* and *Godwrestling—Round 2.* In 1996, Rabbi Waskow was named by the United Nations one of forty "Wisdom Keepers"—religious and intellectual leaders from the world over who met with the Habitat II conference in Istanbul. In 2001, the Jewish Peace Fellowship presented him with its Abraham Joshua Heschel Award.

Rabbi Sheila Peltz Weinberg is a Reconstructionist rabbi who has served as a pulpit rabbi for seventeen years. She is currently outreach director of the Institute for Jewish Spirituality (www.ijs-online.org) and teaches meditation to rabbis, cantors, Jewish educators and community leaders. She is on the board of Rabbis for Human Rights North America. She lives in Amherst, Massachusetts.

Evelyn Wilcock is a British historian and a member of the Institute of Germanic Studies at London University. She explored the history of Jewish pacifism in her book *Pacifism and the Jews: Studies of Twentieth Century Jewish Pacifists.* Her academic publications have focused on questions of the Holocaust and identity as reflected in the work of Theodore Adorno and in the experiences of people of mixed Jewish/non-Jewish descent under Nazism. Her writings have appeared in the *Journal of Holocaust Studies, Journal of European Judaism,* and the *Jewish Quarterly.*

Lawrence S. Wittner is professor of history at the State University of New York at Albany. A former president of the Council on Peace Research in History (now the Peace History Society), his books include the award-winning scholarly trilogy, *The Struggle Against the Bomb,* published by Stanford University Press.

Michael Young is a researcher and writer. His essay, "Facing a Test of Faith" originally appeared in *Peace and Change.*

PHOTOGRAPHERS

Jesse Abrahams is a senior at the University of Delaware.

Leah Green is director of The Compassionate Listening Project.

Tal Hayoun is an Israeli photographer active with New Profile, the Israeli peace group.

Avi Hirshfield is an Israeli photographer whose photos for CHAI appear in this volume.

Stefan Merken co-edited *Peace, Justice and Jews: Reclaiming Our Tradition.*

Deborah Rohan Schlueter is Project Manager for the Institute for the Study of Israel in the Middle East at the University of Denver. She wrote *Moghrabi's Olives*, a historical novel that follows three generations of a Palestinian family throughout the twentiety century.

Paul Tick's photographs have documented homeless Americans, Israelis, Palestinians and Nicaraguans. He is the Clinical Director of a counseling program for people involved in the criminal justice system. Together with this wife, Agnes Zellin, he is a founder of Bethlehem Neighbors for Peace, a local anti-war group as well as the father of Dan, a teenage photographer and filmmaker.

Linda Wolf is the founder and director of Teen Talking Circles and the co-founder of Daughters Sisters, Brothers Sons. Her photographs have appeared in magazines, documentary films, newspapers, and books and been exhibited in the US and Europe.

About the Editors

Murray Polner was the founding and sole editor-in-chief of *Present Tense* magazine, served two terms as interim editor of *Fellowship* magazine and was a book editor and publisher. He served in the US Army. His books include *No Victory Parades: The Return of the Vietnam Veteran; Rabbi: The American Experience* and *Branch Rickey: A Biography.* He co-authored (with Jim O'Grady) *Disarmed and Dangerous: The Radical Lives & Times of Daniel & Philip Berrigan*, edited *When Can I Come Home? A Debate on Amnesty for Exiles, Anti-War Prisoners and Others,* and co-edited (with Naomi Goodman) *The Challenge of Shalom:* The *Jewish Tradition of Peace & Justice.* His writings have appeared in *The New York Times, Washington Monthly, Commonweal, The Nation, Newsday,* and others. He is a history book review editor for www.historynewsnetwork.org, sponsored by George Mason University.

Stefan Merken was a Conscientious Objector in the mid-1960s and a draft counselor and West Coast representative of the Jewish Peace Fellowship from 1978–1995. In addition, he served on the National Council of the Fellowship of Reconciliation for more than twenty years. He was an American Fulbright Scholar in Japan doing postgraduate work from Columbia University. He and Murray Polner served as JPF co-chairs and they co-edited *Wrestling with Your Conscience: a Guide for Jewish Draft Registrants and Conscientious Objectors* and updated and expanded Allan Solomonow's *Roots of Jewish Nonviolence.* With his wife Betty, he wrote *Wall Art* and *Three Plays for Quarter.* He is also a short story writer currently working on his first novel.

A Note on the Type

The text was set 11 point Adobe Garamond with a leading of 14 points space. Garamond is related to the alphabet of Claude Garamond (1480–1561) as well as to the work of Jean Jannon (1580–1635), much of which was attributed to Garamond. This relatively new interpretation of Garamonci, designed by Robert Slimbach, is based on the Original Garamond as a typical Old Face style.

The display fonts are Corvinus Skyline and Engravers' Roman BT. Corvinus Skyline was designed by Ann Pomeroy in 1996 and is owned by FontHaus of Westport, Connecticut. Ann Pomeroy started designing typefaces at Rolling Stone in the late 1970s, where she was the typographer. Engravers' Roman BT is a Bitstream typeface.

Composed by Jean Carbain
New York, New York

Printed and bound in the U.S.A.

PEACE, JUSTICE AND JEWS

JUNGMAN
01/08